Resumes and Cover Letters
For Managers

Anne McKinney, Editor

PREP PUBLISHING

PREP Publishing

1110 ½ Hay Street
Fayetteville, NC 28305
(910) 483-6611

Copyright © 1999 by Anne McKinney

Book design by Katie Severa
Cover design by David W. Turner

Library of Congress Cataloging-in-Publication Data
Resumes and cover letters for managers / Anne McKinney (editor).
      p. cm.
  ISBN 1-885288-10-7 (trade pbk.)
   1. Résumés (Employment) 2. Cover letters. 3. Executives.
I. McKinney, Anne, 1948–
HF5383.R423 1999
808' .06665–dc21

98-56203
CIP

Printed in the United States of America

Also by PREP Publishing

Business and Career Series:

RESUMES AND COVER LETTERS THAT HAVE WORKED

RESUMES AND COVER LETTERS THAT HAVE WORKED FOR MILITARY PROFESSIONALS

GOVERNMENT JOB APPLICATIONS AND FEDERAL RESUMES

COVER LETTERS THAT BLOW DOORS OPEN

LETTERS FOR SPECIAL SITUATIONS

Judeo-Christian Ethics Series:

SECOND TIME AROUND

BACK IN TIME

WHAT THE BIBLE SAYS ABOUT...Words that can lead to success and happiness

A GENTLE BREEZE FROM GOSSAMER WINGS

BIBLE STORIES FROM THE OLD TESTAMENT

Contents

As the editor of this book, I would like to give you some tips on how to make the best use of the information you will find here. Because you are a manager, you will understand the concept of managing your career for maximum enjoyment and self-fulfillment. The purpose of this book is to help you manage your career.

Overview of the Book

Every resume and cover letter in this book actually worked. And most of the resumes and cover letters have common features: all are one-page, all are in the chronological format, and all resumes are accompanied by a companion cover letter. The book is divided into four parts. Part One provides some advice about job hunting. Step One begins with a discussion of why employers prefer the one-page, chronological resume. In Step Two you are introduced to the direct approach and to the proper format for a cover letter. In Step Three you learn the 14 main reasons why jobhunters are not offered the jobs they want, and you learn the six key areas employers focus on when they interview you. Step Four gives nuts-and-bolts advice on how to handle the interview, send a follow-up letter after an interview, and negotiate your salary. At the end of Part One, you'll find advice about how to research and locate the companies and organizations to which you want to send your resume.

Part Two of the book shows you resumes and cover letters that have worked for Junior Managers. You'll find the resumes and cover letters of professionals in fields including accounting, banking, store management, office management, personnel management, property management, purchasing management, and others.

Part Three shows the cover letters and resumes of Mid-Level Managers. These people have more experience than the professionals in Part Two. You will see resumes and cover letters of people in industries and fields including construction, automotive, human resources, manufacturing, restaurants, sports, non-profit management, and many others.

Part Four shows the resumes and cover letters of Self-Employed Managers and Entrepreneurs. You will see resumes and cover letters used by people who founded and managed their own businesses.

Part Five shows the resumes and cover letters of Senior Managers and Executives.

Part Six shows the resumes and cover letter of Top Executives.

But before you proceed further, think about why you picked up this book.
- Are you dissatisfied with the type of work you are now doing?
- Would you like to change careers?
- Are you satisfied with your career field but not with your opportunities for advancement?
- Are you preparing to launch a second career after early retirement?
- Have you been downsized, or do you anticipate becoming a victim of downsizing?
- Do you need expert advice on how to plan and implement a job campaign that will open the maximum number of doors?
- Do you want to make sure you handle an interview to your maximum advantage?
- Would you like to master the techniques of negotiating salary and benefits?
- Do you want to learn the secrets and shortcuts of professional resume writers and employment placement specialists?

Using the Direct Approach

Even if you are not now in a job hunt or career change, you need to be aware that most people end up having at least three distinctly different careers in their working lifetimes, and often those careers are different from each other. Yet people usually stumble through each job campaign, unsure of what they should be doing. Whether you find yourself voluntarily or unexpectedly in a job hunt, the direct approach is the job hunting strategy most likely to yield a full-time permanent job. The direct approach is an active, take-the-initiative style of job hunting in which you choose your next employer rather than relying on responding to ads, using employment agencies, or depending on other methods of finding jobs. You will learn how to use the direct approach in this book, and you will see that an effective cover letter is a critical ingredient in using the direct approach.

The "direct approach" is the style of job hunting most likely to yield the maximum number of job interviews.

Lack of Experience Not a Major Barrier to Entering a New Field

"Lack of experience" is often the last reason people are not offered jobs, according to the companies who do the hiring. If you are an experienced professional changing career fields, you often find that you are selling "potential" rather than experience in a job hunt. Companies often seek personal qualities that they know tend to be present in their most effective professionals, such as communication skills, initiative, organizational and time management skills, and creativity. Frequently companies are trying to discover "personality type," "talent," "ability," "aptitude," and "potential" rather than seeking actual hands-on experience, so your resume should be designed to aggressively present your accomplishments. Attitude, enthusiasm, personality, and a track record of achievements in any field are the primary "indicators of success" which employers are seeking, and you will see numerous examples in this book of resumes written in an all-purpose fashion so that the manager can approach various industries and types of companies.

Using references in a skillful fashion in your job hunt will inspire confidence in prospective employers and help you "close the sale" after interviews.

The Art of Using References in a Job Hunt

You probably already know that you need to provide references during a job hunt, but you may not be sure of how and when to use references for maximum advantage. You can use references very creatively during a job hunt to call attention to your strengths and make yourself "stand out." Your references will rarely get you a job, no matter how impressive the names, but the way you use references can boost the employer's confidence in you and lead to a job offer in the least time. You should ask from three to five people, including people who have supervised you, if you can use them as a reference during your job hunt. You may not be able to ask your current boss since your job hunt is probably confidential. A common question in resume preparation is: "Do I need to put my references on my resume?" No, you don't. And even if you create a page of references at the same time that you prepare your resume, you don't need to mail your references page with the resume and cover letter. The potential employer is not interested in your references until he meets and gets interested in you, so the earliest you need to have references ready is at the first interview. An excellent attention-getting technique is to take to the first interview not just a page of references (giving names, addresses, and telephone numbers) but an actual letter of reference written by someone who knows you well and who preferably has supervised or employed you. A professional way to close the first interview is to thank the interviewer, shake his or her hand, and then say you'd like to give him or her a copy of a letter of reference from a previous employer. Hopefully you already made a good impression during the interview, but you'll "close the sale" in a dynamic fashion if you leave a letter praising you and your accomplishments. For that reason, it's a good idea to ask employers during your final weeks in a job if they will provide you with a written letter of recommendation which you can use in future job hunts. Most employers will oblige, and you will have a letter that has a useful "shelf life" of many years. Such a letter often gives the prospective employer enough confidence in his opinion of you that he may forego checking out other references and decide to offer you the job in the next few days. Whom should you ask to serve as references? References should be people who have known or supervised you in a professional, academic, or work situation. Most employers know that your pastor will almost certainly be your ally, so avoid asking your minister. References with big titles, like school superintendent or congressman, are fine, but remind busy people when you get to the interview stage that they may be contacted soon. Make sure the busy official recognizes your name and has instant positive recall of you! If you're asked to provide references on a formal company application, you can simply transcribe names from your references list. In summary, follow this rule in using references: If you've got them, flaunt them! If you've obtained well-written letters of reference, make sure you find a polite way to push those references under the nose of the interviewer so he or she can hear someone other than you describing your strengths. Your references probably won't ever get you a job, but glowing letters of reference can give you credibility and visibility that can make you stand out among candidates with similar credentials and potential!

With regard to references, it's best to provide the names and addresses of people who have supervised you or observed you in a work situation.

In general, you will find that the approach taken by this book is to (1) help you master the proven best techniques of conducting a job hunt and (2) show you how to stand out in a job hunt through your resume, cover letter, interviewing skills, as well as the way in which you present your references and follow up on interviews.

The best way to "get in the mood" for writing your own resume and cover letter is to select samples from the Table of Contents that interest you and then read them. A great resume is a "photograph," usually on one page, of an individual, and you will meet some talented people between the covers of this book. If you wish to seek professional advice in preparing your resume, you may contact one of the professional writers at Professional Resume & Employment Placement for a brief free consultation by calling 1-910-483-6611.

Part One: Some Advice About Your Job Hunt

What if you don't know what you want to do?

Your job hunt will be more comfortable if you can figure out what type of job you want to do. But you are not alone if you have no idea what you want to do next! You may have knowledge and skills in certain areas but want to get into another type of work. What *The Wall Street Journal* has discovered in its research on careers is that most of us end up having at least three distinctly different careers in our working lives; it seems that, even if we really like a particular kind of activity, twenty years of doing it is enough for most of us and we want to move on to something else!

That's why at PREP we strongly believe that you need to spend some time figuring out *what interests you* rather than taking an inventory of the skills you have. You may have skills that you simply don't want to use, but if you can build your career on the things that interest you, you will be more likely to be happy and satisfied in your job. Realize, too, that interests can change over time; the activities that interest you now may not be the ones that interested you years ago. For example, some professionals may decide that they've had enough of managing people and want a job managing only themselves, even though they have earned a reputation for being an excellent manager of human resources. We strongly believe that interests rather than skills should be the determining factor in deciding what types of jobs you want to apply for and what directions you explore in your job hunt. Obviously one cannot be a lawyer without a law degree or a secretary without secretarial skills; but a professional can embark on a next career as a financial consultant, property manager, plant manager, production supervisor, retail manager, or other occupation if he/she has a strong interest in that type of work and can provide a resume that clearly demonstrates past excellent performance in *any* field and *potential* to excel in another field. As you will see later in this book, "lack of exact experience" is the last reason why people are turned down for the jobs they apply for.

How can you have a resume prepared if you don't know what you want to do?

You may be wondering how you can have a resume prepared if you don't know what you want to do next. The approach to resume writing which PREP has used successfully for many years is to develop an "all-purpose" resume that translates your skills, experience, and accomplishments into language employers can understand. What most people need in a job hunt is a versatile resume that will allow them to apply for numerous types of jobs. For example, you may want to apply for a specific job as a railroad conductor but you may also want to have a resume that will be versatile enough for you to apply for jobs in the construction, electronics, or healthcare industry.

Based on nearly 15 years of serving jobhunters, we at PREP have found that **an all-purpose resume and specific cover letters tailored to specific fields** is your best approach to job hunting rather than trying to create different resumes for different occupational areas. Usually, you will not even need more than one "all-purpose" cover letter, although the cover letter rather than the resume is the place to communicate your interest in a narrow or specific field. An all-purpose resume and cover letter that translate your experience and accomplishments into plain English are the tools that will maximize the number of doors which open for you while permitting you to "fish" in the widest range of job areas.

Figure out what interests you and you will hold the key to a successful job hunt and working career. (And be prepared for your interests to change over time!)

"Lack of exact experience" is the last reason people are turned down for the jobs for which they apply.

Your resume will provide the script for your job interview.

When you get down to it, your resume has a simple job to do: Its purpose is to blow as many doors open as possible and to make as many people as possible want to meet you. So a well-written resume that really "sells" you is a key that will create opportunities for you in a job hunt.

This statistic explains why: The typical newspaper advertisement for a job opening receives more than 245 replies. And normally only 10 or 12 will be invited to an interview.

But here's another purpose of the resume: it provides the "script" the employer uses when he interviews you. If your resume has been written in such a way that your strengths and achievements are revealed, that's what you'll end up talking about at the job interview. Since the resume will govern what you get asked about at your interviews, you can't overestimate the importance of making sure your resume makes you look and sound as good as you are.

> Your resume is the "script" for your job interviews. Make sure you put on your resume what you want to talk about or be asked about at the job interview.

So what is a "good" resume?

Very literally, your resume should motivate the person reading it to dial the phone number you have put on the resume. (If you are relocating, that's one reason you should think about putting a local phone contact number on your resume, if possible, when your contact address is several states away; employers are much more likely to dial a local telephone number than a long-distance number when they're looking for potential employees.)

If you have a resume already, look at it objectively. Is it a limp, colorless "laundry list" of your job titles and duties? Or does it "paint a picture" of your skills, abilities, and accomplishments in a way that would make someone want to meet you? Can people understand what you're saying?

> The one-page resume in chronological format is the format preferred by most employers.

How long should your resume be?

One page, maybe two. Usually only people in the academic community have a resume (which they usually call a *curriculum vitae*) longer than one or two pages. Remember that your resume is almost always accompanied by a cover letter, and a potential employer does not want to read more than two or three pages about a total stranger in order to decide if he wants to meet that person! Besides, don't forget that the more you tell someone about yourself, the more opportunity you are providing for the employer to screen you out at the "first-cut" stage. A resume should be concise and exciting and designed to make the reader want to meet you in person!

Should resumes be functional or chronological?

Employers almost always prefer a chronological resume; in other words, an employer will find a resume easier to read if it is immediately apparent what your current or most recent job is, what you did before that, and so forth, in reverse chronological order. A resume that goes back in detail for the last ten years of employment will generally satisfy the employer's curiosity about your background. Employment more than ten years old can be shown even more briefly in an "Other Experience" section at the end of your "Experience" section. Remember that your intention is not to tell everything you've done but to "hit the high points" and especially hit the employer with what you learned, contributed, or accomplished in each job you describe.

Once you get your resume, what do you do with it?

You will be using your resume to answer ads, as a tool to use in talking with friends and relatives about your job search, and, most importantly, in using the "direct approach" described in this book.

When you mail your resume, always send a "cover letter."

A "cover letter," sometimes called a "resume letter," is a letter that accompanies and introduces your resume. Your cover letter is a way of personalizing the resume by sending it to the specific person you think you might want to work for at each company. Your cover letter should contain a few highlights from your resume—just enough to make someone want to meet you. Cover letters should always be typed or word processed on a computer—never handwritten.

Never mail or fax your resume without a cover letter.

1. Learn the art of answering ads.

There is an "art," part of which can be learned, in using your "best-selling" resume to reply to advertisements.

Sometimes an exciting job lurks behind a boring ad that someone dictated in a hurry, so reply to any ad that interests you. Don't worry that you aren't "25 years old with an MBA" like the ad asks for. Employers will always make compromises in their requirements if they think you're the "best fit" overall.

What about ads that ask for "salary requirements?"

What if the ad you're answering asks for "salary requirements?" The first rule is to avoid committing yourself in writing at that point to a specific salary. You don't want to "lock yourself in."

What if the ad asks for your "salary requirements?"

There are two ways to handle the ad that asks for "salary requirements."

First, you can ignore that part of the ad and accompany your resume with a cover letter that focuses on "selling" you, your abilities, and even some of your philosophy about work or your field. You may include a sentence in your cover letter like this: "I can provide excellent personal and professional references at your request, and I would be delighted to share the private details of my salary history with you in person."

Second, if you feel you must give some kind of number, just state a range in your cover letter that includes your medical, dental, other benefits, and expected bonuses. You might state, for example, "my current compensation, including benefits and bonuses, is in the range of $30,000-$40,000."

Analyze the ad and "tailor" yourself to it.

When you're replying to ads, a finely-tailored cover letter is an important tool in getting your resume noticed and read. On the next page is a cover letter which has been "tailored to fit" a specific ad. Notice the "art" used by PREP writers of analyzing the ad's main requirements and then writing the letter so that the person's background, work habits, and interests seem "tailor-made" to the company's needs. Use this cover letter as a model when you prepare your own reply to ads.

Date

Mr. Arthur Wise
Chamber of Commerce of the U.S.
9439 Goshen Lane
Burke, VA 22105

Dear Mr. Wise:

I would appreciate an opportunity to show you in person, soon, that I am the energetic, dynamic salesperson you are looking for as a Membership Sales Representative of the Chamber of Commerce.

Here are just three reasons why I believe I am the effective young professional you seek:

- *I myself am "sold" on the Chamber of Commerce* and have long been an admirer of its goal of forming a cohesive business organization to promote the well-being of communities and promote business vigor. As someone better known that I put it long ago, "the business of America is business." I wholeheartedly believe that the Chamber's efforts to unite, solidify, and mobilize American business can be an important key in unlocking the international competitiveness and domestic vitality of our economy. I am eager to contribute to that effort.

- *I am a proven salesperson* with a demonstrated ability to "prospect" and produce sales. In my current job as a sales representative, I contact more than 150 business professionals per week and won my company's annual award for outstanding sales performance.

- *I enjoy traveling and am eager to assist in the growth of Texas and vicinity.* I am fortunate to have the natural energy, industry, and enthusiasm required to put in the long hours necessary for effective sales performance.

You will find me, I am certain, a friendly, good-natured person whom you would be proud to call part of the Chamber's "team."

I hope you will call or write me soon to suggest a convenient time when we might meet to discuss your needs further and how I might serve them.

Yours sincerely,

Your Name

Employers are trying to identify the individual who wants the job they are filling. Don't be afraid to express your enthusiasm in the cover letter!

2. Talk to friends and relatives.

Don't be shy about telling your friends and relatives the kind of job you're looking for. Looking for the job you want involves using your network of contacts, so tell people what you're looking for. They may be able to make introductions and help set up interviews.

About 25% of all interviews are set up through "who you know," so don't ignore this approach.

The "direct approach" is a strategy in which you choose your next employer.

3. Finally, and most importantly, use the "direct approach."

More than 50% of all job interviews are set up by the "direct approach." That means you actually send a resume and a cover letter to a company you think might be interested in employing your skills.

To whom do you write?

In general, you should write directly to the <u>exact</u> <u>name</u> of the person who would be hiring you: say, the vice-president of marketing or data processing. If you're in doubt about to whom to address the letter, address it to the president by name and he or she will make sure it gets forwarded to the right person within the company who has hiring authority in your area.

How do you find the names of potential employers?

You're not alone if you feel that the biggest problem in your job search is finding the right names at the companies you want to contact. But you can usually figure out the names of companies you want to approach by deciding first if your job hunt is primarily geography-driven or industry-driven.

In a geography-driven job hunt, you could select a list of, say, 50 companies you want to contact **by location** from the lists that the U.S. Chambers of Commerce publish yearly of their "major area employers." There are hundreds of local Chambers of Commerce across America, and most of them will have an 800 number which you can find through 1-800-555-1212. If you and your family think Atlanta, Dallas, Ft. Lauderdale, and Virginia Beach might be nice places to live, for example, you could contact the Chamber of Commerce in those cities and ask how you can obtain a copy of their list of major employers. Your nearest library will have the book which lists the addresses of all chambers.

In an industry-driven job hunt, and if you are willing to relocate, you will be identifying the companies which you find most attractive in the industry in which you want to work. When you select a list of companies to contact **by industry,** you can find the right person to write and the address of firms by industrial category in *Standard and Poor's, Moody's,* and other excellent books in public libraries. Many web sites also provide contact information.

Many people feel it's a good investment to actually call the company to either find out or double-check the name of the person to whom they want to send a resume and cover letter. It's important to do as much as you feasibly can to assure that the letter gets to the right person in the company.

At the end of Part One, you will find some advice about how to conduct library research and how to locate organizations to which you could send your resume.

What's the correct way to follow up on a resume you send?

There is a polite way to be aggressively interested in a company during your job hunt. It is ideal to end the cover letter accompanying your resume by saying "I hope you'll welcome my call next week when I try to arrange a brief meeting at your convenience to discuss your current and future needs and how I might serve them." Keep it low key, and just ask for a "brief meeting," not an interview. Employers want people who show a determined interest in working with them, so don't be shy about following up on the resume and cover letter you've mailed.

It pays to be aware of the 14 most common pitfalls for job hunters.

STEP THREE: Preparing for Interviews

But a resume and cover letter by themselves can't get you the job you want. You need to "prep" yourself before the interview. Step Three in your job campaign is "Preparing for Interviews." First, let's look at interviewing from the company's point of view.

What are the biggest "turnoffs" for companies?

One of the ways to help yourself perform well at an interview is to look at the main reasons why companies *don't* hire the people they interview, according to companies that do the interviewing.

Notice that "lack of appropriate background" (or lack of experience) is the *last* reason for not being offered the job.

The 14 Most Common Reasons Jobhunters Are Not Offered Jobs *(according to the companies who do the interviewing and hiring)*

1. Low level of accomplishment
2. Poor attitude, lack of self-confidence
3. Lack of goals/objectives
4. Lack of enthusiasm
5. Lack of interest in the company's business
6. Inability to sell or express yourself
7. Unrealistic salary demands
8. Poor appearance
9. Lack of maturity, no leadership potential
10. Lack of extracurricular activities
11. Lack of preparation for the interview, no knowledge about company
12. Objecting to travel
13. Excessive interest in security and benefits
14. Inappropriate background

Department of Labor studies since the 1950's have proven that smart, "prepared" job hunters can increase their beginning salary while getting a job in *half* the time it normally takes. (4½ months is the average national length of a job search.) Here, from PREP, are some questions that can prepare you to find a job faster.

Are you in the "right" frame of mind?

It seems unfair that we have to look for a job just when we're lowest in morale. Don't worry *too* much if you're nervous before interviews (Johnny Carson said he usually was, too!). You're supposed to be a little nervous, especially if the job means a lot to you. But the best way to kill unnecessary fears about job hunting is through 1) making sure you have a great resume and 2) preparing yourself for the interview. Here are three main areas you need to think about before each interview.

Do you know what the company does?

Don't walk into an interview giving the impression that, "If this is Tuesday, this must be General Motors."

Research the company before you go to interviews.

Find out before the interview what the company's main product or service is. Where is the company heading? Is it in a "growth" or declining industry? (Answers to these questions may influence whether or not you want to work there!)

Information about what the company does is in annual reports as well as newspaper and magazine articles. Just visit your nearest library and ask the reference librarian to guide you to materials on the company. Internet searches may also yield valuable information. At the end of Part One you will find many suggestions about how to research companies.

Do you know what you want to do for the company?

Before the interview, try to decide how you see yourself fitting into the company. Remember, "lack of exact background" the company wants is usually the <u>last</u> reason people are not offered jobs.

Understand before you go to each interview that the burden will be on you to "sell" the interviewer on why you're the best person for the job and the company.

How will you answer the critical interview questions?

Anticipate the questions you will be asked at the interview, and prepare your responses in advance.

Put yourself in the interviewer's position and think about the questions you're most likely to be asked. Here are some of the most commonly asked interview questions:

Q: "What are your greatest strengths?"
A: Don't say you've never thought about it! Go into an interview knowing the three main impressions you want to leave about yourself, such as "I'm hard-working, loyal, and an imaginative cost-cutter."

Q: "What are your greatest weaknesses?"
A: Don't confess that you're lazy or have trouble meeting deadlines! Confessing that you tend to be a "workaholic" or "tend to be a perfectionist and sometimes get frustrated when others don't share my high standards" will make your prospective employer see a "weakness" that he likes. Name a weakness that your interviewer will perceive as a strength.

Q: "What are your long-range goals?"
A: If you're interviewing with Microsoft, don't say you want to work for IBM in five years! Say your long-range goal is to be <u>with</u> the company, contributing to its goals and success.

Q: "What motivates you to do your best work?"
A: Don't get dollar signs in your eyes here! "A challenge" is not a bad answer, but it's a little cliched. Saying something like "troubleshooting" or "solving a tough problem" is more interesting and specific. Give an example if you can.

Q: "What do you know about this company?"

A: Don't say you never heard of it until they asked you to the interview! Name an interesting, positive thing you learned about the company recently from your research. Remember, company executives can sometimes feel rather "maternal" about the company they serve. Don't get onto a negative area of the company if you can think of positive facts you can bring up. Of course, if you learned in your research that the company's sales seem to be taking a nose-dive, or that the company president is being prosecuted for taking bribes, you might politely ask your interviewer to tell you something that could help you better understand what you've been reading. Those are the kinds of company facts that can help you determine whether you want to work there or not.

Go to an interview prepared to tell the company why it should hire you.

Q: "Why should I hire you?"

A: "I'm unemployed and available" is the wrong answer here! Get back to your strengths and say that you believe the organization could benefit by a loyal, hard-working cost-cutter like yourself.

In conclusion, you should decide in advance, before you go to the interview, how you will answer each of these commonly asked questions.

Have some practice interviews with a friend to role-play and build your confidence.

STEP FOUR: Handling the Interview and Negotiating Salary

A smile at an interview makes the employer perceive of you as intelligent!

Now you're ready for Step Four: actually handling the interview successfully and effectively. Remember, the purpose of an interview is to get a job offer.

Eight "do's" for the interview
According to leading U.S. companies, there are eight key areas in interviewing success. You can fail at an interview if you mishandle just one area.

1. *DO Wear Appropriate Clothes.*
   You can never go wrong by wearing a suit to an interview.

2. *DO Be Well Groomed.*
   Don't overlook the obvious things like having clean hair, clothes, and fingernails for the interview.

3. *DO Give a Firm Handshake.*
   You'll have to shake hands twice in most interviews: first, before you sit down, and second, when you leave the interview. Limp handshakes turn most people off.

4. *DO Smile and Show a Sense of Humor.*
   Interviewers are looking for people who would be nice to work with, so don't be so somber that you don't smile. In fact, research shows that people who smile at interviews are perceived as more intelligent. So, smile!

5. *DO Be Enthusiastic.*
   Employers tell PREP they are "turned off" by lifeless, unenthusiastic job hunters who show no special interest in that company. The best way to show some enthusiasm for the employer's operation is to find out about the business beforehand.

6. *DO Show You Are Flexible and Adaptable.*

An employer is looking for someone who can contribute to his organization in a flexible, adaptable way. No matter what skills and training you have, employers know every new employee must go through initiation and training on the company's turf. Certainly show pride in your past accomplishments in a specific, factual way ("I saved my last employer $50.00 a week by a new cost-cutting measure I developed"). But don't come across as though there's nothing about the job you couldn't easily handle.

7. *DO Ask Intelligent Questions about the Employer's Business.*

An employer is hiring someone because of certain business needs. Show interest in those needs. Asking questions to get a better idea of the employer's needs will help you "stand out" from other candidates interviewing for the job.

8. *DO "Take Charge" when the Interviewer "Falls Down" on the Job.*

Go into every interview knowing the three or four points about yourself you want the interviewer to remember. And be prepared to take an active part in leading the discussion if the interviewer's "canned approach" does not permit you to display your "strong suit." You can't always depend on the interviewer's asking you the "right" questions so you can stress your strengths and accomplishments.

Employers are seeking people with good attitudes whom they can train and coach to do things their way.

An important "don't"

Don't ask questions about salary or benefits at the first interview.

Employers don't take warmly to people who look at their organization as just a place to satisfy salary and benefit needs. Don't risk making a negative impression by appearing greedy or self-serving.

The place to discuss salary and benefits is normally at the second interview, and the employer will bring it up. Then you can ask any questions you like without appearing excessively interested in what the organization can do for you.

"Sell yourself" before talking salary

Make sure you've "sold" yourself before talking salary. First show you're the "best fit" for the employer and then you'll be in a stronger position from which to negotiate salary.

Interviewers sometimes throw out a salary figure at the first interview to see if you'll accept it. Don't commit yourself. You may be able to negotiate a better deal later on. Get back to finding out more about the job. This lets the interviewer know you're interested primarily in the job and not the salary.

Don't appear excessively interested in salary and benefits at the interview.

Now...negotiating your salary

You must avoid stating a "salary requirement" in your initial cover letter, and you must avoid even appearing **interested** in salary before you are offered the job.

Never bring up the subject of salary yourself. Employers say there's no way you can avoid looking greedy if you bring up the issue of salary and benefits before the company has identified you as its "best fit."

When the company brings up salary, it may say something like this: "Well, Mary, we think you'd make a good candidate for this job. What kind of salary are we talking about?"

Never name a number here, either. Give the ball back to the interviewer. Act as though you hadn't given the subject of salary much thought and respond something like this: "Ah, Mr. Jones, salary. . .well, I wonder if you'd be kind enough to tell me what salary you had in mind when you advertised the job?" Or ... "What is the range you have in mind?"

Don't worry, if the interviewer names a figure that you think is too low, you can say so without turning down the job or locking yourself into a rigid position. The point here is to negotiate for yourself as well as you can. You might reply to a number named by the interviewer that you think is low by saying something like this: "Well, Mr. Lee, the job interests me very much, and I think I'd certainly enjoy working with you. But, frankly, I was thinking of something a little higher than that." That leaves the ball in your interviewer's court again, and you haven't turned down the job, either, in case it turns out that the interviewer can't increase the offer and you still want the job.

Salary negotiation can be tricky.

Last, send a follow-up letter
Finally, send a letter right after the interview telling your interviewer you enjoyed the meeting and are certain (if you are) you are the "best fit" for the job.

Again, employers have a certain maternal attitude toward their companies, and they are looking for people who want to work for *that* company in particular.

A follow-up letter can help the employer choose between you and another qualified candidate.

The follow-up letter you send might be just the deciding factor in your favor if the employer is trying to choose between you and someone else.

A sample follow-up letter prepared for you by PREP is shown at the end of this section. Be sure to modify it according to your particular skills and interview situation.

And, finally, from all of us at PREP, best wishes in your job hunt and in all your future career endeavors. We hope we may have the pleasure of serving you as a customer in the future should you find yourself in a job hunt or in a career transition.

Company Information Available at Libraries
Figuring out the names of the organizations to which you want to mail your resume is part of any highly successful job campaign. Don't depend on just answering ads, waiting for the ideal job to appear in a newspaper or magazine. Aggressively seek out a job in the companies you want to work for. Here is some information which you can use in researching the names of organizations for which you might be interested in working.

Most libraries have a variety of information available on various organizations throughout the U.S. and worldwide. Most of these materials are only available for use in the reference room of the library, but some limited items may be checked out. Listed below are some of the major sources to look for, but be sure and check at the information desk to see if there are any books available on the specific types of companies you wish to investigate.

The Worldwide Chamber of Commerce Directory

Most chambers of commerce annually produce a "list of major employers" for their market area (or city). Usually the list includes the name, address, and telephone number of the employer along with information about the number of people employed, kinds of products and services produced, and a person to contact about employment. You can obtain the "list of major employers" in the city where you want to work by writing to that chamber. There is usually a small charge.

The *Worldwide Chamber of Commerce Directory* is an alphabetical listing of American and foreign chambers of commerce. It includes:

> All U.S. Chambers of Commerce (with addresses and phone numbers)
> American Chambers of Commerce abroad
> Canadian Chambers of Commerce
> Foreign Chambers of Commerce in principal cities worldwide
> Foreign Embassies and Consulates in the U.S.
> U.S. Consulates and Embassies throughout the world

Standard and Poor's Register of Corporations, Directors, and Executives

Standard and Poor's produce three volumes annually with information concerning over 77,000 American corporations. They are:

Volume I—**Corporations.** Here is an alphabetical listing of a variety of information for each of over 77,000 companies, including:
- name of company, address, telephone number
- names, titles, and functions of several key officers
- name of accounting firm, primary bank, and law firm
- stock exchange, description of products or services
- annual sales, number of employees
- division names and functions, subsidiary listings

Volume 2—**Directors and Executives.** This volume lists alphabetically over 70,000 officers, directors, partners, etc. by name. Information on each executive includes:
- principal business affiliation
- business address, residence address, year of birth
- college and year of graduation, fraternal affiliation

Volume 3—**Index.**

Moody's Manuals

Moody's Manuals provide information about companies traded on the New York and American Stock Exchanges and over the counter. They include:

Moody's Industrial Manual

Here, Moody's discusses detailed information on companies traded on the New York, American, and regional stock exchanges. The companies are listed alphabetically. Basic information about company addresses, phone numbers, and the names of key officers is available for each company listed. In addition, detailed information about the financial and operating data for each company is available. There are three levels of detail provided:

Complete Coverage. Companies in this section have the following information:
- *financial information* for the past 7 years (income accounts, balance sheets, financial and operating data).
- *detailed description of the company's business* including a complete list of subsidiaries and office and property sites.
- *capital structure information,* which includes details on capital stock and long-term debt, with bond and preferred stock ratings and 2 years of stock and bond price ranges.
- *extensive presentation of the company's last annual report.*

Full Measure Coverage. Information on companies in this section includes:
- *financial information for the past 7 years* (income accounts, balance sheets, financial and operating data).
- *detailed description of company's business,* with a complete list of subsidiaries and plant and property locations.
- *capital structure information,* with details on capital stock and long term debt, with bond and preferred stock ratings and 2 years of stock and bond price changes.

Comprehensive Coverage. Information on companies in this section includes:
- *5 years of financial information* on income accounts, balance sheets, and financial and operating ratios.
- *detailed description of company's business,* including subsidiaries.
- *concise capital structure information,* including capital stock and long term debts, bond and preferred stock ratings.

Moody's OTC Manual
Here is information on U.S. firms which are unlisted on national and regional stock exchanges. There are three levels of coverage: complete, full measure, and comprehensive (same as described above). Other Moody's manuals include: *Moody's Public Utility Manual, Moody's Municipal and Government Manual,* and *Moody's Bank and Finance Manual.*

Dun's Million Dollar Directory
Three separate listings (alphabetical, geographic, and by products) of over 120,000 U.S. firms. There are three volumes:
Volume 1—The 45,000 largest companies, net worth over $500,000
Volume 2—The 37,000 next largest companies
Volume 3—The 37,000 next largest companies

U.S. industrial directories
Ask your librarian to guide you to your library's collection of industrial directories. Almost every state produces a manufacturing directory, for example, and many libraries maintain complete collections of these directories. You may find information on products and the addresses and telephone numbers of industrial companies.

Thomas' Register of Manufacturers
16 volumes of information about manufacturing companies.
Volumes 1-8—Alphabetical listing by product.

Volumes 9-10—Alphabetical listing of manufacturing company names, addresses, telephone numbers, and local offices.
Volumes 11-16—Alphabetical company catalog information.

Information About Foreign Companies
If you'd like your next job to be overseas or with an international company, you can find much helpful information in the library. You approach these companies in the same way as you would approach U.S.-based companies.

Directory of Foreign Manufacturers in the U.S.
Alphabetical listing of U.S. manufacturing companies which are owned and operated by parent foreign firms. The information provided includes the name and address of the U.S. firm, the name and address of the foreign parent firm, and the products produced.

Directory of American Firms Operating in Foreign Countries
Alphabetical listing of the names, addresses, chief officers, products, and country operated in of U.S. firms abroad.

International Firms Directory
This lists foreign corporations.

Hoover's Handbook of World Business
This lists corporations in Asia and Europe.

Principal International Businesses
This is a comprehensive directory of international businesses.

Information Available From The Internet
Information about companies is also available through the Internet. You can use all the search engines to help you in your search for company information and company website addresses.

Date

Exact Name of Person
Title or Position
Name of Company
Address (number and street)
Address (city, state, and zip)

Dear Exact Name:

I am writing to express my appreciation for the time you spent with me on 9 December, and I want to let you know that I am sincerely interested in the position of Controller which you described.

I feel confident that I could skillfully interact with your 60-person work force in order to obtain the information we need to assure expert controllership of your diversified interests, and I would cheerfully travel as your needs require. I want you to know, too, that I would not consider relocating to Salt Lake City to be a hardship! It is certainly one of the most beautiful areas I have ever seen.

As you described to me what you are looking for in a controller, I had a sense of "déjà vu" because my current boss was in a similar position when I went to work for him. He needed someone to come in and be his "right arm" and take on an increasing amount of his management responsibilities so that he could be freed up to do other things. I have played a key role in the growth and profitability of his multi-unit business, and he has come to depend on my sound financial and business advice as much as my day-to-day management skills. Since Christmas is the busiest time of the year in the restaurant business, I feel that I could not leave him during that time. I could certainly make myself available by mid-January.

If you felt you needed me to work with you during my vacation from the 26th until I go back to handle the New Year's business on the 29th, I would be happy to work with you as you close the books and handle end-of-year matters. Please note that I will be out of town from Saturday 19th until Monday 22nd visiting relatives.

It would be a pleasure to work for a successful individual such as yourself, and I feel I could contribute significantly to your business not only through my accounting and business background but also through my strong qualities of loyalty, reliability, and trustworthiness. I am confident that I could learn Quick Books rapidly, and I would welcome being trained to do things your way. I send best wishes for the holidays, and I'd like to send a special compliment to your wife for the delicious cookies she baked!

Yours sincerely,

Jacob Evangelisto

Follow-up Letter

A great follow-up letter can motivate the employer to make the job offer, and the salary offer may be influenced by the style and tone of your follow-up letter, too!

PART TWO
JUNIOR
MANAGERS

In this section, you will find resumes and cover letters of junior managers. How does a junior manager differ from the managers in the other sections of this book? In general, junior managers have less experience, manage fewer people, and handle less responsibility than the managers in the other sections of this book. However, many of the junior managers shown in this section have shouldered extensive responsibility. Therefore, whether to show a resume in the Mid-Level Managers' Section or the Junior Managers' Section was frequently a judgment call by the editor.

Junior managers have advantages over more experienced managers.
In a job hunt, junior managers often have an advantage over their more experienced counterparts. Junior managers have usually not made a 15-year commitment to an industry or type of work, so prospective employers often view them as "more trainable" and "more coachable" than their seniors. This makes it easier for the junior manager to "change careers" and transfer skills to other industries.

Junior managers have disadvantages compared to their seniors.
Almost by definition, the junior manager is less tested and less experienced than senior or mid-level managers, so the resume and cover letter of the junior manager may often have to "sell" his or her potential to do something he or she has never done before. Lack of experience in the field she wants to enter can be a stumbling block to the junior manager, but remember that many employers believe that someone who has excelled in one field can excel in many other fields.

Junior Managers are often still experimenting in their careers, and they have more freedom than older job hunters to try new fields and change careers. They are not "locked in" to their career of choice.

Some advice to junior managers...
If senior managers could give junior managers a piece of advice about careers, here's what they would say: Manage your career and don't stumble from job to job in an incoherent pattern. Try to find work that interests you, and then identify prosperous industries which need work performed of the type you want to do. Learn early in your working life that a great resume and cover letter can blow doors open for you and help you maximize your salary.

Date

Exact Name of Person
Exact Title
Exact Name of Company
Address
City, State, Zip

Dear Exact Name of Person (or Dear Sir or Madam if answering a blind ad):

Notice the fourth paragraph. In a gracious way, this junior professional is announcing her desire to become a part of an organization which will use her in sales management roles. Here's a tip about employers: they like people who know what they want to do, because if you are in a job doing what you want to do, you are more likely to excel — and make money for the company.

I would appreciate an opportunity to talk with you soon about how I could contribute to your organization through my demonstrated skills in sales management as well as my exceptional communication, organizational, and time management abilities.

As you will see from my enclosed resume, I am presently excelling as a Corporate Account Manager with Quality Rent-a-Car. When I assumed responsibility for corporate accounts, monthly sales were an average of $27,000. Due to my initiative in developing new accounts and maximizing existing accounts, sales have risen to $98,000 per month, and I have received numerous awards for sales excellence.

Joining this national company three weeks after graduating from college, I quickly mastered all aspects of branch management, customer service, sales, and administration during the management training program. As Assistant Branch Manager, I was the top seller in the region in both outside and inside sales, and my branch was the top office in the region in Customer Satisfaction scores. In addition, two employees whom I trained were promoted through two levels of advancement, to Assistant Branch Manager positions. Since joining this company, I have earned a reputation as a talented and articulate sales professional with strong managerial abilities.

Although I am highly respected in my present job and achieving results in all areas of performance, I feel that my abilities would be better utilized in a sales management role than in the administrative positions for which Quality is grooming me.

If you can use an intelligent, enthusiastic, and results-oriented professional, I hope you will contact me to suggest a time when we might meet to discuss your needs. I can assure you in advance that I could rapidly become an asset to your organization.

Sincerely,

Elizabeth Hyland

ELIZABETH HYLAND

1110½ Hay Street, Fayetteville, NC 28305 • preppub@aol.com • (910) 483-6611

OBJECTIVE	To benefit an organization that can use an articulate young sales and management professional with exceptional communication, time management, and organizational skills and a background in multi-unit sales management and staff development.
EDUCATION	B.S., Psychology and Business Administration, University of Las Vegas, 1994.

- Maintained a cumulative 3.5 GPA while working 30 hours per week and completing this rigorous degree program in three years.
- Was elected Panhellenic Chairwoman (1993) and Pledge Class Vice President (1991), Psi Alpha chapter of Chi Omega Sorority.
- Played first-string goalie on women's water polo team (1992-94); participated on the PSU women's cross country team (1993); counseled a special needs child with Tourette's Syndrome (1992); placed 2nd in a scholarship pageant.

EXPERIENCE

Am advancing in a track record of promotion with Quality Rent-a-Car (1995-present):

CORPORATE ACCOUNT MANAGER. Las Vegas, NV (1997-present). Design and sell corporate account programs to business and government clients; increased monthly sales to $160,000 from $45,000 since taking over corporate accounts for this 12-store area.

- Provide government and private industry representatives with information on the advantages of a corporate rental car program in their travel plans.
- Generate business through a combination of client visits and employee referrals.
- Prepare and submit bids used in obtaining federal, state, and local government contracted business from 12 rental car offices throughout Nevada.
- Created and implemented a corporate business training manual; responsible for all corporate training for 52 current employees and new hires.
- Organize and coordinate corporate presence at events such as corporate trade shows, business expos, and career fairs.
- Was recognized with the **Employee Excellence Award** in December 1999.
- Received the **#1 Corporate Class Performance Award** for the western region in March 1999.

ASSISTANT BRANCH MANAGER. Tempe, AZ (1996-97). Set sales records in several areas while also supervising a staff of four full-time and three part-time employees.

- Earned recognition as "Top Seller" in both inside and outside sales for the Arizona region and established the highest number of corporate accounts of any manager in the area.
- Trained and motivated manager trainees in daily branch rental business.
- Managed and collected branch receivables and vehicle repossessions.
- Devised a new method for the reservations process which streamlined branch operations and increased productivity.
- Provided exceptional customer service which enabled the branch to place first in customer satisfaction scores for the region in 1997.

MANAGEMENT TRAINEE. Monterey, CA (1995-96). Mastered all aspects of branch office management, customer service, sales, and administration; achieved sales in the top 5% of my training groups.

- Orchestrated a branch delivery service project which involved a staff of 12 and 225 vehicles.

PERSONAL

Affiliations and professional memberships include the Las Vegas Chamber of Commerce, Las Vegas Business Network, and National Defense Transportation Association. Excellent personal and professional references on request.

Exact Name of Person
Title or Position
Name of Company
Address (number and street)
Address (city, state, and zip)

Accounting Manager

Dear Exact Name of Person: (or Dear Sir or Madam if answering a blind ad.)

This is a young professional who had advanced to an accounting position with the Army and Air Force Exchange Service in Germany. She left her great job because her husband got transferred. Now she is in a small town where accounting jobs are not plentiful. PREP tried to make her resume and cover letter as versatile as possible since she may have to take a job outside her accounting field.

With the enclosed resume, I would like to make you aware of my strong accounting, office management, and finance experience as well as my desire to put my expertise to work within your organization.

With a background which includes knowledge of numerous software programs as well as experience in both retail and industrial accounting, I have become known as a versatile and adaptable young professional. As you will see from my enclosed resume, my most recent experience was as an Accounting Manager for the Army and Air Force Exchange System (AAFES), the retail store system which supports military personnel and families throughout the world. After receiving several performance awards as a Lead Accounting Clerk, I was promoted ahead of older and more experienced personnel to supervise 52 employees and provide financial advice, guidance, and support for 105 facilities.

My husband has recently resigned from military service, and we are making our permanent home in Bessemer, Oregon, where he grew up and where most of his family lives. I am eager to make Bessemer my personal and professional home, too. A dedicated hard worker known for attention to detail and unflagging commitment to excellence, I can provide outstanding references. It is my hope that I can find an employer to whom I can make a long-term contribution.

I hope you will welcome my call soon to arrange a brief meeting to discuss your current and future needs and how I might serve them. Thank you in advance for your time.

Sincerely,

Orietta Hallock

ORIETTA HALLOCK

1110½ Hay Street, Fayetteville, NC 28305 • preppub@aol.com • (910) 483-6611

OBJECTIVE   To offer a reputation as a highly knowledgeable and dedicated manager with expertise in finance and accounting to an organization which can benefit from my attention to detail, initiative, enthusiasm, and dedication to excellence.

EDUCATION   Completed schooling in Germany which is the equivalent of two years of college coursework in the U.S., 1989-91.

Earned certification as a commercial employee in a two-year apprenticeship program with a concentration in economics and social studies, Chamber of Industry and Commerce, Wuerzburg and Schweinfurt, Germany, 1993.

EXPERIENCE   *Advanced to a managerial role in an international organization, AAFES (the Army and Air Force Exchange System), based on my knowledge, skills, and abilities, Wuerzburg, Germany:*

ACCOUNTING MANAGER. (1997-99). Officially evaluated as a key player in the implementation of new programs and consolidation of support facilities, was promoted to this job supervising 52 employees in March 1997 ahead of more experienced employees.

- Provided financial advice and guidance to 105 facilities while inspecting and balancing their accounts as well as reconciling accounts payable and receivable.
- Earned praise for my attention to detail and time management skills while handling the hiring and training of personnel for a new accounting office at an outlying site.
- Attended corporate-sponsored workshops on subjects which included EEO (Equal Employment Opportunity) for managers and how to deal with a diverse work force.
- Was recognized with a second "Sustained Superior Accomplishment Award" for my role in implementing and supervising four accounting offices.

LEAD ACCOUNTING CLERK. (1992-97). During a period of rapid change due to military post closings and the consolidation of many services, earned several superior service awards in recognition of my support for a multimillion-dollar retail store and 105 additional stores.

- Became aware of problems in the Purchase-in-Transit procedures which led to their identification by the national headquarters and resulted in their revamping.
- Received a "Sustained Superior Accomplishment Award" as well as Service and Excellence Awards in recognition of my professionalism, sound judgment, and five years of devoted service.

Began as a student apprentice and was hired on a permanent basis by Weifenbach of Germany, a mechanical engineering company:

PAYROLL AND ACCOUNTING SPECIALIST. (1991). Assigned to the payroll office to assist in payroll and direct labor cost accounting, used automated data processing systems while adjusting differences using the attendance lists and production figures to find and correct discrepancies.

- Learned procedures for calculating large corporation payroll and labor costs.
- **INTERN.** (1989-91). Excelled in a training program which acquainted me with the inner workings of every type of commercial business in a large industrial firm from purchasing, to operations, to sales, to financial control.

PERSONAL   Bilingual in German and English. Supportive and concerned manager.

Date

Mr. George Brown
Senior Vice President
First Union National Bank
2391 Augusta Street SW
Atlanta, Georgia 89012

Dear Mr. Brown:

I would appreciate an opportunity to talk with you soon about my strong interest in receiving consideration for the position of Public Relations Manager. I believe I offer the enthusiasm, talent, and knowledge that make me a professional who can make important contributions to First Union National Bank in this area.

As you will see from my enclosed resume, I am presently a Client Services Manager who consistently places at the top of my peer group in internal performance evaluations. I rapidly advanced from Administrative Assistant in the consumer banking department, gained experience as a Teller, and then advanced to this position where I represent the bank while opening new accounts and selling bank products to our clients. While excelling in my full-time positions, I have worked hard in my spare time to complete my college degree.

My ability to develop interesting and informative written materials was discovered in high school when I edited the yearbook. While attending Peace College in Raleigh for my first two years of studies, I was selected to edit the college yearbook and was credited with producing an attractive and well-organized publication. I went on to earn a degree in Mass Communications from the University of North Carolina at Charlotte where I wrote for the college newspaper. I have become involved in the Junior League and am now serving this organization as the Public Relations chairman in a role which includes preparing all newspaper releases about the organization and its civic activities.

I believe that through my enthusiasm, experience, and talent I can make valuable contributions in preparing products which will enhance the bank's ability to sell services to the public and gain new clients through informative and interesting written materials.

I hope you will call or write me soon to suggest a time convenient for us to discuss how I would fit into the bank's public relations efforts and how I might continue to serve most effectively. Thank you in advance for your time.

Sincerely,

Kerry Zaeske

KERRY ZAESKE

1110½ Hay Street, Fayetteville, NC 28305 • preppub@aol.com • (910) 483-6611

OBJECTIVE	To benefit an organization through my dynamic personality and strong communication skills, my sophisticated understanding of banking services, my background in mass communications and public relations, as well as my ability to effectively market ideas, services, and products.

EDUCATION

B.S. in Mass Communications, University of North Carolina at Charlotte, NC, 1997.
- Completed this degree in my spare time while excelling in my full-time job.
- Maintained a cumulative GPA of above 3.5.
- Wrote interesting and informative articles for the college newspaper.

Attended Peace College, Raleigh, NC, for my first two years of basic studies in the Liberal Arts.
- Selected by faculty advisors to edit the college yearbook during my sophomore year, applied my communication skills and creativity to write copy for and produce a well-organized and attractive publication.

EXPERIENCE

CLIENT SERVICES MANAGER. First Union National Bank, Charlotte, NC (1995-present). After a short time as an Administrative Assistant in the consumer banking department, received training as a Teller and was then selected for the bank's Financial Management Development Training Program; subsequently advanced to this key role which involves extensive public relations as I communicate the bank's products and services.
- Have become skilled at understanding people's financial needs and requirements in order to recommend products such as Certificates of Deposit, MasterCard and VISA credit cards, savings accounts, equity lines, and investment instruments.
- Consistently place at the top of my peer group within the region according to the bank's system of internal performance ratings.

SALES REPRESENTATIVE. Carlyle & Co., Charlotte, NC (1994-1995). Consistently met aggressive sales goals through both my patience and persistence in public relations and customer service; became known as a goal-driven, skilled professional who could be counted on to always deliver customer satisfaction.

ADMINISTRATIVE ASSISTANT. First Union National Bank, Charlotte, NC (1993-94). Gained valuable experience in banking procedures and all phases of the loan process while providing clerical and administrative support to two regional vice presidents specializing in the area of consumer credit.
- Used my talent for organization and attention to detail while creating spreadsheets, coordinating word processing support, and maintaining files for two busy executives.
- Improved the filing system for increased efficiency.
- Refined my communication skills dealing with banking professionals on a regular basis.
- Advanced my knowledge of computer operations using Word, WordPerfect, Lotus, and Excel software while preparing correspondence and handling financial record keeping.

LEGAL OFFICE INTERN. Office of the District Attorney, Charlotte, NC (1990-92). Gained valuable exposure to the legal system while aiding assistant district attorneys in activities which included contacting witnesses to remind them of court appearances; became familiar with legal procedures while working with a wide range of elected officials.
- Wrote guilty pleas; advised people pleading "guilty" about how to respond to questioning.
- Earned a reputation for the maturity and judgment I displayed while relating to a variety of people from all socio-economic and age groups.

PERSONAL

Single; will cheerfully relocate. Am an articulate speaker and skilled writer. Offer a creative and enthusiastic approach to project development and the organizational skills to see them to completion. Enjoy dealing with the public and making contributions to my community.

Date

Exact Name of Person
Title or Position
Name of Company
Address (no., street)
Address (city, state, zip)

Bookstore Assistant Manager

This junior professional likes bookselling, but the resume and cover letter are designed so that he can seek employment in a wide range of industries. The skills ("communication and organizational skills") and the knowledge of "purchasing, financial management, and inventory control" which he mentions in his Objective are transferrable to many fields. As a general rule, it's best to keep the Objective on your resume versatile and all-purpose.

Dear Exact Name of Person: (or Dear Sir or Madam if answering a blind ad.)

I would appreciate an opportunity to talk with you soon about how I could contribute to your organization through my purchasing, financial management, and inventory control experience, along with my excellent public relations and writing skills.

As you will see from my resume, I excelled in the business administration program at Mercer University, graduating *cum laude.* My coursework emphasized personnel, financial, and production management in addition to business policy and strategic planning.

You would find me to be an organized, results-oriented professional who works well with others and who also has a special knack for working with numbers. I sincerely enjoy contributing to my employer's "bottom line."

I hope you will welcome my call soon to arrange a brief meeting at your convenience to discuss your current and future needs and how I might serve them. Thank you in advance for your consideration.

Sincerely yours,

Larry Bass

Alternate last paragraph:
I hope you will call or write me soon to suggest a time convenient for us to meet and discuss your current and future needs and how I might best serve them. Thank you in advance for your time.

LARRY BASS

1110½ Hay Street, Fayetteville, NC 28305 • preppub@aol.com • (910) 483-6611

OBJECTIVE

To benefit an organization through my purchasing, financial management, and inventory experience along with my excellent communication and organizational skills.

EDUCATION

B.S. in Business Administration/Finance, Mercer University, Mercer, GA, 1994.
- Completed a rigorous degree program in 3 1/2 years with a 3.33 GPA, graduating *cum laude*.
- Awarded a **Certificate of Achievement** for maintaining an exceptional standard of scholarship.

EXPERIENCE

ASSISTANT STORE MANAGER. Waldenbooks, Atlanta, GA (1991-present).
In this fast-paced position, conducted day-to-day financial transactions and supervised up to 10 employees at one of the nation's largest retail booksellers.
- Responsible for store operations, including loss prevention, in-store audits, cash handling and reconciliation.
- Assisted with setup and opening of new stores.
- Developed an effective style in dealing fairly and patiently with the public in both sales and customer relations.
- Acquired skills in marketing, merchandising displays, and personnel administration.
- Gained professional poise while learning to use my time effectively.

MERCHANDISE MANAGER. Dress to the Nines, Atlanta, GA (1989-91).
Played a key role in the setup and opening of this popular retail clothing store.
- Gained valuable "hands-on" experience in business administration, cash flow, and inventory control management.
- Supervised up to eight employees in planning and executing daily operations.
- Acquired skills in clothing merchandising and marketing.

RETAIL MANAGER. Paper Peddler, Burlington, VT (1986-1988).
Supervised day staff and managed inventory while developing a loyal clientele for this retail business.
- Assisted management in most facets of branch operation.
- Applied my creative design skills in developing decorations for both individual customers and business promotions.
- Gained valuable skills in buying, ordering, and merchandising store product.

MANAGER'S AIDE. Shed House, South Burlington, VT (1986).
With little or no supervision, handled numerous details in the daily operations of this retail business; supervised and managed a small staff of 3 to 4 people.
- Handled cash transactions; responsible for daily bank deposits and drawer reconciliations.

Highlights of other experience:
- Tutor, Pine Ridge School, Williston, VT (1985). Created and used lesson plans to teach three dyslexic children.
- Special events volunteer, Chittenden County United Way, Burlington, VT (1988). Refined my public relations and communication planning and coordinating special events.

COMPUTERS

Have experience with Word, Lotus 1-2-3, and WordPerfect software programs.

PERSONAL

Am a self-directed innovative thinker with high personal and professional standards. Work well under pressure and enjoy working closely with others to achieve a common goal.

Date

Exact Name of Person
Title or Position
Name of Company
Address (no., street)
Address (city, state, zip)

**Grocery Store Manager &
Department Manager**

Notice the aggressive and dynamic
first sentence of his cover letter.
What employer couldn't use an
employee who could improve sales
and profitability? Also notice the
similar nature of the Objective on
his resume. It is specific without
"nailing him down" to a particular
industry. (He is actually seeking a
change from grocery retailing.)

Dear Exact Name of Person: (or Dear Sir or Madam if answering a blind ad.)

Can you use a hard-working professional who offers a track record of promotion based on accomplishments in increasing sales, boosting productivity, improving morale, reducing costs, lowering employee turnover, improving merchandising, and strengthening customer service?

As you will see when you look over my enclosed resume, I gained expertise in most aspects of retailing and business management while excelling in a history of promotion with the Winn-Dixie Corporation at locations in North Carolina and Georgia. I can say proudly, but without boasting, that I have increased sales in every job I have ever held, from department manager to store co-manager. In my most recent job with Winn-Dixie I was promoted from co-manager of a $135,000 weekly store to co-manage a store with weekly revenues of $285,000. In three separate jobs as a Department Manager, I either doubled or tripled weekly sales by implementing new training programs coupled with prudent inventory ordering and control techniques.

I offer a strong working knowledge of computers and cash registers, and I have utilized computerized inventory ordering and control systems. I believe I offer a talent, refined by experience, for retailing and operations management. I can provide excellent personal and professional references, and I offer a reputation as a tactful and sensitive communicator who is skilled at solving customer, employee, and vendor problems.

I hope you will welcome my call next week when I try to arrange a brief meeting at your convenience to discuss your needs and goals and how I might help you fulfill them. Thank you in advance for your time.

Sincerely,

Walter King

Alternate last paragraph:
I hope you will call or write me soon to suggest a time when we might meet to discuss your needs and goals and how I might serve them. Thank you in advance for your time.

WALTER KING

1110½ Hay Street, Fayetteville, NC 28305 • preppub@aol.com • (910) 483-6611

OBJECTIVE

To contribute to the profitability and growth of a company that can use a skilled manager who offers a track record of accomplished results related to increasing sales, reducing employee turnover, boosting productivity, cutting costs, and improving merchandising.

EXPERIENCE

DEPARTMENT MANAGER. Kroger Sav-On, Raleigh, NC (1999-present). After relocating to NC to be closer to my ailing father, took a job supervising a three-person produce department; instituted changes in ordering, buying, stocking, and merchandising that led to a $2,000 weekly increase in sales and made my department the second most profitable of its kind within the chain.
- Am applying my skill in adjusting buying patterns according to local supply and demand.
- Have established excellent relationships with local customers and vendors.

Excelled in the following pattern of promotion and advancement within the Winn-Dixie Corporation, GA and NC (1980-99).
STORE CO-MANAGER. Atlanta, GA (1995-99). Shared management responsibilities of a 100-employee store; was credited with increasing store sales and developing an internal working environment that reduced friction between labor and management, resulting in lower employee turnover, better morale, and higher productivity.
- Was promoted to co-manager of a store grossing $285,000 weekly after excelling as the co-manager of a store grossing $135,000 weekly in another Atlanta location.
- Personally oversaw all aspects of customer relations, employee relations, and vendor relations; became known for my sensitive and tactful communication style.
- Hired, trained, and scheduled all employees; monitored planning, ordering, receiving, stocking, displaying, and rotation as well as cashiering, bookkeeping, and payroll administration.

STORE CO-MANAGER. Atlanta, GA (1992-95). Was promoted to the job above after solving numerous inventory control problems caused by customer and employee theft at this 60-person store; was selected for this job because of my proven ability to troubleshoot internal problems.

ASSISTANT MANAGER. Atlanta, GA (1991-92). Oversaw these areas in a 60-person store: cashiering, budgeting/bookkeeping, receiving/stocking, and organizing and training a crew.
- In a store with few operational problems, developed and implemented a more in-depth training program which improved employee skills and strengthened customer service.

DEPARTMENT MANAGER. Stone Mountain, GA (1990-91). Took over management of a four-person dairy/frozen food department and increased sales from $14,000 weekly to $45,000 weekly in just six months; hired and trained new employees.
- From hands-on experience, learned the sensitivity of sales to proper display.

DEPARTMENT MANAGER. Raleigh, NC (1988-90). Shouldered a heavy workload at this fast-growing Winn-Dixie; doubled weekly sales from $9,000 to $19,000 while managing four people.

Other Winn-Dixie experience: At Winn-Dixies in GA and NC, was trained in grocery, dairy, seafood, deli, frozen foods, produce, cashiering, and bookkeeping.

TRAINING

Graduated from Alpharetta High School in Alpharetta; have completed numerous training courses sponsored by Winn-Dixie related to management, supervision, and retailing.

PERSONAL

Believe I offer a knack, refined by experience, for retailing and operations management. Offer a strong working knowledge of computers and cash registers. Have utilized the MSI ordering system. Can provide excellent personal and professional references.

Date

Exact Name of Person
Title or Position
Name of Company
Address (number and street)
Address (city, state, and zip)

This junior manager gained some
experience in the broadcasting
industry after college graduation.
Now she seeks to transfer her
skills and knowledge to the
corporate world. Notice the Skills
Section on her resume. Do you see
the "environmental issues and
trends" bullet? The environmental
industry is where she wants
to work, so she is making a
subtle "pitch" in this bullet.

Dear Exact Name of Person: (or Dear Sir or Madam if answering a blind ad.)

With this letter, I would like to make you aware of my skills related to corporate communications and media liaison. Please consider this letter and my accompanying resume as a formal expression of my interest in utilizing my talents for the benefit of your organization.

As you will see from my enclosed resume, I offer a background in broadcasting which includes working as a news director, reporter, and public affairs producer. Through that experience, I have learned how to prepare press kits and publicity materials that attract media attention, and I offer a proven ability to communicate technical information in a way the public can understand. As a Reporter with Tar Heel Broadcasting, I have developed stories about environmental issues which sparked the public's interest in saving natural resources and which responded to public fears about a proposed new incinerator. Although I have excelled in a track record of promotion with Tar Heel Broadcasting and am being groomed for further promotion in my current job as Assistant News Director, I am interested in transferring my knowledge and talents to the corporate sector. I am certain that my broadcasting industry background could be very helpful to an organization seeking to improve its public image and aggressively pursue positive media relations.

I hope you will welcome my call soon to arrange a brief meeting at your convenience to discuss your current and future needs and how I might serve them. With a reputation as a dynamic communicator and skillful writer, I can provide outstanding personal and professional references at the appropriate time. Thank you in advance for your time.

Sincerely yours.

Lynette Underwood

Alternate last paragraph:
I hope you will call or write me soon to suggest a time convenient for us to meet and discuss your current and future needs and how I might serve them. Thank you in advance for your time.

LYNETTE UNDERWOOD

1110½ Hay Street, Fayetteville, NC 28305 • preppub@aol.com • (910) 483-6611

OBJECTIVE   I want to contribute to the public relations image and activities of an organization that can use an experienced young news reporter who offers an excellent understanding of the media and how companies can maximize media relations.

EDUCATION   **Bachelor of Science** degree in English with a minor in Journalism, N.C. State University, Raleigh, NC; 1988.
- Staff writer for *The Technician*, NC State University.

Studied English, Atlantic Christian College, Wilson, NC; 1984-86.
- Copywriter for *The Pineknot*, Atlantic Christian College Annual.

SKILLS
- Offer the ability to prepare publicity materials and press kits.
- Knowledgeable of how to write press releases, public service announcements, as well as feature, news, and sports articles for publication and broadcast.
- Knowledgeable of environmental issues and trends.
- Familiar with the Associated Press (AP) News Desk and the AP database.
- Have earned a reputation as a creative professional with a knack for making complex issues understandable to the public.
- Skilled in video, writing, and production.

EXPERIENCE   **ASSISTANT NEWS DIRECTOR**. Tar Heel Broadcasting, Raleigh, NC (1993-present). Was promoted to this job after excelling as a reporter, and am in charge of making assignments for a three-person staff in the news room of this radio station; handle numerous administrative responsibilities related to maintaining the news room's productivity and efficiency.
- As a **Reporter**, cover local government and other issues.
- Am respected for my skills in identifying, researching, and developing interesting stories.
- Have learned how to manage a news operation.
- Have covered a wide variety of environmental issues.

REPORTER. Tar Heel Broadcasting, Raleigh, NC (1989-93). Sharpened my creative writing skills and interpersonal/interviewing abilities in building news beats.
- Covered county/community issues; developed stories about education and environmental issues for use in regular newscasts; generated much public awareness/discussion based on stories I produced on saving natural resources and a proposal for a new incinerator.
- Anchored and occasionally produced special reports on a wide range of issues of local interest.

REPORTER/NEWS DIRECTOR. WCEC-AM, Rocky Mount, NC (1988-89). Was solely responsible for local news production and anchoring.
- Through my hard work and initiative, greatly strengthened this station's coverage of local government issues, educational matters, and spot news events.
- Was commended for my soothing voice and professional manner of delivering the news.

NEWS ASSISTANT and **PUBLIC AFFAIRS PRODUCER**. WTRG-FM, Raleigh, NC (1987-88). Developed and produced stories of local interest to morning news casts.
- Originated the concept for and produced a weekly public affairs show focusing on issues in the station's city of license.

PERSONAL   Offer excellent interpersonal skills which have helped me build solid working relationships with government officials, politicians, business people, and citizens. Have developed an easy-going style of interviewing people. Excellent references.

Administrator
Muncy Medical Center
P.O. Box 449
Muncy, IN 89053

Medical Accounts Manager

Dear Sir or Madam:

In the first job on her resume, her skills are shown with a functional emphasis. Even though her previous jobs were not in the medical field, she shows her work experience without gaps. Don't leave off experience which you feel is unrelated. The employer is curious about all of your work experience. (The general rule is that you should go back at least ten years.)

I would appreciate an opportunity to talk with you soon about how I could contribute to your organization through my experience in the area of medical accounts management.

As you will see from my resume, I currently handle accounting and data entry for a company which has recently computerized its operations while experiencing a 20% growth in patient volume. I am skilled at accounts receivable/payable, billing/collections, insurance liaison, data entry, and customer service within a medical environment.

In previous jobs I excelled in a field dominated by fire and rescue professionals. I started out as a Fire Dispatch Operator for the City of Raleigh and was promoted to Telecommunications Supervisor of Wake County's Emergency Operation Center based on strong work performance and professional recommendations. A hard-working and highly motivated individual, I am always seeking to refine my skills and knowledge. I am certified as an Emergency Medical Technician and trained to provide CPR and other medical support.

You would find me to be a dedicated person who would pride myself on contributing to your goals and objectives. I can provide outstanding personal and professional references.

I hope you will call or write me soon to suggest a time convenient for us to meet and discuss your current and future needs and how I might best serve them. Thank you in advance for your time.

Sincerely yours,

Katie Eubanks

KATIE EUBANKS

1110½ Hay Street, Fayetteville, NC 28305 • preppub@aol.com • (910) 483-6611

OBJECTIVE

To contribute to an organization that can use a well-organized young professional who offers outstanding medical accounts management skills along with extensive data entry experience and expert understanding of medical terminology.

EXPERIENCE

MEDICAL ACCOUNTS MANAGER. U.S. Health Services, Raleigh, NC (1995-present). While balancing accounts totaling $190,000 monthly, mastered new computerized accounting procedures as the company expanded to a new automated accounting and billing system; continuously increased my efficiency as patient volume increased by 20%.
- *Accounts receivable:* Receive and post payments to patients' accounts.
- *Accounts payable*: Prepare a wide range of bills for companies and individuals.
- *Billing/collections*: Bill more than 150 patients monthly; follow up on past due accounts.
- *Insurance billing*: Prepare paperwork for Medicare, Medicaid, and commercial companies for insurance billing purposes.
- *Data entry*: Perform data entry for hundreds of accounts which require numerous entries weekly.
- *Customer service/public relations*: Have earned a reputation as a hard-working professional with a cheerful disposition and a helpful attitude toward the public.

TELECOMMUNICATIONS SUPERVISOR III. Wake County Emergency Operation Center, Raleigh, NC (1987-95). Was promoted to this job because of my excellent performance in the job below; was commended for remaining calm in emergencies and for my ability to soothe people in stressful situations while supervising the Emergency Operation Center.
- At a time when the emergency dispatch field was dominated by fire and rescue professionals, became a respected supervisor because of my significant contributions to the city/county when they were enhancing their 911 system.
- Monitored electronic telecommunications equipment; maintained detailed dispatch records for all emergency response.

FIRE DISPATCH OPERATOR. City of Raleigh Fire Department, Raleigh, NC (1985-87). Learned to operate complex communications equipment and acquired transcriptionist skills while monitoring multi-channel fire and rescue dispatch equipment.
- Made decisions about appropriate equipment to dispatch to emergencies.
- Received a Letter of Congratulations from the Chief of Police and was promoted.

INSURANCE CLERK. Mainline Insurance Company, Dallas, TX (1981-85). While operating a wide range of office equipment and learning internal operations of an insurance company, determined correct charges for patients' premiums and distributed correct insurance policies to both companies and individuals.

EDUCATION

Studied Computer Programming, Wake Technical College, Raleigh, NC, 1998-99.
Completed Supervisory School, Wake Technical College, Raleigh, NC, 1986.
Certified Emergency Medical Technician; completed Basic Life Support studies, 1985.

SKILLS

Medical equipment: Skilled in oxygen setup and knowledgeable of equipment used to record vital signs; operate traction equipment.
Medical skills: Can provide basic life support, CPR, airway management, splinting, bandaging, hemorrhage control, and shock management.

CERTIFICATIONS Certified as an EMT and in CPR, State of North Carolina, since 1985.

PERSONAL

Am a highly motivated person who strives to make a contribution in my job.

Date

Exact Name of Person
Title or Position
Name of Company
Address (no., street)
Address (city, state, zip)

Dear Exact Name of Person: (or Dear Sir or Madam if answering a blind ad.)

I would appreciate an opportunity to talk with you soon about how I could contribute to your organization through my versatile skills related to medical office operations and financial services, as well as through my proven sales ability, initiative, and creativity oriented toward improving the "bottom line."

As you will see from my resume, most recently I played a key role in the start-up of a new orthopedics practice. While developing office systems and office procedures "from scratch," including designing all forms, I used and trained other employees to use UNIX software and made valuable suggestions which the UNIX vendor applied to refine and upgrade the system. Skilled in bookkeeping and insurance claims administration, I have filed insurance claims and performed ICD-9 and CPT-4 coding. I also handled accounts payable/receivable and payroll and acted as Credit Manager. In my previous job at Scotland Memorial Hospital, I was rapidly promoted to coordinate business office systems and supervised a large staff while acting as the "internal expert" on the computer system and software problems.

In earlier experience in the banking field, I was involved in loan administration, supervised teller transactions, and managed credit card accounts. I am skilled in dealing with the public.

I am confident you would find me in person to be a poised communicator and dynamic personality who enjoys solving technical and business problems. I have been told that I am a "natural" for sales, although I personally believe that the ability to sell a product has a lot to do with the salesperson's product knowledge. A fast learner with the ability to rapidly master new areas of knowledge, I am always eager to learn new things and accept new challenges.

I hope you will welcome my call soon to arrange a brief meeting at your convenience to discuss your current and future needs and how I might serve them. Thank you in advance for your time.

Sincerely yours,

Rosalind Rulnick

ROSALIND RULNICK

1110½ Hay Street, Fayetteville, NC 28305 • preppub@aol.com • (910) 483-6611

OBJECTIVE

To add value to a company that can use a creative professional and dynamic communicator who offers proficiency with computer software, expertise in managing offices and developing business systems, as well as knowledge of the medical and financial fields.

EXPERIENCE

OFFICE MANAGER. Gravelley & Associates, Chapel Hill, NC (1996-present). Worked with UNIX software and made numerous suggestions which the UNIX vendor used to upgrade and refine the system; supervised six clerical employees in medical office operations and trained the entire staff in the operation of the computer system.

- *Business development*: Joined this practice during its initial setup and played a key role in helping it become a profitable operation; developed office systems and internal procedures "from scratch" including designing all forms.
- *Insurance claims administration*: Filed insurance claims and performed ICD-9 and CPT-4 coding.
- *Customer service*: Acted as Patient Accounts Representative and Receptionist.
- *Accounting/bookkeeping*: Handled accounts payable/receivable and payroll and acted as Credit Manager.
- *Written communication*: Composed reports, memos, and correspondence.

BUSINESS OFFICE SYSTEM COORDINATOR. Scotland Memorial Hospital, Scotland, NC (1993-96). Began with this hospital as a **Patient Account Representative** and was promoted to coordinate all systems in the business office; earned a reputation as a creative problem-solver who could develop efficient and simple new procedures and work flows.

- *Office systems coordination*: Supervised a large staff composed of insurance clerks, file room clerks, mail room personnel, cashiers, and switchboard operators; worked closely with the business manager to interview, hire, and train employees.
- *Customer service*: Supervised four people while overseeing the process of interviewing patients, determining sources of financial aid, collecting past due accounts, and filing insurance claims.
- *Computer consulting*: Acted as the internal expert/consultant on the operations of the computer system used to maintain patient information; performed keying and batching and continuously found innovative new ways of managing data.

PERSONAL BANKER. Cape Fear Bank & Trust Company, Raleigh, NC (1989-93). Began with this financial institution as a Sales Finance Secretary and earned rapid promotions in succession to Assistant to Installment Loan Manager; Senior Teller; and Personal Banker.

- *Loan administration*: Approved loan applications, conducted credit history investigations, sold and opened new accounts, and became skilled in solving banking problems.
- *Teller transactions*: Ordered currency and coin from the Federal Reserve, sold financial services, balanced vault and teller windows, trained tellers.
- *Credit card accounts*: Managed Ready Reserve and Master Charge Accounts and computed terms for payment.

EDUCATION

Completed two years of college coursework, Raleigh Community College, Raleigh, North Carolina, 1990-92; attended college at night while excelling in my full-time job.

PERSONAL

Outstanding personal and professional references on request. Am an adaptable team player who works well under pressure. Creative person who welcomes new learning opportunities. Single; will cheerfully relocate and travel as my employer's needs require.

Exact Name of Person
Title or Position
Name of Company
Address (number and street)
Address (city, state, and zip)

**Mental Health Program
Manager**

Dear Exact Name of Person: (or Dear Sir or Madam if answering a blind ad.)

There are a couple of things you can learn from this resume. Notice that the address line on the resume has two addresses —the address where he currently resides, and the address to which he will be moving shortly. In the first paragraph of the cover letter, he alerts his reader to the fact that he is relocating because of his wife's job. This will reassure the prospective employer that he is not leaving his current position because of work-related problems.

With the enclosed resume, I would like to indicate my interest in your organization and my desire to explore employment opportunities. My wife and I have recently relocated to Atlanta because my wife has been promoted and relocated by her employer, Farmington Industries. We have bought a house and are hoping to make Atlanta our permanent home.

As you will see from my enclosed resume, I have excelled in a track record of outstanding results within the social services and human services field. I am a dedicated social worker who "found my field" after a distinguished "first career" serving in the Air Force in the recreational and transportation fields. As a manager in the Air Force, I thoroughly enjoyed the challenges involved in training and counseling young soldiers, and I was successful in helping many troubled young people turn their lives around and become positive, contributing, and well-adjusted members of society. After military service I earned my Bachelor of Science in Social Work (magna cum laude). As a Social Worker, I have discovered that I have a "gift" for comforting both the young and elderly, and I have been enriched by work experience in hospice, hospital, and mental health environments.

I hope you will welcome my call soon to arrange a brief meeting at your convenience to discuss your current and future needs and how I might serve them. I can provide excellent references. Thank you in advance for your time.

Sincerely yours.

Frederick Hallgarth

Alternate last paragraph:
I hope you will call or write me soon to suggest a time convenient for us to meet and discuss your current and future needs and how I might serve them. Thank you in advance for your time.

FREDERICK HALLGARTH

Until 12/15/99: 1110½ Hay Street, Decatur, GA 28305   (910) 483-6611

After 12/16/99: 538 Pittsfield Avenue, Atlanta, GA 58401   (805) 483-6611

OBJECTIVE

I want to contribute to an organization that can use a dedicated social worker who is known for my caring manner and for my belief that the elderly as well as children deserve to be honored and given a helping hand by sincere, empathetic professionals.

EDUCATION

Earned a Bachelor of Science in Social Work (B.S.W.) **magna cum laude** with a 3.83 GPA, Georgia College, Decatur, GA, 1996.

CERTIFICATIONS

Certified in CPR and First Aid by the American Red Cross
Received Certification of Completion from a Personal Intervention Course (PIC)

EXPERIENCE

MENTAL HEALTH PROGRAM MANAGER. Decatur County Mental Health, Decatur, GA (1997-99). In a group home for nine male juvenile sex offenders aged 14-18, monitored and assisted children on a 24-hour-a-day basis.

- Administered prescription medicine for charts; was responsible for safety of my clients.
- Transported clients to appointments and to outings as deemed appropriate by Decatur County Mental Health.
- Became very knowledgeable of the special needs of this particular client population, and excelled in handling and diffusing hostile situations with clients.
- Learned how important it is to assure proper administration of prescription medicines to clients.

HOSPICE INTERN. Home Health Care of Decatur, Decatur, GA (Sept-Dec 1996). Derived enormous satisfaction from this four-month internship in a hospice environment.

- It gave me a great feeling of accomplishment to help someone through his last journey in life in a peaceful way; I also learned that the dying still have much to contribute to those around them, and I greatly enjoyed listening and providing a comforting presence to the little children and the elderly whom I saw die.
- Learned how gratifying it is for people to die in their own natural surroundings.

SOCIAL WORKER TRAINEE/VOLUNTEER. Veterans Administration Hospital, Decatur, GA (1993-96). While earning my B.S.W. degree, worked more than 3,000 hours with older people in the Intermediate Ward; became skilled in working with older people with AIDS, Hepatitis C, cancer, and with amputees.

- Functioned as the personal assistant to many elderly people, and took them to doctors' appointments, on outings, and to activities.
- Became a favorite assistant of the nursing staff; often assisted them in various activities.

TRANSPORTATION SPECIALIST. U.S. Air Force, various locations (1982-92). Worked in the purchasing, logistics, and transportation field training and managing up to six individuals; became skilled in purchasing items ranging from paper clips to heavy industrial equipment.

- Developed excellent supervisory and personnel administration skills.

RECREATIONAL SPECIALIST. U.S. Air Force, various locations (1972-82). Developed a recreational program which was voted "best" in the parent organization while advancing to top management positions in the recreational management field.

- Supervised up to eight recreational assistants while supervising athletic events, overseeing the maintenance of athletic fields, and overseeing a wide range of athletic events, competitions, tournaments, and activities.

PERSONAL

Can provide outstanding personal and professional references. Have a true love of geriatric patients and children and feel that they are often the "throwaway citizens" in society.

Exact Name of Person
Title or Position
Name of Company
Address (no., street)
Address (city, state, zip)

Motel Manager

This junior manager is actually seeking his first job after college graduation. Although he doesn't emphasize that he has worked for his family's business throughout college, that is how he has gained the managerial skills which he is now "shopping around" to various industries and companies.

Dear Exact Name of Person: (or Dear Sir or Madam if answering a blind ad.)

I would appreciate an opportunity to talk with you soon about how I could contribute to your organization through my education in biology and experience in business management.

As you will see from my enclosed resume, I will receive my bachelor's degree in Biology from The University of Georgia in December. I have completed more than 300 hours as a Lab Technician in biology, chemistry, and organic chemistry labs while in college and earlier while studying Organic Chemistry at Atlanta Technical Institute.

Through my experience in helping a family-owned business grow to increased profitability, I have gained valuable exposure to bookkeeping and finance, customer service, and public relations. During the past eight years, beginning while I was still in high school and part-time throughout my college years, I have been involved in making decisions and advanced with the business as profits increased at a 20% growth over the last five years.

I am a fast learner with knowledge of several languages. Through my adaptability, friendly personality, and initiative I have always been able to quickly earn the respect and admiration of people from employees, to peers, to members of the public.

I hope you will welcome my call soon to arrange a brief meeting at your convenience to discuss your current and future needs and how I might serve them. Thank you in advance for your time.

Sincerely yours,

Boyd Strickland

Alternate last paragraph:
I hope you will call or write me soon to suggest a time convenient for us to meet and discuss your current and future needs and how I might serve them. Thank you in advance for your time.

BOYD STRICKLAND

1110½ Hay Street, Fayetteville, NC 28305 • preppub@aol.com • (910) 483-6611

OBJECTIVE

To contribute to an organization through my education in biology, my experience in small business management, as well as my exposure to public relations, customer service, and financial/accounting functions.

EDUCATION

Bachelor's degree in Biology, The University of Georgia, December 1999.
Studied Organic Chemistry, Atlanta Technical Institute, 1998.

TRAINING

Completed more than 100 hours as a Lab Technician in university laboratory settings such as: chemistry lab and biology lab — University of Georgia
organic chemistry lab — Atlanta Technical Institute

EXPERIENCE

While earning my college degree in my spare time in the evenings and on weekends, gained experience in all phases of small business operations and made important contributions to the growth of a family-owned motel, Traveler's Inn, Atlanta, GA, in this track record of advancement:
MANAGER. (1992-present). Refined my managerial skills and learned to oversee the work of others while becoming familiar with the financial aspects of taking care of the company's bookkeeping activities.
- Quickly learned the details of handling financial activities; prepared the daily figures for the accountants and wrote checks to pay various operating expenses.
- Was praised for my decision-making skills and ability to develop ideas which led to increased profitability and smoother daily operations.
- Made suggestions which helped ease the transition to a new name after the motel had operated as the Georgia Motor Inn for several years.
- Refined my interpersonal communication skills dealing with a wide range of customers and employees.
- Have been recognized as a key figure in the motel's record of annual increases in income — over the past five years the business has seen a 20% increase.

DESK CLERK and **REPAIRMAN**. (1990-92). Advanced to take on a more public and active role in day-to-day operations as a front-desk clerk responsible for providing helpful and courteous service to customers and handling large sums of money.
- Maintained the swimming pool which included seeing that the proper chemical balances were reached and that the pool was clean and safe to use.
- Displayed my versatility by doing painting, roofing, and minor electrical repairs on air conditioning systems and TVs which resulted in decreasing costs of outside repairs.

Highlights of other experience: As a **Patient Care Volunteer** at the VA Hospital, Atlanta, GA 1994), helped the nursing staff in emergency room care such as transporting patients and assisting in preliminary check-ups.
- Learned how to operate vital computer systems and hook up equipment such as heart monitors and blood sugar checking devices as well as preparing records.

COMPUTERS

Am proficient in using Windows for word processing and recordkeeping.

LANGUAGES

As a native of India who came to the U.S. as a young teenager, can speak, read, and write in English, Hindu, and the Gujarati dialect. Also have basic knowledge of French.

HONORS

As a high school student, was named to Who's Who Among High School Students, graduated in the top 5% of my class with a 3.8 GPA, and earned Algebra Excellence Awards.

PERSONAL

Lived in three countries and attended 15 schools while growing up: rapidly adapted to new cultures and ways of life and earned the respect of those around me.

Date

Mr. William Monroe
Gruber Properties
222 McPherson Church Rd.
Charlotte, NC 27803

Dear Mr. Monroe:

I would appreciate an opportunity to talk with you soon about how I could contribute to your organization through my sales and management experience along with my formal education and technical training related to real estate.

As you will see from the enclosed resume, I am licensed by the North Carolina Real Estate Commission as a sales person and am currently completing Brokers Certification courses. I completed the "North Carolina Fundamentals of Real Estate Course" at The Charlotte School of Real Estate.

My resume also will show you my "track record" of achievement in sales and management. Although I was born and raised in the Charlotte area and am living here permanently, most recently I worked in Ft. Lauderdale and Jacksonville, FL, as a Store Manager for Camelot Music. I managed other employees, decreased inventory shrinkage, opened new stores, converted acquisition stores to Camelot systems and procedures, and was specially selected to manage a new "superstore" of more than 10,000 square feet.

I am sending you this resume because, after conducting extensive research of real estate companies, your company is the one I would most like to be associated with. I hope you will find some time in your schedule for us to meet at your convenience to discuss your needs and goals and how I might serve them. I shall look forward to hearing from you, and thank you in advance for your time.

Yours sincerely,

Michael Jenkins

MICHAEL JENKINS

1110½ Hay Street, Fayetteville, NC 28305 • preppub@aol.com • (910) 483-6611

OBJECTIVE	To contribute to an organization that can use a resourceful and congenial sales professional with excellent customer relations skills who offers a proven "track record" of accomplishment in both sales and operations management.
REAL ESTATE	• Licensed by North Carolina Real Estate Commission. • Currently completing Brokers Certification courses. • Completed "North Carolina Fundamentals of Real Estate Course" at the Charlotte School of Real Estate.
EXPERIENCE SUMMARY	• Eight years of restaurant and retail management experience. • Skilled in hiring, training, scheduling, and maintaining sales staff dedicated to superior customer relations. • Proven commitment to meeting deadlines and serving customers. • Exceptionally strong analytical and problem-solving skills. • Known for my positive attitude and cheerful disposition.

EXPERIENCE

STORE MANAGER. Camelot Music, Jacksonville, FL, and Ft. Lauderdale, FL (1993-99). Earned a reputation as a skilled store manager who was equally effective in starting up new retail operations, "turning around" existing stores experiencing sales and profitability problems, and managing "superstores."

• After managing three Camelot Music retail stores in Jacksonville and Ft. Lauderdale, was selected to manage a new 10,000 square foot free-standing "superstore."
• Was responsible for opening new stores and converting acquisition stores to Camelot's procedures, methods, and systems.
• Devised and implemented effective merchandising techniques.
• Specialized in maintaining superior inventory conditions.
• Achieved consistent sales increases and ranked among the chain's highest volume stores.
• Diminished shrinkage and substantially increased profits.
• Implemented effective off-site sales locations utilizing radio and television as well as popular musicians and bands at successful local events.

Other experience:

After earning my Associate of Arts degree, excelled in restaurant management and was selected for management training programs.

• Worked in Hardee's and was selected for their corporate training program; was selected as co-manager of a Hardee's at Myrtle Beach.
• Worked in Quincy's Restaurant as an assistant manager after completing their corporate training program.

EDUCATION

Associate of Arts (A.A.) degree in Restaurant and Hotel Management, Baltimore's International Culinary College, 1987-89.

• Completed renowned management training programs with established restaurants, Hardee's and Quincy's.
• Completed high school at Hargrave Military Academy and Flora McDonald Academy.

PERSONAL

Am an accomplished guitarist and musical collector. Born 1969. Excellent health. Single.

Exact Name of Person
Title or Position
Name of Company
Address (number and street)
Address (city, state, and zip)

**Non-Profit Organization
Director**

This junior professional offers
experience in managing a non-
profit organization. However, she is
yearning to get back into the kind
of work she was doing several
years ago — as a culinary
instructor and marketer of
consumer products related to
cooking. The resume and cover
letter slightly emphasize culinary
arts and the cooking field, but they
are versatile and all-purpose. She
has moved frequently with her
husband, who is an airline
executive, and she has often
found herself in towns where
she could not find employment
in her chosen field.

Dear Exact Name of Person: (or Dear Sir or Madam if answering a blind ad.)

With the enclosed resume, I would like to indicate my interest in your organization and my desire to explore employment opportunities.

As you will see from my enclosed resume, my recent experience is as a non-profit manager with skills in volunteer recruitment and training, fundraising and budgeting, as well as media relations and community liaison. With a reputation as an outstanding writer and public speaker, I have become knowledgeable of grant writing.

You will also see that I have an extensive background in consumer products marketing and public relations. In one job as a Market Research Analyst, I was instrumental in the launch of new products marketed by Fortune 500 companies.

My culinary background is also extensive. I have developed and conducted consumer education related to the products of major manufacturers.

I hope you will welcome my call soon to arrange a brief meeting at your convenience to discuss your current and future needs and how I might serve them. Thank you in advance for your time.

Sincerely yours.

Judith Leopard, MSED

Alternate last paragraph:

I hope you will call or write me soon to suggest a time convenient for us to meet and discuss your current and future needs and how I might serve them. Thank you in advance for your time.

JUDITH LEOPARD, MSED

1110½ Hay Street, Fayetteville, NC 28305 • preppub@aol.com • (910) 483-6611

OBJECTIVE	To benefit an organization that can use my background in training and consulting, my experience related to the marketing and selling of consumer products, as well as my food knowledge and culinary expertise.
EDUCATION	Masters of Science in Education (MSED), University of Delaware, Dover, DE, 1998. • Achieved a 3.9 GPA with a major in Vocational Education. Bachelor of Science in Consumer Studies, University of Dayton, Dayton, OH, 1974.
EXPERIENCE	**RESOURCE CENTER MANAGER.** The Women's Center of Dover, Dover, DE (1998-present). Coordinate and supervise the recruitment, training, and retention of a volunteer staff which provides helpful resources to disadvantaged women. • Organize and manage special projects. • Perform liaison with a wide range of agencies and private organizations which offer opportunities related to employment, counseling, and other areas. • Maintain a high profile within the community while representing the Center at community events, meetings, workshops, and functions. • Have assisted in the research of grant proposals. **TEACHER.** Delaware School System, Dover, DE (1993-97). Coordinated classroom activities and designed innovative lesson plans as a Substitute Teacher in all academic and vocational areas. **MARKET RESEARCH ANALYST.** Business Systems, Inc., Dover, DE (1990-93). Was promoted from **Phone Bank Manager**, to **Executive Interviewer**, to **Market Research Analyst** in charge of a wide range of consulting, project management, and consumer education activities for a consulting company which provided focus group testing and other services to Fortune 100 and Fortune 500 companies. • Hired, supervised, trained, and scheduled a 30-person staff at the Consumer Testing Center; trained employees in data collection, executive telephone interviewing, intercept surveying, and product demonstrations • Conducted surveys to test new product lines for national companies. • Acted as a Public Relations Representative in preparing fact sheets, researching data, and handling communication with companies. • Test marketed new products for client companies; prepared visual aid materials for the demonstration of assigned products, organized and conducted consumer education pertaining to the product lines. **CULINARY INSTRUCTOR & EDUCATOR.** Cannonfield Culinary Equipment, Dover, DE (1978-83). Instructed auditorium-size classes of hundreds of people in microwave, conventional, and general cooking; formulated and tested recipes and developed menus. • Demonstrated appliance products and their capabilities and features. • Organized and conducted consumer education pertaining to food and major cooking appliances for Cuisinart, Braun, Krups, Toastmaster, GE, Litton, Amana, Caphalon, Romertopf, and others.
CERTIFICATION	Certified in Food Safety by The National Restaurant Association Completed Culinary Update Certification, Culinary Institute of America
PERSONAL	Can provide outstanding personal and professional references.

Date

Exact Name of Person
Title or Position
Name of Company
Address (number and street)
Address (city, state, and zip)

Nursing Supervisor

Dear Exact Name of Person: (or Dear Sir or Madam if answering a blind ad.)

This young nurse is seeking advancement. Notice that, instead of leaving a gap on the resume related to the two years when she was in nursing school, we show her as a "Full-Time Nursing Student" so that it will be obvious to employers that there was no two-year gap in her employment history.

With the enclosed resume, I would like to indicate my interest in your medical center and my desire to explore employment opportunities.

As you will see from my enclosed resume, I offer experience as a Head Nurse and am known for my compassionate style when dealing with patients and their families. I decided on a career in nursing after working in administrative support roles at two medical offices and discovering my strong desire to become more involved in patient care.

I hope you will welcome my call soon to arrange a brief meeting at your convenience to discuss your current and future needs and how I might serve them. Thank you in advance for your time.

Sincerely yours.

Belinda Warren

Alternate last paragraph:
I hope you will call or write me soon to suggest a time convenient for us to meet and discuss your current and future needs and how I might serve them. Thank you in advance for your time.

BELINDA WARREN

1110½ Hay Street, Fayetteville, NC 28305 • preppub@aol.com • (910) 483-6611

OBJECTIVE   To contribute to an organization that can use a skilled nursing professional who offers effective communication skills along with a reputation as a hard-working and compassionate person.

EDUCATION   **Associate's degree in Nursing,** Towson Technical Community College (TTCC), MD, 1995. Certificate in **Surgical Technology,** TTCC, 1984; completed extensive on-the-job training at Towson Medical Center.
Certified CPR Instructor.

EXPERIENCE   **HEAD NURSE.** Cliffdale Primary Care, Towson, MD (1995-present). In addition to supervising the clinic staff of nine LPNs, lab technicians, and phlebotomists, order supplies and equipment while overseeing and controlling the completion of numerous tests and procedures which include:

pulmonary function testing	flex sigmoidoscopy
stress testing	visual acuity testing
peak flow meter usage	immunizations/vaccinations
monitoring EKGs	sterilization of equipment

- Acted as liaison between pharmaceutical company representatives and physicians; accepted samples and stocked pharmaceutical supplies for clinic use.
- Assisted during in-office surgical procedures.
- Made insurance referrals and authorizations along with referrals to other doctors.

FULL-TIME NURSING STUDENT. Towson Technical Community College, MD (1993-95). Placed on the President's List in recognition of my academic achievements.

CLINICAL STAFF MEMBER and **ADMINISTRATIVE ASSISTANT.** Medical Drive Obstetrics and Gynecology, Towson, MD (1987-93). Handled support activities ranging from taking patients' vital signs, to answering phones and routing messages, to setting up appointments and making referrals to other medical practices.

- Called in prescriptions; also conducted telephone triage by advising patients and helping determine how urgent their situation was.
- Developed mutually beneficial relations with pharmaceutical representatives including acting as liaison between them, the physicians, and the nursing staff.

SURGICAL ASSISTANT. Dr. Dennis Michaels, Towson, MD (1984-87). Provided chairside assistance in periodontal surgeries as well as handling office support activities including making appointments, preparing surgical instruments, taking X-rays, and working with ultrasound equipment.

Highlights of earlier experience: Gained skills in sales, office operations, credit application processing, and letters/contract preparation.

SPECIAL SKILLS   Am proficient with various office machines including typewriters, copy machines, personal and office computers, and X-ray and ultrasound equipment.

PERSONAL   Offer exceptionally strong communication skills. Excellent references.

Date

Exact Name of Person
Title or Position
Name of Company
Address (number and street)
Address (city, state, and zip)

Office Manager,
Real Estate Company

This junior professional was the
victim of "downsizing" when the
real estate and construction
industries fell on hard times. That's
why her first job shows an ending
date expressed as a year. Notice
that nearly all these resumes show
just the "year dates" of
employment; it is usually not
necessary to show the dates of
employment with month-by-month
details. Sometimes this allows you
to "edit" your career and leave a
job off your resume which you held
for only a few months.

Dear Sir or Madam:

With the enclosed resume, I would like to make you aware of the considerable business, management, and customer service skills I could put to work for you.

As you will see from my resume, I am skilled in all aspects of office management and am proficient with software including accounting programs such as Quicken Pro as well as WordPerfect and the Windows 95 programs including Word, Excel, and Access. In one of my first professional positions, I was promoted rapidly by a children's entertainment company to responsibilities which involved traveling to conventions to book shows and negotiate contracts. The youngest person ever promoted to vice president, I am still a member of the Board of Directors of that company and am respected for my business insights and marketing instincts.

I offer exceptionally strong management skills and have contributed significantly to the bottom line in every job I have ever held. In my most recent position with a real estate company, I handled office responsibilities which had previously been the responsibility of two people, and I made valuable contributions to profitability by reorganizing numerous office systems for greater efficiency. I can provide outstanding personal and professional references from all employers for whom I have worked.

In every job I have held, I have played a key role in the development and implementation of sound business plans while also creating and coordinating innovative marketing and advertising programs. I have also been involved in financial analysis, projections, and business plan modeling as well as the preparation and analysis of reports used for strategic and operational business purposes.

You will see from my resume that I have completed three years of college with a cumulative GPA of 3.87. I am pursuing completion of that degree in my spare time. I am a highly motivated individual with a reputation as am ambitious self-starter, and much of my college work was completed while I excelled in sales and other jobs.

If you can use a versatile young professional known for outstanding management, marketing, customer service, organizational, communication, and public relations skills, I hope you will contact me to suggest a time when we might meet.

Sincerely,

Claudine Walbert

CLAUDINE WALBERT

1110½ Hay Street, Fayetteville, NC 28305 • preppub@aol.com • (910) 483-6611

OBJECTIVE

To benefit an organization that can use a hard worker and fast learner with extensive computer operations experience, a background in business management and business development, along with skills in marketing and advertising.

EDUCATION

With a 3.87 GPA, have completed three years of college studies in Economics, Indiana University, Bloomington, IN; am pursuing completion of the degree in my spare time.

SPECIAL SKILLS

Skilled in utilizing a variety of software for maximizing business performance:

WordPerfect (3.1, 5.0)	Quicken Pro	One Write Plus
Windows 95, including Word, Excel, and Access		Quick Books

- Experienced in accounts receivable and payable as well as inventory control
- Operate multi-line telephone systems
- Excel in newsletter development and graphic layout

EXPERIENCE

OFFICE MANAGER. Craven and Associates, Tampa, FL (1997-99). For a real estate company, functioned as the "right arm" to the owner as he concentrated his energies in sales while I managed all business and office functions; completed Real Estate School.

- Performed strategic business planning and development while also coordinating all marketing and advertising activities; designed effective advertising.
- Handled all areas of accounting including payables and receivables.
- Processed all the company's real estate contracts and performed liaison with customers.
- Scheduled appointments for clients with the builder, interior decorator, insurance company, and closing attorney.
- As Office Manager, performed work previously done by two people; saved the company money by reorganizing office procedures and the filing system for greater efficiency.

MANAGER. Fred Astaire Dance Studio, Tampa, FL (1996-97). Made significant contributions to the bottom line of this company which specialized in teaching the art of Ballroom dancing; handled all accounting matters, including the preparation of weekly and monthly reports, while also planning and implementing innovative campaigns to boost the numbers of students.

- Developed and implemented business plans that increased the customer base.
- Coordinated marketing and advertising activities.
- Prepared/analyzed reports pertaining to business development and strategic planning.
- Hired, trained, and supervised new employees including dance instructors.
- Played a key role in diversifying the types of dance instruction offered to include Country Western and Latin as well as Ballroom.
- Planned dance competitions and special events including parties; became known for my meticulous attention to detail in all matters.

MANAGER. Common Sense Business Systems, Tampa, FL (1995-96). For a small wholesale distribution company, excelled in handling numerous roles simultaneously; in this one-person office, handled sales, customer service, accounting, inventory control, and liaison with the parent company.

PERSONAL

Have a cheerful, outgoing personality that is well suited to customer service.

Exact Name of Person
Title or Position
Name of Company
Address (number and street)
Address (city, state, and zip)

**Personnel Management
Assistant**

This junior professional got her start in the personnel field while serving in the military. Now in a personnel job in the retail business, she is seeking advancement and will be sending her resume and cover letter to companies in all types of industries, not just retail.

Dear Exact Name of Person: (or Dear Sir or Madam if answering a blind ad)

Can you use a hard-working and energetic young professional who offers a background in personnel administration along with outstanding office operations and management skills?

As you will see by my enclosed resume, I most recently have worked in the personnel administration field in the administrative offices of the Target Stores location in Raleigh, NC. As the Assistant Personnel Manager, I played a role in setting up procedures for and organizing the personnel department. I oversaw the management of personnel records, time cards, and scheduling for around 150 employees with direct supervision over six people. While excelling in my full-time job, I have used my spare time to complete my college degree in Human Resources.

In earlier jobs, I was cited for my customer service and managerial abilities and placed in positions of responsibility usually reserved for older, more experienced managers. For instance, at the Peachtree Plaza Hotel in downtown Atlanta, GA, I directed a staff of 18 people at one of the hotel's popular restaurants. While serving my country in the U.S. Army I worked in the personnel administration field while using state-of-the-art automated equipment to maintain personnel records for over 15,000 people at Ft. Bragg, NC, the world's largest U.S. military base.

With exceptional organizational, motivational, and communication skills and a reputation as a fast learner, I am proficient in utilizing many popular software programs.

I hope you will welcome my call soon to arrange a brief meeting at your convenience to discuss your current and future needs and how I might serve them. Thank you in advance for your time.

Sincerely yours.

Gail Davies

Alternate last paragraph:
I hope you will call or write me soon to suggest a time convenient for us to meet and discuss your current and future needs and how I might serve them. Thank you in advance for your time.

GAIL DAVIES

1110½ Hay Street, Fayetteville, NC 28305 • preppub@aol.com • (910) 483-6611

OBJECTIVE	To contribute through my reputation as a hard-working, enthusiastic, and energetic young professional with a broad base of experience related to personnel management, human resources management, employee relations, and customer service.
SPECIAL SKILLS	Offer outstanding office skills such as the following: *Computer skills:* am familiar with Word and WordPerfect *General office skills:* type approximately 55 wpm and am experienced in filing and using standard office equipment including multi-line phones, faxes, and copiers
EXPERIENCE	**ASSISTANT PERSONNEL MANAGER.** Target Stores, Raleigh, NC (1995-present). Was commended for my planning and organizational skills as well as my attention to detail while assuring efficient personnel administration for 150 employees working for a major retail business in its first year of operation in this city.

- Directly supervised six people; maintained personnel records for all 150 employees and was solely responsible for employee scheduling, timekeeping, and payroll preparation.
- Contributed to the store's reputation for customer service by issuing "rain checks" promptly when advertised merchandise became available.
- Played a key role in establishing personnel department policies.
- Learned ISIS and HOST computer systems which are specialized pricing systems and mastered software used in merchandising.

PERSONNEL ADMINISTRATIVE ASSISTANT. U.S. Army, Ft. Bragg, NC (1993-95). Refined my general office, administrative, and customer service skills while handling dual roles as an Administrative Assistant and Personnel Specialist in a department maintaining personnel records for more than 15,000 people.

- Received, analyzed, and entered data into an army-wide data base at a personnel headquarters located at the nation's largest military base.
- Was singled out for my exceptional public relations skills demonstrated while assisting customers with personal and financial matters.
- Applied my writing, proofreading, and typing/word processing abilities while preparing correspondence, documentation for awards, and narratives for personnel evaluations.

ASSISTANT MANAGER. The Cafe, Westin Hotels, Atlanta, GA (1992-93). Was hired at the age of 20 to manage a staff of 18 people and coordinate a wide range of daily activities in the restaurant at Peachtree Plaza, a major downtown hotel.

- Learned what to look for and how to investigate overages or shortages in cash drawers and in inventory; trained, scheduled, and supervised six employees.

ASSISTANT MANAGER. Burger King, Decatur, GA (1988-89). Originally hired as a Cashier, was soon promoted on the basis of my maturity and ability to lead others and contribute to the sense of team work necessary in the fast-paced environment of fast food.

- Supervised nine people while overseeing day-to-day activities and emphasizing quick, friendly customer service; handled cash deposits/cash drops and balanced cash drawers.

EDUCATION	Completed B.S. degree in Human Resources, Webster University, St. Louis, MO, 1998.

- Completed this degree at night at an adjunct campus while excelling in my full-time job. Excelled in approximately 724 hours of professional development training in management information systems and personnel information systems management.

PERSONAL	Am a quick learner who strongly believes in always giving 100%. Have an outgoing personality and well-developed motivational abilities. Excellent references.

Date

Exact Name of Person
Title or Position
Name of Company
Address (number and street)
Address (city, state, and zip)

Property Manager

Dear Exact Name of Person: (or Dear Sir or Madam if answering a blind ad.)

Although the Objective on the resume is versatile and all-purpose, just in case she wishes to job-hunt outside the property management field, this junior professional likes what she does and is simply looking for advancement to greater responsibilities.

With the enclosed resume, I would like to indicate my interest in your organization and my desire to utilize my management skills for your benefit.

As you will see from my resume, I offer extensive experience in property management and am known for my strong bottom-line orientation. You will notice that I have handled all aspects of property management including administration, maintenance management, public relations, inspection and inventory control, as well as collections and delinquency management.

I hope you will welcome my call soon to arrange a brief meeting at your convenience to discuss your current and future needs and how I might serve them. Thank you in advance for your time.

Sincerely yours.

Dianne Jones Weaver

Alternate last paragraph:

I hope you will call or write me soon to suggest a time convenient for us to meet and discuss your current and future needs and how I might serve them. Thank you in advance for your time.

DIANNE JONES WEAVER

1110½ Hay Street, Fayetteville, NC 28305 • preppub@aol.com • (910) 483-6611

OBJECTIVE   I want to contribute to an organization that can use a highly motivated self-starter who offers strong public relations and communication skills along with experience in managing people, property, finances, and daily business operations.

EXPERIENCE   **PROPERTY MANAGER.** Bladenboro Apartment Community, Canby, OR (1997-present). While managing this large apartment complex, raised and maintained occupancy by 17% in a 6-month interval.
- Collect rent, make deposits, and balance books at end of each month.
- Prepare activity, occupancy, and market reports for Broker-in-Charge and property owner.
- Maintain a monthly operating budget and explain any variances; manage a budget of $82,000.
- Coordinate with contractors and oversee all maintenance on units; lease apartment, process applications, and expedite lease agreements.

Began with The Affiliated Real Estate Consortium in 1992, and excelled in handling both sales/marketing and property management responsibilities on a large scale:
PROPERTY MANAGER. The Affiliated Real Estate Consortium, Property Management Department, Canby, OR (1992-1997). Excelled as a property manager for one of the area's most well-known real estate/property management firms; was responsible for an inventory of between 180 to 200 residences.
- *Maintenance Management*: Supervised maintenance activities; coordinated and scheduled staff and independent contractors; obtained estimates for work to be performed and monitored major repairs as work proceeded.
- *Public Relations*: Screened potential residents and conducted rental showings.
- *Inspections and Inventory*: Conducted biannual inspections of every property and conducted house inventories; ordered goods and materials as needed.
- *Administration*: Prepared reports for top management while also preparing lease renewals, inspection reports, and other paperwork.
- *Court Liaison*: Handled evictions and represented the company in small claims court.
- *Negotiation*: Mediated between owners and tenants as needed in situations where disputes arose over damages, security deposits, or rent owed.
- *Accomplishments*: Made significant contributions to office operations through my talent for organizing office policies and procedures; brought more than 125 new properties into management.

REALTOR. The Johnson Agency Realtors, Canby, OR (1990-92). Became a $1.2 million dollar producer within 12 months!
- Gained valuable skills in sales, marketing, and contract negotiating while acquiring expert knowledge of most aspects of the real estate business.

OFFICE ADMINISTRATOR. Killeen Real Estate Corp., Killeen, TX (1989-90). Handled a wide range of activities for this real estate company.
- Processed sales contracts and revisions; verified sales prices, financing, option pricing, and lot premiums with approved documents; deposited and accounted for all earnest money received; prepared sales, closings, and construction reports; maintained land files including settlement statements and title insurance commitments.
- Compiled information on approved houses for start of construction; handled building permits, color selections, and related matters; ordered trusses, brick, and cable; issued job assignments and construction schedules; assembled and evaluated plans and specifications for use by real estate appraisers.

PERSONAL   Can provide outstanding personal and professional references on request.

Date

Exact Name of Person
Title or Position
Name of Company
Address (number and street)
Address (city, state, and zip)

Dear Exact Name of Person: (or Sir or Madam if answering a blind ad.)

In the first paragraph, this junior professional makes it clear that he is relocating to Seattle. Although his background will be of interest to food companies, his experience in sales and purchasing is transferable to many fields. Notice that, although he has a license to sell Life and Health insurance, he doesn't plan on approaching the insurance industry, so his license is shown in a low-key fashion in the Personal section of his resume rather than in a separate License section.

With the enclosed resume, I would like to make you aware of the considerable sales and purchasing experience which I could put to work for your company. I am in the process of relocating to Seattle, and I believe my background is well suited to your company's needs.

As you will see from my resume, since 1989 I have been excelling as the purchasing agent for a large wholesale food distributor with a customer base of schools, restaurants, and nursing homes throughout the western states. While negotiating contracts with vendors and handling the school lunch bid process, I have resourcefully managed inventory turnover in order to optimize inventory levels while maximizing return on investment. I have earned a reputation as a prudent strategic planner and skillful negotiator.

In a prior position as a Sales Trainer and Sales Representative with a food industry company, I increased sales from $250,000 to $1.3 million and won the Captain Max award given to the company's highest-producing sales representative.

With a B.S. degree, I have excelled in continuous and extensive executive training in the areas of financial management, purchasing, contract negotiation, and quality assurance.

I can provide outstanding personal and professional references at the appropriate time, and I hope you will contact me if you can use a resourceful hard worker with a strong bottom-line orientation. I am in the Seattle area frequently and could make myself available to meet with you at your convenience. Thank you in advance for your time.

Sincerely,

Benjamin Brainerd

BENJAMIN BRAINERD

Until 12/15/99: 1110½ Hay Street, Fayetteville, NC 28305   (910) 483-6611
After 12/16/99: 538 Pittsfield Avenue, Seattle, WA 89023   (805) 483-6611

OBJECTIVE

To contribute to an organization that can use my exceptionally strong sales and marketing skills as well as my background in purchasing, inventory management, and contract negotiation.

EDUCATION

Bachelor of Science Degree, Denver University, Denver, CO, 1980.
- Majored in Health and Physical Education
- Minor in Business Administration

Graduated from W.G. DuBois High School, Denver, CO.
- Was named one of the "Ten Most Outstanding Seniors."
- Was selected to receive the Cayman Sportsmanship Award during my senior year. This award is presented annually to only one athlete in the Denver area.
- Earned varsity letters in football, basketball, and baseball.

EXPERIENCE

PURCHASING MANAGER. Culloughby Co., Denver, CO (1989-present). For this wholesale food distributor with a customer base of schools, nursing homes, and restaurants throughout the western states, purchase $750,000 of canned, dry, and staple goods.
- Am responsible for turning the inventory and maximizing return on investment (ROI); have resourcefully developed methods of purchasing products in a timely manner in order to optimize inventory turnover and ROI.
- Have earned a reputation as a skilled negotiator in the process of negotiating contract pricing as well as other terms and conditions with vendors.
- Have acquired eight years of experience with school lunch bid process; conduct product availability research, secure guarantee bid pricing, handle bid quoting.
- Utilize a computer with Target software for purchasing activities.

SALES REPRESENTATIVE. Mason Brothers, Denver, CO (1987-1988). Sold portion control meat and seafood to established and newly developed accounts.

SALES REPRESENTATIVE. PYA/Monarch, Denver, CO (1986-87). Sold full-line food service products to restaurants, hospitals, and military procurement offices.

SALES REPRESENTATIVE & SALES TRAINER. Bryan Foods, Bodega Bay, CA (1979-1986). Excelled in numerous positions of responsibility related to sales and sales management during my eight years with this company.
- As a Sales Representative, boosted annual sales from $250,000 to $1.3 million.
- As "Equipment and Supplies Specialist," initiated sales efforts in the western California region and helped produce sales in excess of $200,000 during the first quarter of the 1985 fiscal year.
- As "Sales Representative," produced growth of over $900,000 in annual sales revenue between 1979 and 1984, which resulted in my winning the "Captain Max" Award, presented to the company's most outstanding salesperson.
- Managed and coordinated divisional sales meeting; trained sales personnel.

Other experience:
- As **Co-Manager** of a seafood restaurant in Denver, was in charge of hiring, training, scheduling, and supervising all employees.
- Worked as a **Sales Representative and Staff Manager** for Pilot Life Insurance Company in Los Angeles; sold life and health insurance products and served as Staff Manager at the Smithfield Branch.

PERSONAL

Can provide outstanding references. Have been licensed to sell **Life and Health** insurance.

Date

Exact Name of Person
Title or Position
Name of Company
Address (number and street)
Address (city, state, and zip)

Purchasing Manager, Industrial Materials

This junior professional is approaching a wide range of companies, including some companies in her industry. Although it is not likely that a company she approaches will contact her current employer before talking with her, she explicitly requests in the second paragraph of her letter that the reader hold her initial expression of interest in confidence.

Dear Exact Name of Person: (or Dear Sir or Madam if answering a blind ad.)

I would appreciate an opportunity to talk with you soon about how I could contribute to your organization through my extensive background in purchasing parts and services for a manufacturing firm.

You will see from my enclosed resume that I have been with Goodyear Consumer Products, Inc., in St. Louis, MO, for several years. Although I enjoy this position and have advanced with the company from a Materials Buyer position to Purchasing Manager, I am interested in confidentially exploring opportunities within your company.

Because of my ability to reduce costs and negotiate product contracts with a wide variety of vendors, I have received numerous awards and honors recognizing my purchasing expertise and management ability. I believe that you would find me to be an enthusiastic and outgoing professional who offers strong organizational abilities and attention to detail.

I hope you will welcome my call soon to arrange a brief meeting at your convenience to discuss your current and future needs and how I might serve them. Thank you in advance for your time.

Sincerely yours.

Dean Hardwick

Alternate last paragraph:
I hope you will call or write me soon to suggest a time convenient for us to meet and discuss your current and future needs and how I might serve them. Thank you in advance for your time.

DEAN HARDWICK

1110½ Hay Street, Fayetteville, NC 28305 • preppub@aol.com • (910) 483-6611

OBJECTIVE

To offer my extensive background in purchasing and my aggressive bottom-line orientation to an organization that can use a positive and enthusiastic professional known for attention to detail as well as expertise in all aspects of purchasing both parts and services.

EXPERIENCE

PURCHASING MANAGER & MATERIALS BUYER. Goodyear Consumer Products, Inc., St. Louis, MO (1984-present). Began as a Materials Buyer and was promoted to Purchasing Manager in charge of a five-person department; provide oversight of the purchasing of a wide range of products valued at six million annually.

- Received a letter of appreciation from the company president in recognition of my accomplishments and contributions including my ability to continually reduce costs, January 1999.
- Wrote the standard operating procedures (SOPs) used by all purchasing department personnel, not only at the St. Louis central office but also at the 12 field offices.
- Oversee MRO (Maintenance, Repair, and Operating) purchasing contracts for plant services at 16 plants; negotiate contracts valued at $25 million annually.
- In 1999, negotiated a contract for additional commodities including labels and instruction books.
- Have acquired expertise in commodity buying including the purchasing of all electrical and electronic parts, fasteners, screw machine, and imported parts including finished goods.
- In 1998, chaired a task force which developed a new line of ceiling fans: the project was successfully completed ahead of schedule and within corporate budget guidelines and restrictions.
- On my own initiative, established a new buyer training program which has led to numerous efficiencies; set up a complete how-to system and oversaw the implementation of a new automated system used for tracking inventory and purchasing.

Highlights of previous experience: Refined skills as a Clerk/Typist and Secretary for a Human Relations/Equal Opportunity Office and the Director of Personnel and Community Affairs for an Army post in Germany.

- Earned several letters and certificates of commendation and a Sustained Performance Award in recognition of my professionalism and accomplishments as a government employee.

Became familiar with the functions of a purchasing office as a Departmental Secretary, Goodyear Industries, Inc., St. Louis, MO.

Gained experience in jobs as a Office Clerk/Claims Handler/Dispatcher for a trucking company and Real Estate Salesperson.

EDUCATION

Associate's degree in **Industrial Management Technology,** St. Louis Technical Community College, MO, 1996.
Completed 60 credit hours in **Personnel Management** through a correspondence course.
Attended Bohecker's Business College, Ravenna, OH: received training in the field of executive secretarial duties.

PERSONAL

Active in church activities, have served as vice president and secretary of the women's organization; served on the finance committee. Am a friendly and enthusiastic individual.

Date

Exact Name of Person
Title or Position
Name of Company
Address (number and street)
Address (city, state, and zip)

If you have been promoted ahead of your peers, or "ahead of schedule," according to company tradition, go ahead and say so! In the "conceptual statement" for her first job, this young professional points out that she was promoted quickly into a job "usually reserved for someone with much more experience." Notice her "personal guarantee" in paragraph three of her cover letter. This is designed to inspire confidence in prospective employers!

Dear Sir or Madam:

I would appreciate an opportunity to talk with you soon about how I could contribute to your organization through my exceptionally strong "track record" in management and sales.

As you will see from my resume, I have been promoted rapidly in every job I have ever held because of my proven leadership ability and willingness to assume responsibility. A self-starter and fast learner, I have excelled most recently in retail management and was promoted to Sales Area Manager by the Army & Air Force Exchange Service after beginning as a stocker and advancing rapidly to reorder associate. As Sales Area Manager I supervised a department of 13 employees and became skilled in hiring and interviewing.

I believe that my exceptionally strong management "track record" is due to a combination of natural ability, excellent training which I received from my employers, and a "hard-charging" personality that thrives on a fast pace. I offer a talent for training and motivating people, and experience has taught me how to handle "problem" employees and how to motivate marginal workers. I guarantee you can trust me to produce outstanding results with little or no supervision.

I hope you will welcome my call soon to arrange a brief meeting at your convenience to discuss your current and future needs and how I might serve them. Thank you in advance for your time.

Sincerely yours,

Patricia Cresswell

PATRICIA CRESSWELL

1110½ Hay Street, Fayetteville, NC 28305 • preppub@aol.com • (910) 483-6611

OBJECTIVE

To offer my proven management, organizational, and sales skills to an organization that can use a fast learner and hard worker who thrives on serving customers and solving problems in a fast-paced, competitive environment in which I am handling lots of responsibility.

EDUCATION

Completed extensive executive development training sponsored by Army & Air Force Exchange Service (AAFES) in these and other areas:
- Managing a department of employees
- Ordering/reordering merchandise throughout the U.S.
- Using the AAFES computer system for retail sales, accounting, and control
- Was selected to attend specialized OSHA training for supervisors

EXPERIENCE

SALES AREA MANAGER. Army & Air Force Exchange Service (AAFES), Germany (1995-99). Began with AAFES as a stocker and after two months was promoted to Reorder Associate; after less than ten months in that job was selected as Sales Area Manager, a position usually reserved for someone with much more experience.
- Received a cash bonus and Excellence Awards for superior performance, 1994.
- Was recommended through a formal letter from my supervisor for selection as Sales and Merchandise Manager because of my trustworthiness, ability to motivate a team, and willingness to tackle any responsibility.
- Supervised a department of 13 employees and learned how to adopt a neutral attitude with "problem" employees; became skilled in hiring and interviewing.
- Acquired considerable skills related to merchandise ordering, shipping, and markdowns.
- Was commended on my flair for creating eye-catching displays.
- Learned valuable techniques for maximizing the turnover of seasonal merchandise.
- Continuously assured correct merchandise pricing and stocking; set plan-o-grams.
- Gained extensive experience with retail hard lines.

ASSISTANT MANAGER. Biscuit Kitchen, Dallas, TX (1995). Learned "the ropes" of managing a fast food service business.

STORE MANAGER. The Pantry, Inc., Houston, TX (1991-94). Always exceeded sales and inventory turnover goals, and earned a bonus with every paycheck I received from this company; responsible for making daily deposits of up to $8,000.
- Learned to do every job in this store including cashiering, ordering merchandise, controlling inventory, cleaning the store, hiring/firing/training employees, closing the store, and completing extensive paperwork.

ASSISTANT MANAGER. The Pantry, Inc., Houston, TX (1987-89).
Was groomed for eventual store management, and became knowledgeable about every job in this convenience store.
- Acted as cashier and made deposits; learned to order inventory and stock shelves; prepared plan-o-grams; trained and scheduled employees; handled all the paper work required of shift managers; was responsible for vendor check-ins; sold gas; handled customer relations.

COMPUTERS

Rapidly master new software and have used numerous AAFES programs to check mail, assess inventory levels in the warehouse, and determine location of products in route to their final destination.

PERSONAL

Sincerely thrive on a fast pace and work well under deadlines and pressures. Enjoy applying my talent for organizing and training people. Am a self-starter and can be trusted to do an outstanding job with little or no supervision. Am skilled at producing team results.

Date

Exact Name of Person
Title or Position
Name of Company
Address (no., street)
Address (city, state, zip)

Sales Manager, Agricultural Industry

Sometimes the Objective on a resume emphasizes personal qualities, as this one does. Since his job titles are nearly identical in each of his three jobs, he has a chance to reveal something about his strong personal characteristics in his Objective. Remember that a great resume helps an employer "get to know you."

Dear Exact Name of Person: (or Dear Sir or Madam if answering a blind ad.)

I would appreciate an opportunity to show you soon in person that I am the young, energetic, dynamic salesperson you are looking for.

As you can see from my resume, I am a proven professional with a demonstrated ability to "prospect" and produce sales. Under my direction, The Tobacco Warehouse was able to maintain a sales volume of $3.5 million despite a depressed agricultural economy. As a salesman and warehouse supervisor with Industrial Agricultural Cooperative, I increased sales from $500,000 to $1.5 million in two years. I have earned a reputation for my dedication and hard work in addition to a sincere concern for the customers I serve.

I feel certain you would find me to be a well-organized, reliable professional with a genuine customer service orientation. I pride myself on my ability to make "cold calls" and relate to people at all levels of any organization, from the mail clerk to the president. I can provide excellent personal and professional references.

I hope you will welcome my call soon to arrange a brief meeting at your convenience to discuss your current and future needs and how I might serve them. Thank you in advance for your time.

Sincerely yours,

Larry McPhail

Alternate last paragraph:
I hope you will call or write me soon to suggest a time convenient for us to meet and discuss your current and future needs and how I might best serve them. Thank you in advance for your time.

LARRY MCPHAIL

1110½ Hay Street, Fayetteville, NC 28305 • preppub@aol.com • (910) 483-6611

OBJECTIVE
To offer my leadership, problem-solving ability, and public relations skills to an organization that can use a hard-working young professional who is known for unquestioned integrity, unflagging enthusiasm, and tireless dedication to excellence.

EXPERIENCE
SALES MANAGER. The Agricultural Market, Inc., Marietta, GA (1995-present).
Applied my financial expertise and excellent public relations/communication skills to contribute to the "bottom line" of this agricultural chemical and fertilizer manufacturer.
- Performed "cold calls" within a 30-mile sales territory; established and maintained approximately 175-200 accounts with dealers and individual customers.
- Ensured timely delivery of products and services.
- Billed customers and collected on delinquent accounts.
- Supervised three employees in administration/distribution.

SALES SUPERVISOR. The Tobacco Warehouse, Graceland, KY (1990-1995).
Built "from scratch" this successful tobacco sales and distribution center with sales totaling $3.5 million even though the agricultural economy was at a low point.
- As co-owner, managed all administrative and financial aspects of operations.
- Hired, supervised, and trained 12 employees, including floor workers, secretaries, and bookkeepers.
- Developed and maintained a loyal customer network of local farmers.
- Organized and conducted auctions to sell the product to tobacco companies.

SALESMAN and **WAREHOUSE SUPERVISOR**. Industrial Agricultural Cooperative, Lexington, KY (1986-90).
Excelled in a variety of roles because of my versatile management skills.
- Was accountable for warehouse inventory; determined product line and ordered fertilizers and agricultural chemicals.
- Performed collections and made bank deposits.
- Astutely managed finances and purchasing, meeting the company's budget goals each year.
- Through exceptional customer service to approximately 200 accounts, was able to increase sales from $500,000 to $1.5 million in two years.

SALESMAN. Best Seed Co., North Carolina (1990).
As a "sideline" to my other sales positions, applied my top-notch customer service skills to introduce this company's cotton seed line to 12 distributors throughout the state.

SPECIALIZED TRAINING
Attend more than 36 hours of instruction on pesticides each year at Georgia State University, Kentucky University, and North Carolina State University to maintain GA, NC, and KY Dealers Association licenses.

PERSONAL
Am a hard worker with a high energy level. Enjoy the challenge of motivating a team of employees while contributing to my organization's "bottom line" and serving customers.

In this section, you will find resumes and cover letters of mid-level managers. Many of these resumes could have been placed in the Junior Managers section and some could have been shown in the Senior Managers and Executives sections. So if you are a "middle manager," you should also consult the other sections of this book.

What can you learn from resumes and cover letters of middle managers?

If you consider yourself a mid-level manager, it would be in your best interest to examine the resumes and cover letters of managers in this section, even if they are not in your field. For example, resumes and cover letters in this section will help you learn the language to use if you're in a career change. They will help you see how to choose the most effective words to let employers know that you're relocating. You will gain valuable insights into people who are aggressively managing their careers, even if they are in a different field than you. For example, you will see a service station manager who is yearning to get out of management and back into the technical, hands-on activities he likes. You will see examples of managers who don't enjoy managing people and who want to restructure their career along the lines of consulting and training management.

What's different about mid-level managers?

What differentiates a junior manager from a mid-level manager? In general, a mid-level manager has learned more about himself or herself professionally, and the mid-level manager usually has more distinct preferences than junior managers. Many of the resumes for junior managers were written to help the junior manager "branch out" and "try new things." On the other hand, many of the resumes in this section were written for people who have worked long enough that they have gained some insights into what they want to do next—or what they definitely do not want to do. A mid-level manager has usually had experience in managing people and assets, and he knows if he likes it. The junior manager often has not been tested on as many different kinds of management soil. Sometimes the best way to advance in your career is to seek advancement within your own company, and mid-level managers know that; therefore, some of the resumes in this section are written for people who seek advancement with their current employer.

Mid-level managers aggressively manage their careers.

By the time a manager is at the middle management level, she usually has gained insights into what interests her and what she's good at. Making sure she places herself in a job which truly interests her is a distinctive feature of the middle manager. So even if the mid-level manager is in a career change, she is usually quite targeted in her job preferences and career choices. The mid-level manager has a longer "won't do" list than the junior manager because the mid-level manager has usually "been there, done that," and experience has taught her whether or not she's good at it and whether or not she likes it. (You can be good at doing things which you don't enjoy, but that's no reason to keep doing them. It's very important to enjoy your work, and mid-level managers understand this concept.)

Exact Name of Person
Title or Position
Name of Company
Address (number and street)
Address (city, state, and zip)

Accountant and CPA

Dear Exact Name of Person: (or Dear Sir or Madam if answering a blind ad.)

As every experienced professional knows, it is a sobering reality that often one must change companies in order to increase one's pay and range of responsibilities. This CPA is seeking a larger firm which can offer her a wider range of involvements.

With the enclosed resume, I would like to indicate my interest in your organization and my desire to explore employment opportunities.

As you will see from my enclosed resume, I have excelled in my first job as a Staff Accountant after passing the CPA exam, and I have worked with corporations, partnerships, sole proprietors, pension and profit-sharing plans, and individuals. Although I am held in high regard by my current employer, I am selectively exploring opportunities with larger firms involved in more diversified accounting activities.

I hope you will welcome my call soon to arrange a brief meeting at your convenience to discuss your current and future needs and how I might serve them. Thank you in advance for your time.

Sincerely yours.

Joan Mackler

Alternate last paragraph:
I hope you will call or write me soon to suggest a time convenient for us to meet and discuss your current and future needs and how I might serve them. Thank you in advance for your time.

JOAN MACKLER

1110½ Hay Street, Fayetteville, NC 28305 • preppub@aol.com • (910) 483-6611

OBJECTIVE	To contribute to an organization that can use a resourceful CPA candidate with excellent problem-solving skills as well as a background in accounting and financial planning.
EDUCATION	B.S. in Business Administration with a concentration in Accounting, University of San Diego, CA. A.A., San Diego Community College, San Diego, CA.
LICENSURE	Passed CPA exam, November 1996. Enrolled in Certified Financial Planner program, The American College, Bryn Mawr, PA.
EXPERIENCE	**STAFF ACCOUNTANT.** Cary & Sharp CPAs, Anchorage, AK (1997-present). Compile financial statements, prepare payroll and sales tax reports, and prepare tax returns for corporations, partnerships, sole proprietors, pension and profit-sharing plans, and individuals.

- Set up companies on QuickBooks accounting software.
- Prepare year-end tax projections for clients; conduct audits of non-profit organizations.
- For one company, identified and resolved client recordkeeping discrepancies which resulted in a reduction of taxable income to client; designed and implemented a new "daily report" system to monitor sales, receivables, and expenses, simplifying verification of cash flow and providing accountability.
- Identified illegal acts occurring within one client's accounting office, designed internal control procedures for implementation by management.

FINANCE MANAGER. Barrington, Wells, and Company, San Diego, CA (1995-97). Contributed knowledge and problem-solving skills in ways which increased cash flow and the effectiveness of financial support operations in this dealership while handling the full range of financial activities including accounts payable and receivable and payroll accounting for 15 employees.

- Solved cash flow problems after investigating auto parts department procedures: designed and implemented inventory and accounts receivable activities.
- On my own initiative, mastered computer applications unique to this industry such as dealership warranties, sales reporting, and marketing programs.
- Handled bank reconciliations, sales tax processing for the dealership and a separate auto parts business, vehicle warranty repair administration, and employee insurance.
- Maintained daily reports, ledgers, and computer records on dealership operations.

CLIENT CONTACT SPECIALIST. USPA & IRA, San Diego, CA (1990-95). Became recognized as a top-notch communicator and sales/customer service professional while calling on prospective and existing clients of this financial planning company which supports a clientele made up predominantly of military officers with a full range of financial planning and investment services.

- Received recognition from the highest levels of the company as part of one of the most productive teams of Brokers, Administrative Assistants, and Client Specialists.
- Made it possible for two agents to set new sales records due to the increased level of appointments made through my skill in describing the company's services.

Highlights of earlier experience: Gained versatile skills and abilities in previous jobs:

- As **PROJECT ACCOUNTANT,** handled the costing of an average of $25 million worth of construction projects.
- As **ACCOUNTING MANAGER,** supervised two employees while handling retail accounting including inventory, accounts receivable and payable, general ledger, financial statements, payroll, and sales tax.

PERSONAL	Offer excellent analytical skills and the ability to develop workable strategies.

Date

Exact Name of Person
Title or Position
Name of Company
Address (number and street)
Address (city, state, and zip)

Apartment Complex Manager

You will find resumes and cover letters of other property managers in the Junior Managers' Section. In the Personal Section of her resume, this manager mentions that Ashland is home. She is in the process of relocating to Ashland and wants prospective employers to view her as a potential long-term employee and not a "fly-by-night" individual.

Dear Exact Name of Person: (or Dear Sir or Madam if answering a blind ad.)

With the enclosed resume, I would like to indicate my interest in your organization and my desire to explore employment opportunities. I am in the process of relocating permanently to the Ashland area, where my family lives.

As you will see from my enclosed resume, I offer extensive experience in all aspects of apartment rentals management. In my current job, on my own initiative I directed the set-up of 35 corporate apartments and personally marketed the concept to area businesses. This concept has been so successful that the owners of the complex have decided to double the number of corporate rentals by next year.

I hope you will welcome my call soon to arrange a brief meeting at your convenience to discuss your current and future needs and how I might serve them. Thank you in advance for your time.

Sincerely yours.

Annette Chase

Alternate last paragraph:
I hope you will call or write me soon to suggest a time convenient for us to meet and discuss your current and future needs and how I might serve them. Thank you in advance for your time.

ANNETTE CHASE

1110½ Hay Street, Fayetteville, NC 28305 • preppub@aol.com • (910) 483-6611

OBJECTIVE   To benefit an organization that can use an articulate, motivated professional with exceptional communication, organizational, and negotiation skills who offers experience in accounts payable, accounts receivable, and office management.

EXPERIENCE   **APARTMENT COMPLEX MANAGER.** Grant's Village, Portland, OR (1998-present). Supervise all aspects of the operation of this exclusive 200-unit apartment complex, including overseeing leasing and maintenance as well as coordinating the fitness center and landscaping efforts.

- Process accounts payable, making disbursements for corporate utility bills; maintenance and other upkeep; advertising and promotions; and other expenses.
- Manage accounts receivable, taking in monthly lease payments from existing residents and security deposits from new residents, as well as other payments.
- Develop and maintain excellent relationships with local vendors, setting up new accounts and preserving connections with existing suppliers.
- Supervise one office employee and a three-person maintenance crew.
- Direct the rental and set-up of 35 corporate apartments.
- Inspect units being vacated and schedule cleaning and maintenance to ensure apartments are prepared for incoming residents.

Excelled in the following track record of advancement to increasing responsibilities with UDC of Oregon (1995-98).

MARKETING ASSOCIATE. The Village at Smithfield, Portland, OR (1996-98). Was promoted by UDC to a job equivalent to Assistant Manager with this 356-unit complex; credited with decreasing the number of delinquent accounts through my collections skill and knowledge in handling cases through Small Claims Court.

- Performed accounts payable and receivable, processing bills from vendors and utility companies for property and receiving lease payments and security deposits from residents.
- Processed lease applications and familiarized new residents with our lease and policies; conducted move-in and move-out inspections.
- Supervised and trained one employee; processed weekly reports promptly.
- Oversaw two corporate accounts.

LEASING MANAGER/ASSISTANT MANAGER. Morganton & Associates, Portland, OR (1995-96). Began with the company as a floating leasing agent and was assigned for two months to the 253-unit Cumberland Trace Apartments complex and then to The Village at Cliffdale before being promoted to Assistant Manager of the 280-unit Morganton Place Apartments.

- Collected accounts receivable and disbursed accounts payable for the property.
- Leased apartments and processed applications; handled lease signings; conducted move-in and move-out inspections; processed weekly reports; wrote a monthly newsletter.

AFFILIATION   Received NALP designation, Portland County Apartment Association.

COMPUTERS   Experienced with Rent Roll and Prentice Hall property management programs.

PERSONAL   Excellent references upon request. Known for my strong work ethic. Am single (never married). Have family in the Ashland area, which I consider home.

Date

Exact Name of Person
Title or Position
Name of Company
Address (number and street)
Address (city, state, and zip)

Dear Exact Name of Person: (or Dear Sir or Madam if answering a blind ad.)

I would appreciate an opportunity to talk with you soon about how I could benefit your organization through my outstanding abilities gained in a multifunctional business where I oversaw activities including training and supervision, merchandising and promotion, sales and customer service, as well as administrative and fiscal operations.

As the Store Manager of a Southern Auto location which had $2.5 million in sales its last fiscal year, I have become very efficient at managing my time while dealing with three different operational areas — parts, tires and service, and automotive accessories. This store averages from 1,500 to 1,700 transactions a week with average weekly sales in the $40-60,000 range. In my five years as Store Manager I have achieved consistently high levels of productivity, sales, and customer satisfaction.

As you will see from my enclosed resume, before joining Southern Auto I earned rapid advancement with Quality Auto Parts. In my five years with this organization I was promoted to Store Manager after starting as a part-time sales person and then becoming a Merchandiser, a Parts Specialist, and Assistant Manager. As Store Manager I was involved in making decisions concerning merchandising, computer operations and fiscal control, inventory control, and public relations as well as internal employee counseling and supervision.

A dedicated and hard-working professional, I can be counted on to find ways to ensure customer satisfaction and productivity while always impacting favorably on the organization's bottom line.

I hope you will welcome my call soon to arrange a brief meeting at your convenience to discuss your current and future needs and how I might serve them. Thank you in advance for your time.

Sincerely yours,

Eugene Lobato

EUGENE LOBATO

1110½ Hay Street, Fayetteville, NC 28305 • preppub@aol.com • (910) 483-6611

OBJECTIVE   To benefit an organization in need of an experienced manager with a strong background in inventory control/parts ordering, merchandising and sales, public relations, and fiscal operations along with specialized knowledge of the automotive parts business.

EXPERIENCE   **STORE MANAGER.** Southern Auto, Atlanta, GA (1991-present). Direct and oversee all phases of daily operations in an established store with 28 employees and with average weekly sales of from $40,000 to $60,000; motivate employees to achieve high levels of productivity, sales, and customer satisfaction.
- Played an important role in the success of a location with $2.5 million in annual sales and from 1,500 to 1,700 transactions a week.
- Received an Award of Excellence as an Auto Parts Specialist in recognition of my professionalism and knowledge of the inventory control aspect of the business (1997).
- Received Customer Service Award Pin for my exceptional customer relations.
- Earned certification in tires and parts in recognition of my expertise in providing customer service in these areas (1997).
- Was chosen to attend a corporate training program for store managers in 1997.
- Participated in setting up and running a job fair booth in order to recruit management trainees for Southern Auto at technical colleges throughout the southeast (1998).
- Carried out interesting sales merchandising and promotional activities which helped to increase sales of additional services once customers entered the store.
- Became skilled in time management while overseeing the operation of distinctly different areas within one location — parts, tires and service, and automotive accessories.

STORE MANAGER. Quality Auto Parts, Macon, GA (1986-91). Earned rapid promotion with this business and was placed in charge of overseeing all aspects of store operations from personnel, to sales, to inventory control.
- Advanced from a part-time sales position to Merchandiser, then to Parts Specialist and Assistant Manager, and in 1990 was promoted to Store Manager.
- Became familiar with management unique to the automotive parts industry involving public relations, computer operations/fiscal controls, and parts and inventory control.
- Supervised as many as 14 employees in a location which averaged from $15,000 to $18,000 in sales a week.

EDUCATION   Completed one semester of Business Administration, Priory College, Atlanta, GA.
Studied Electronic Engineering and Business Management, Atlanta Technical Community College, GA.

TRAINING   Was selected for corporate-sponsored training including:
"Introduction to Management" — a part of the Southern Auto Management School
Technical Electronic Ignition Course — Wells Manufacturing Corp.

CERTIFICATIONS Received ASE (Automotive Service Excellence) certification as a Parts Specialist and Western Auto certification as a Master Tire Specialist and Parts Specialist.

PERSONAL   Am a well-rounded professional with excellent communication skills in all areas — dealing with the public and with employees. Have a pleasant and friendly personality.

Date

Exact Name of Person
Title or Position
Name of Company
Address (number and street)
Address (city, state, and zip)

Automobile Adjuster

There are many different formats for showing a track record of progression within a single company. Look at the first job on his resume and you will see one approach for showing a pattern of involvement in increasingly more complex assignments. He may be approaching competitors of his current employer, so notice how he emphasizes his desire for confidentiality.

Dear Exact Name of Person: (or Dear Sir or Madam if answering a blind ad.)

With the enclosed resume, I would like to indicate my interest in your organization and my desire to explore employment opportunities.

As you will see from my enclosed resume, I am an expert appraiser and licensed insurance adjuster with a proven commitment to outstanding customer service. I also offer a reputation for unquestioned integrity and reliability. You will notice that I have excelled in a track record of advancement with my current employer.

Although I am held in high regard by my employer and enjoy both my work and my colleagues, I am selectively exploring opportunities in other companies which have earned a reputation for quality. Although I can provide excellent references at the appropriate time, please keep my interest in your company confidential until after we have a chance to talk.

I hope you will welcome my call soon to arrange a brief meeting at your convenience to discuss your current and future needs and how I might serve them. Thank you in advance for your time.

Sincerely yours,

Daniel Naidoo

Alternate last paragraph:
I hope you will call or write me soon to suggest a time convenient for us to meet and discuss your current and future needs and how I might serve them. Thank you in advance for your time.

DANIEL NAIDOO

1110½ Hay Street, Fayetteville, NC 28305 • preppub@aol.com • (910) 483-6611

OBJECTIVE   To benefit a company that can use an expert automobile appraiser and licensed insurance adjuster who offers a proven commitment to outstanding customer service along with a reputation for unquestioned honesty, strong negotiating skills, and technical knowledge.

LICENSE   Licensed by the state of South Carolina as an Auto Damage Adjuster and Auto Appraiser; also licensed as a Notary Public.
- Was previously licensed in New York as an Automobile Damage Adjuster/Appraiser.
- Hold a valid South Carolina Driver's License with a violation-free record.

EXPERIENCE   **AUTO DAMAGE ADJUSTER**. Nationwide Insurance Company, Columbia, SC (1993-present) and various locations in New York State (1984-present).
Began with Nationwide as a part-time security guard on weekends, and was offered a chance to train as an adjuster; excelled in all schools and training programs, and have exceeded corporate goals and expectations in every job I have held within Nationwide.
- *1995-present*: Was the first adjuster sent into South Carolina, and have played a key role in implementing the company's strategic plan to do more business inland selling auto policies; in a highly competitive market, opened the Columbia office "from scratch," which now includes two drive-in locations as well as a guaranteed repair shop which I monitor while averaging 100-125 claims monthly as the only adjuster within a 50-mile area.
- *1991-95*: Built a six-adjuster territory into a 14-adjuster territory in Queens.
- *1989-91*: Worked in Suffolk County, a huge territory 30 miles wide and 100 miles long, where I made a significant contribution to building the territory; when I left as the only adjuster in Suffolk County, I was replaced with four adjusters in this rapidly expanding territory where I had helped Nationwide earn a name for excellent service.
- *1987-89*: Relocated to Nassau County, Long Island, where I trained new adjusters while also working the field and drive-in.
- *1986-87*: After initial training as an adjuster, worked in Brooklyn and the Bronx, NY: averaged five claims per day while helping the company earn a reputation for outstanding customer service.

Technical knowledge: Skilled at utilizing Mitchell Estimate System and CCC Total Loss Evaluation as well as guide books including NADA and the Red Book; routinely use equipment including a CRT and personal computer.
- Known for my excellent negotiating skills and ability to settle claims quickly and fairly.
- In the Columbia area, have improved customer relations and reduced loss ratio 15%.
- Skilled at evaluating total losses, coordinating removal of salvage, and handling titles.

NAVAL PETTY OFFICER. (1980-86). After joining the Navy, advanced rapidly through the ranks to E-5 in four years while managing people as well as inventories of ammunition, missiles, and nuclear fuel; was strongly urged to make a career out of the Navy because of my exceptional management ability, leadership skills, human relations know-how, and technical knowledge of supply and logistics.

EDUCATION & TRAINING   Completed college course work in Business Administration and Management, Farmingdale State University, NY, 1991-92.
Completed technical training in Risk & Insurance and Insurance Law as well as numerous courses conducted by companies such as General Motors and Honda pertaining to refinishing, principles of four-wheel steering, transmission repair, computer operation, other areas.

PERSONAL   Offer an unusual combination of exceptional organizational and communication skills, along with technical knowledge of auto adjusting and the insurance industry. Strongly believe in delivering outstanding customer service.

Exact Name of Person
Title or Position
Name of Company
Address (no., street)
Address (city, state, zip)

**Automobile Dealership
Business Manager**

This manager enjoys her work;
she is simply seeking a larger
dealership with a commensurate
increase in responsibility and pay.
Compare this resume and cover
letter of Willa Clark, who wants
to stay in the auto industry, to
the resume and cover letter
on the next two pages of
William Wright, who wants
to get out of the industry.

Dear Exact Name of Person: (or Dear Sir or Madam if answering a blind ad.)

I would appreciate an opportunity to talk with you soon about how I could contribute to your organization through my well-rounded experience in managing automobile dealership business operations. Although I am held in high regard by my current employer, I am interested in selectively exploring business office management opportunities with larger dealerships.

In my position as the Business Manager for Honda—Isuzu in Raleigh, NC, I have become adept at handling details which ensured that everything was done correctly and on time in order to complete sales and delivery to the customer. Some of my main areas of responsibility included running credit checks, negotiating loan agreements, assuring that sales personnel complete proper documentation, and selling warranties and additional products.

As you will see from my resume, my prior experience included jobs which called for strong sales and customer service skills as well as a base of knowledge in all phases of automobile dealership operations.

With a degree in Marketing, I have earned a reputation as a dependable and honest professional. I enjoy the challenge of learning new methods and procedures. Known for a high degree of self motivation, I offer a strong ability to motivate others through my enthusiasm and dedication. I can provide excellent personal and professional references.

I hope you will welcome my call soon to arrange a brief meeting at your convenience to discuss your current and future needs and how I might serve them. Thank you in advance for your time.

Sincerely yours,

Willa Clark

Alternate last paragraph:
I hope you will call or write me soon to suggest a time convenient for us to meet and discuss your current and future needs and how I might serve them. Thank you in advance for your time.

WILLA CLARK

1110½ Hay Street, Fayetteville, NC 28305 • preppub@aol.com • (910) 483-6611

OBJECTIVE To offer my experience as a professional with a broad base of knowledge of automobile dealerships along with experience in managing a business department and supporting areas in order to make the greatest positive impact on the bottom line.

EXPERIENCE **BUSINESS MANAGER.** Honda—Isuzu, Raleigh, NC (1994-present). In a busy dealership, oversee a wide range of behind-the-scenes activities which guarantee support for the sales force as well as completion of contracts after automobiles were sold.
- Handle sales support functions ranging from running credit checks, to assisting the sales personnel in completing documents necessary for bank approval and ultimate vehicle delivery, to completing all paperwork needed to get contracts approved.
- Use my communication skills and knowledge to negotiate with lending institutions, find the best rates, and secure loan approval.
- Deal closely with customers while selling them additional services such as extended warranties, credit life insurance, A & H, and security systems.
- Prepare documentation in case of warranty cancellations; research problems and assure that corrections are made.

Advanced to a position of increased responsibility based on my accomplishments and performance with Kelly Ford, Inc., Charlotte, NC:
BUSINESS MANAGER. (1992-94). Advanced to this position after displaying an aptitude for quickly learning new aspects of dealership support operations.
- Gained experience in daily activities which included running credit checks, assisting sales personnel in document preparation, negotiating with lending institutions, selling extended warranties and other services, and preparing regular reports.

GENERAL OFFICE CLERK. (1990-92). Was cross-trained in a wide range of areas including cashier for the parts and service departments, service dispatcher, and receptionist while assisting with warranty claims processing and inventory control.
- Adapted to every area of operations quickly and easily and became known for my willingness to take on new responsibilities.

SALES ASSOCIATE. The Closet/Maurice's, Charlotte, NC (1991-92).
Consistently set sales records for these popular clothing stores which have different types of clientele: helped customers make decisions on styles and colors as well as on accessories to complement the items they selected.
- Placed on the "Shining Star" list for six consecutive months for having the top volume of sales.
- Gained additional experience in inventory control and stocking.

CASHIER/CLERK. Lafayette Ford, Charlotte, NC (1989-90).
Became familiar with the background support needed to keep an automobile dealership running smoothly while learning to prepare bank deposits, stock car parts, provide customer service in the service area and parts department, and file records.

EDUCATION & TRAINING Associate's degree in Marketing, South Central Technical Community College, St. Elmo's Ridge, NV, 1992.
Completed corporate training seminars on the following topics: Ford Motor Company's leasing programs and a Heritage Insurance program on management techniques.

PROFESSIONAL AFFILIATION Hold membership in the Ford ESP Professional Sales Guild; maintained the sales warranty penetration rate above 50% and passed an examination.

PERSONAL Am a very hard-working individual with a reputation for dependability, honesty, and integrity.

Exact Name of Person
Exact Title
Exact Name of Company
Address
City, State, Zip

Automobile Dealership Business Manager

Sometimes a detour in our career makes us realize what we really like to do! This "middle manager" on the fast track was recruited for a business management position in the automobile industry. Although he excelled in the work, he didn't find it as satisfying and stimulating as the work he'd done in banking and financial institutions. Hence, this resume and cover letter are designed to help him change industries.

Dear Exact Name of Person (or Dear Sir or Madam if answering a blind ad):

With the enclosed resume, I would like to make you aware of my background as an experienced professional with exceptional supervisory, communication, and analytical skills as well as a strong bottom-line orientation and a proven ability to maximize profits and sales.

I was recruited by AutoMax for my present position as Business Manager, and my rapid success in that position resulted in my being entrusted with the responsibility for overseeing the finance departments at both of their locations. I supervise three finance managers as well as a sales force of 15 automotive sales representatives. Through my efforts in promoting finance and warranty products, the dealership's average aftermarket profit has increased from $300 per vehicle to $500 per vehicle.

In my previous position with Virginia Bank & Trust, I was promoted rapidly, achieving a position as Assistant Vice President after only 33 months. I began with the company as a Credit Analyst and was promoted to Commercial Relationship Manager at the end of seven months of service. In this position, I actively recruited new commercial accounts and serviced existing accounts. During my tenure, my commercial accounts portfolio grew from $15 million to $25 million, and I doubled non-interest (fee-based) income from $20,000 per year to $40,000 per year.

I have earned Master of Business Administration and Bachelor of Science in Business Administration degrees from Virginia University.

If you can use a hard-working young manager with proven business savvy, I would enjoy an opportunity to meet with you in person to discuss your needs. Although I can provide outstanding references at the appropriate time, I would appreciate your holding my interest in your company in confidence at this point. I can assure you in advance that I have an exceptional reputation and could become a valuable asset to your company.

Sincerely,

William Wright

WILLIAM WRIGHT

1110½ Hay Street, Fayetteville, NC 28305 • preppub@aol.com • (910) 483-6611

OBJECTIVE To benefit an organization that can use an enthusiastic, experienced manager with exceptional supervisory, communication, and analytical skills who offers a track record of success in maximizing profitability and increasing sales.

EDUCATION **Master of Business Administration**, Virginia University, Greenville, VA, 1993 — GPA 3.6. **Bachelor of Science in Business Administration** concentration in Finance, Virginia University, 1992.

EXPERIENCE **BUSINESS MANAGER.** Somerville AutoMax, Somerville, VA (1997-present). Was recruited for this position by this automotive dealership; oversee sales force of 15 employees.
- After excelling as Business Manager at one of AutoMax's locations, was entrusted with the additional responsibility of managing the finance departments at both locations.
- Supervise three finance managers, ensuring accurate and efficient preparation, processing, and completion of loan documentation.
- Communicate directly with lenders by phone and fax to obtain financing for customers; process loan applications for nearly 200 customers per month.
- Maximize the dealership's profit by selling and promoting the sale of aftermarket products such as extended warranties and credit life insurance.
- Established a secondary finance program for customers with past credit problems.
- Increased the dealership's average profit on aftermarket sales from $300 per vehicle to more than $500 per vehicle.

At Virginia Bank & Trust, was promoted in the following "track record" of increasing responsibility by this large national bank:
1994-1997: **COMMERCIAL RELATIONSHIP MANAGER.** Greenville, VA. Was rapidly promoted within the organization; advanced to Commercial Relationship Manager after seven months with Virginia Bank & Trust, and to Assistant Vice President after only 33 months.
- Actively recruited new commercial accounts while providing the highest level of customer service to established accounts.
- Communicated the advantages of Virginia Bank & Trust and promoted our products and services to new and existing customers.
- Through my efforts, my commercial accounts portfolio grew from $15 million to $25 million during my tenure.
- Doubled fee-based (non-interest) income from $20,000 per year to $40,000 per year for accounts that I managed.

1994: **CREDIT ANALYST.** Various locations in VA.. Started with Virginia Bank & Trust upon completion of my MBA program; quickly mastered skills related to loan pricing and the making of credit decisions.
- Underwrote loan requests for Relationship Managers throughout VA.
- Analyzed financial statements including balance sheets and income statements; gained valuable knowledge related to cash flow management.
- Completed Relationship Manager Development Course, November, 1994.

AFFILIATIONS Rotary International — Finance Committee Chairperson
Member, Chamber of Commerce

PERSONAL Excellent personal and professional references are available upon request.

Mr. Dale Sweeney
Regional Operations Manager
Cableton
498 Manzanita Road, Suite 234
Fairfax, VA 22033

Automobile Service Manager

There's an old saying, "A change is as good as a rest." In some instances in our careers, that's true, too. Here you see the resume and cover letter of an automobile industry professional seeking to transfer his industry knowledge from a management position inside a dealership to a consulting and training role inside a specialized training organization. Notice in the first paragraph of his letter that he "drops a name" of an industry colleague and provides a reference. The position he seeks requires extensive travel, so he clarifies that he would welcome extensive travel.

Dear Mr. Sweeney:

At the encouragement of Jim West, I am sending you the enclosed resume. I am very interested in becoming a member of the Cableton district management team through my versatile background in service, parts, and sales management.

As you will see from my resume, I am presently employed as a Service Manager with Thurston Chrysler Plymouth Suzuki, Inc., in Canby, OR. Although I am well respected for my expertise and professionalism by this company, I would very much like to move into a corporate position in which I can apply my strong consulting and communication skills.

I am confident that my extensive experience in all areas of service, parts, and warranty operations, along with my ability to consistently maintain high customer satisfaction scores in service and sales, would allow me to become a valuable part of your team. In addition, I am certain that you would find me to be a hard-working and reliable professional who prides myself on doing every job to the best of my ability.

I welcome the opportunity for additional training and am willing to travel according to your needs.

I hope you will contact me soon to arrange a time convenient for us to meet and discuss your current and future needs and how I can help serve them. Thank you in advance for your time and consideration.

Sincerely,

Lee Southerland

LEE B. SOUTHERLAND

1110½ Hay Street, Fayetteville, NC 28305 • preppub@aol.com • (910) 483-6611

OBJECTIVE

To benefit a progressive automotive organization through my experience in service, parts, and sales as well as through my proven ability to train and motivate others to achieve the highest levels of job knowledge and productivity.

EXPERIENCE

Excelled in a track record of promotions with Thurston Chrysler Plymouth, Suzuki, Inc., Canby, OR (1991-present):
SERVICE MANAGER (Suzuki) and **ASSISTANT SERVICE MANAGER** (Chrysler/ Plymouth). Oversee service operations including performing service write ups, dispatching, effectively explaining recommended repairs, conducting sales, as well as handling special orders and inventory control.

- Process warranty claims; help launch new vehicles through creative advertising and marketing of accessories.
- Refined management and administrative skills while managing employees, handling weekly and monthly financial and inventory reports, and performing daily computer operations.
- Demonstrate effective public relations and communication skills while maintaining excellent customer and dealer relations.
- Earned several performance awards while handling service write ups, dispatching, explaining recommended repairs, as well as conducting sales, warranty counseling, and customer relations.
- Sold new and used vehicles as a **Sales Representative** (1991-92) while becoming skilled at the minute details of contracting and inventory control; became a 1991 Chrysler Certified Sales Representative.
- Was recognized as **"Employee of the Month"** on several occasions and **"Employee of the Year,"** 1999.

SPECIAL SKILLS

Offer detailed knowledge of computers along with industry-specific software programs including the ADP and SCAT systems. Offer strong communication, time management, and customer relations skills.

EDUCATION and TRAINING

Excelled at various corporate-sponsored training programs and seminars including these:
- American Suzuki Electronic Fuel Injection 95-97 EFI, June 1999
- American Suzuki warranty seminar, 1997
- Product Introduction Technical Training — an overview of Suzuki automobiles, service, and repairs, 1997
- SME-SMO1, SM The Essential Service Management System, 1996
- SME-SMO2, SM Work Distribution, Work Performance, 1994
- Studied Business at Maryland University and Gaithersburg Technical Community College.

PERSONAL

Know the importance of being willing to be flexible and versatile when working in service industries. Effective decision maker with strong administrative and public relations skills.

Date

Exact Name of Person
Title or Position
Name of Company
Address (number and street)
Address (city, state, and zip)

**Automobile Service
Station Manager**

A service station manager does
not frequently need a resume,
but this particular manager
decided he wanted out of daily
management activities and
back into full-time technical
activities. He is seeking a
highly paid position as a
mechanic in a foreign location.

Dear Exact Name of Person: (or Dear Sir or Madam if answering a blind ad.)

With the enclosed resume, I would like to indicate my interest in your organization and my desire to explore employment opportunities.

As you will see from my enclosed resume, I am experienced in all aspects of managing an automotive business, and I offer strong knowledge of accounting, finance, and purchasing as well as automotive repair. I am selling my ownership in the service station which my partner and I started "from scratch" in order to make myself available for worldwide relocation with a company that can utilize my expert mechanical and maintenance knowledge. An experienced industrial mechanic, welder, and automotive mechanic, I have received numerous awards and honors for technical expertise.

I hope you will welcome my call soon to arrange a brief meeting at your convenience to discuss your current and future needs and how I might serve them. Thank you in advance for your time.

Sincerely yours.

Conrad Kael

Alternate last paragraph:
I hope you will call or write me soon to suggest a time convenient for us to meet and discuss your current and future needs and how I might serve them. Thank you in advance for your time.

CONRAD KAEL

1110½ Hay Street, Fayetteville, NC 28305 • preppub@aol.com • (910) 483-6611

OBJECTIVE

To contribute to an organization that can use a skilled operations manager with a proven ability to establish and manage successful new ventures along with extensive expertise in every aspect of the automotive business.

COMPUTERS

Highly proficient in utilizing a variety of software programs to enhance bottom-line efficiency and profitability; experienced with Windows 95 and with various types of software used for accounting and inventory control including ShopPro.

EXPERIENCE

GENERAL MANAGER. ALL AMERICAN BP, Lawrence, KS (1994-present). With a partner, established "from scratch" and now manage a service station which has gained an excellent reputation for quality repairs and honest business dealings.

- *Accounting:* On my own initiative, created a completed computerized system which allows us to instantly track all work orders, inventory levels, and account balances; personally prepare all final work orders and initiate estimates for customer approval before work begins.
- *Customer Service:* Have become respected for my ability to clearly explain technical repair needs to customers; handle customer complaints and problems which occur.
- *Automotive Repairs:* Perform mechanical repairs and troubleshooting including engine replacement, cylinder head replacement, timing belts, brakes, and other jobs.
- *Finance and Purchasing*: Make all decisions regarding equipment/tools purchasing.
- *Advertising and Marketing:* Plan and implement advertising and special promotions designed to attract new customers and interest existing customers in our full line of services.
- *Special Skills:* Offer extensive experience related to these and other areas:
  - Repair fuel and brake systems
  - Operate tractor-trailers up to 10 tons
  - Emergency dispatching and repairs
  - Driving, troubleshooting, and repairing wheeled vehicles
  - Operate five-ton wreckers, front-end loaders, buses,
  - Troubleshoot and repair vehicles of all types and sizes
  - Operate tire machine, brake lathe, wheel balancer
  - Troubleshoot/repair vehicles of all types and sizes

INDUSTRIAL MECHANIC. Kelly Industries, Lawrence, KS (1993-94). In this large, state-of-the-art plant of a Fortune 500 company, solved numerous quality problems through my individual initiative while implementing changes which made machine set-ups more efficient.

WELDER & FABRICATOR. Melrose, Inc., Lawrence, KS (1989-92). Designed fixtures for some of the drilling processes while excelling in fabrication layout of materials used in building air control systems; performed final welding of systems frames and other devices.

WELDER & AUTOMOTIVE MECHANIC. U.S. Army, locations worldwide (1980-89). Became a welder and mechanic on wheeled and track vehicles.

EDUCATION

Studied Welding, Scarlet Oaks School, Sharonville, OH, 1978-80.
Completed U.S. Army training related to automotive repair/maintenance.

Exact Name of Person
Title or Position
Name of Company
Address (number and street)
Address (city, state, and zip)

**Automobile Parts
Department Manager**

Great minds think alike, as they
say, and Mr. Conrad Kael from the
preceding page and Jeremiah
Horenkamp have similar
objectives: Both want to work for
a large international company
which will send them to an exotic
location, probably in the Middle
East, where they can apply their
hands-on skills in automotive
repair and maintenance.

Dear Exact Name of Person: (or Dear Sir or Madam if answering a blind ad.)

With the enclosed resume, I would like to indicate my interest in your organization and my desire to explore employment opportunities.

As you will see from my enclosed resume, I am experienced in all aspects of parts management and maintenance shop supervision. Prior to my current job with AutoMax, I reduced costs and improved customer satisfaction in jobs managing up to seven mechanics maintaining a fleet of vehicles. Although I am excelling in my current position and am held in high regard by my employer, I am interested in exploring opportunities with international companies that can use a maintenance expert available for worldwide relocation.

I hope you will welcome my call soon to arrange a brief meeting at your convenience to discuss your current and future needs and how I might serve them. Thank you in advance for your time.

Sincerely yours.

Jeremiah Horenkamp

Alternate last paragraph:
I hope you will call or write me soon to suggest a time convenient for us to meet and discuss your current and future needs and how I might serve them. Thank you in advance for your time.

JEREMIAH HORENKAMP

1110½ Hay Street, Fayetteville, NC 28305 • preppub@aol.com • (910) 483-6611

OBJECTIVE

To benefit an organization that can use a motivated young professional with strong problem-solving and organizational skills who offers a background as an automotive maintenance supervisor, parts manager, mechanic, and retail merchandiser.

EXPERIENCE

PARTS MANAGER. AutoMax, El Paso, TX (1997-present). Manage all operational aspects of the parts department of this busy automotive supply wholesaler.
- Supervise seven employees; daily utilize a computer with customized software.
- Reset displays throughout the store, merchandising all areas according to the plan-o-gram as well as district and regional guidelines.
- Oversee and direct the stocking, merchandising, and recovery of the sales floor.
- Open and close the store, balancing the safe and completing all daily operational paperwork, shortage/overage reports, etc.
- Control inventory shrinkage; implement and train staff in the implementation of loss prevention procedures and guidelines.
- Increase average sales per customer by reminding staff of our target average and encouraging "plus selling" of related items.

MAINTENANCE SHOP SUPERVISOR. U.S. Army, Fort Buffalo, TX (1996-1997). Ensured that the shop workers under my supervision followed proper maintenance, safety, and hazardous material handling and disposal procedures.
- Supervised a staff of 7-10 mechanics.
- Scheduled work assignments and training cycles for staff.
- Ensured security and maintenance of more than $150,000 worth of equipment.
- Developed streamlined procedures for common repairs, reducing labor time by 50%.

VEHICLE MAINTENANCE TECHNICIAN. U.S. Army, Fort Buffalo, TX (1994-1996). Performed major and minor repairs as well as preventive maintenance on wheeled vehicles.
- Operated welding equipment, brake lathes, battery testers, impact wrenches, winches, and overhead cranes.
- Utilized computer diagnostic equipment to troubleshoot vehicle malfunctions.
- Completely rebuilt engines and transmissions.

SHOP SUPERVISOR. MotorWorld, Tempe, AZ (1994). Opened and closed the shop, balancing the safe, and preparing the cash register tills for the next day's business. Supervised and trained four employees. Assisted mechanics with repairs and prepared bills for customers.

TRAINING

Excelled in a number of military and civilian training courses, including the following:
- Oral Communication and Emergency Lifesaver courses, Buffalo Technical Community College, Buffalo, TX, 1996-1997.
- Junior Leadership Course, Distinguished Honor Graduate (Top student in class), 1995.
- Wheeled Vehicle Repair, Distinguished Honor Graduate (Top student in class), 1995.
- Driver Training Course; trained in the operation of medium and heavy duty trucks, as well as the transportation of hazardous materials, 1995.
- Wrecker Operator Course; trained to operate rollback, winch, and block-and-tackle wreckers to recover stalled vehicles, 1995.
- Licensed to operate 6,000- and 10,000-lb. forklifts and other heavy power equipment.

PERSONAL

Excellent personal and professional references are available upon request.

Date

Exact Name of Person
Exact Title or Position
Name of Company
Address (number and street)
Address (city, state, and zip)

Banking
Assistant Vice President

This aggressive young professional
is on the "fast track" in his
company, but he is feeling
restless and wants to "see what's
out there." The resume and cover
letter are designed to interest
employers in numerous fields.

Dear Exact Name of Person: (or Dear Sir or Madam if answering a blind ad.)

With the enclosed resume, I would like to formally initiate the process of being considered for a position within your organization which can use my exceptionally strong marketing, communication, and consulting skills.

As you will see from my resume, since earning my B.S. degree in Business Administration with a Marketing major, I have enjoyed a track record of success in highly competitive banking and consumer product environments. Most recently I was named the top producer in my region based on my results in establishing the most new accounts, achieving the highest loan volume, and obtaining the most referrals. In an earlier position, I consistently led my office in sales and received the Sales Leadership award as well as other honors recognizing my aggressive marketing orientation and highly refined customer service skills.

Even in summer and part-time jobs while earning my college degree, I was selected for highly responsible positions at companies including R.J. Reynolds/Nabisco, where I managed 30 employees. My summer jobs prior to college graduation helped me acquire excellent skills in merchandising, marketing, and sales.

If you can use an ambitious, results-oriented marketing professional, I hope you will contact me to suggest a time when we might meet to discuss your needs and goals and how I might help you achieve them.

Sincerely,

Jason Vetter

JASON VETTER

1110½ Hay Street, Fayetteville, NC 28305 • preppub@aol.com • (910) 483-6611

OBJECTIVE

To offer strong marketing, managerial, and sales experience to an organization in need of a professional with the ability to motivate others to exceed expectations through excellent communication and consulting skills.

EXPERIENCE

ASSISTANT VICE PRESIDENT, CONSUMER BANKING. FirstBank, N.A., Seattle, WA (1996-present). In May, 1997, was ranked the Top Consumer Banker in the Central Washington Region based on my results in establishing the most new accounts, achieving the highest loan volume, and obtaining many referrals.
- Have achieved a record productivity for two years in a row.
- Assisted customers while educating them on the merits of different products such as checking and savings accounts, Certificates of Deposit, and IRAs.
- As a loan officer, met with customers and explained differences between types of loans available and made decisions on their qualifications for loans.

PERSONAL BANKER and **RETAIL MANAGEMENT ASSOCIATE.** Nations Bank of Washington, N.A., Seattle, WA (1995-1996). Achieved record productivity while completing a comprehensive management training program with this major financial institution; maintained and managed a portfolio of approximately 1,000 customers.
- Increased the size of my customer base by 30%.
- Played a key role in achieving the highest number of loan and credit card sales and the highest dollar volume of any branch in the Sandhills region (April and May).
- Learned all aspects of banking from teller operations to becoming familiar with investment and loan procedures as well as account management; continued to attend training classes to refine and add to my store of knowledge.
- Emphasized quality customer service and set an example for other bank employees while helping existing customers and selling the bank's services to new ones.
- Supervised teller staff and daily operations; conducted staff sales meetings.

ACCOUNT REPRESENTATIVE. Dictaphone Corporation/Pitney Bowes, Midlands, WA (1994-95). Managed more than 300 new and existing accounts while selling communications equipment including Dictaphone, voice mail, and time management equipment in a three-county area.
- Consistently led the office in sales: received the "Sales Leadership" award for achieving 206% of my quota two months ahead of schedule and later received recognition in the "Achievement Club" for 210% of quota.
- Worked mainly with medical and legal accounts while selling systems valued from $400 to more than $100,000 in a generally long-term sales process.
- Opened more than 25 accounts.

EDUCATION

B.S. in Business Administration, Seattle State University, Seattle, WA, 1993.
- Majored in Marketing; was a member of the American Marketing Association.
- Held leadership roles in Delta Chi Fraternity including vice president and rush coordinator; was honored as "Brother of the Year"; and currently serve as a trustee on the alumni board.

Completed professional development programs related to consumer finance and consumer loans sponsored by FirstBank, 1996-present.

PERSONAL

Have volunteered with the United Way, Hospitality House, and Watauga Hunger Coalition. Knowledgeable of Microsoft Word, Lotus 1-2-3, dBase III.

Date

Mr. David Smith
District Manager
Quality Booksellers
88 Independence Avenue
New York, NY 12367

**Bookseller and
Store Manager**

Mid-level managers are often
distinguished from junior managers
by their ability to manage their
careers. In the case of Delaine
Baughman, he is aggressively
pursuing a management
opportunity with a prestigious
bookseller who is coming to town
to compete. He's now commuting
more than 40 minutes each way
to work, and a job with the new
company would mean only a
five-minute commute.

Dear Mr. Smith:

With the enclosed resume, I would like to make you aware of my background as an experienced retail bookstore manager whose proven communication, organizational, and leadership skills have been tested in a high-volume, large-format environment.

As you will see, I have been with Books-A-Million for some time and have served in a managerial capacity in the Charleston store. Supervising 18 employees in a store that averages $2.5 million dollars a year, I have consistently received high marks on all employee evaluations. Since my promotion to Store Manager, I am responsible for all aspects of personnel recruitment, staff development, and scheduling.

As Manager, I also act as operations manager, directing day-to-day functions of the store and assigning tasks to employees. In addition to administering payroll, benefit and personnel programs, I handle all aspects of the hiring process, and I am proud of the low turnover I have achieved in a job market with a very high transient rate.

Although I am highly regarded by my present employer and can provide excellent references at the appropriate time, I would like to take on the challenge of a larger store. I could benefit Quality Booksellers as they enter the Charleston market through my enthusiasm, high energy level, and "can-do" attitude as well as through my strong management, staff development, and organizational skills.

If you can use a manager with a strong commitment to providing the highest possible levels of customer service and the proven ability to motivate employees to achieve excellence, then I hope you will contact me soon. I can assure you that I have an excellent reputation within the community and could quickly become a valuable addition to your organization.

Sincerely,

Delaine Baughman

DELAINE BAUGHMAN

1110½ Hay Street, Fayetteville, NC 28305 • preppub@aol.com • (910) 483-6611

OBJECTIVE

To benefit an organization that can use an energetic, self-motivated, and highly experienced bookstore manager with exceptional communication skills as well as the proven ability to positively impact the attitude and performance of employees.

EXPERIENCE

Started with Books-A-Million as a Bookseller and was promoted in the following "track record" of increasing responsibility in this high-volume, large-format store:

1996-present: **STORE MANAGER.** Books-A-Million #4326, Charleston, SC. Advanced to this position when the increase in our sales volume prompted home office to re-classify this as a large-format store; perform all my previous duties while assuming increased responsibilities.
* Direct all aspects of operations of a large-format store averaging $2.5 million per year; supervise an average of 18 employees.
* Develop weekly schedules and prioritize daily tasks, directing each employee's work so that all assignments are accomplished in a timely and accurate manner.
* Promote the highest possible standards of customer service by ensuring compliance with Customer Service Standards and providing a strong example for other employees.
* Oversee and direct ordering, receiving, and returns, ensuring a strong in-stock position on fast-moving titles in spite of the store's small size for its volume and high turn rate.
* Solely responsible for all recruiting, interviewing, hiring, and training of staff members; administer payroll, personnel, and benefit programs; perform employee evaluations.
* Conduct coaching, counseling, and motivational sessions, maintaining employee morale and assisting employees to improve in areas of marginal performance.
* Coordinate special events; actively seeking institutional sales and arranging off-site Book Fairs and in-store Author Appearances to raise community awareness of Books-A-Million.

1987-1992: **ASSISTANT MANAGER.** Books-A-Million #4326, Charleston, SC. Advanced to Assistant Manager from Senior Sales Clerk.
* Assisted the Manager in all aspects of the operations of this high-volume store.
* Prepared and maintained the accuracy of all management-level paperwork to include daily, weekly, and monthly sales reports; completed time sheets and schedules; price changes; book, non-book, and magazine receiving and returns logs, etc.
* Merchandised all areas of the store according to district, region, and chain guidelines; changed weekly best-sellers and power aisles; maintained full and attractive displays throughout the store.

1986-87: **SENIOR SALES CLERK.** Books-A-Million #2102, Charleston, SC. Was promoted to Senior Sales Clerk after only four months with Books-A-Million.
* Performed all the duties of a key holder, opening and closing the store.
* Provided direction to booksellers when no Managers were present.
* Stocked, shelved and merchandised all assigned areas of the store, creating effective displays and keeping all display areas full and attractive.

1985-1986: **BOOKSELLER.** Books-A-Million #4109, Charleston, SC. Responsible for customer service; ringing sales, assisting customers in locating and selecting their purchases, and special ordering titles which were out of stock.

PERSONAL

Excellent personal and professional references are available upon request.

Date

Exact Name of Person
Title or Position
Name of Company
Address (number and street)
Address (city, state, and ZIP)

This is an excellent example of an all-purpose resume and cover letter. The cover letter is designed to make this individual appealing to employers in numerous industries, and the Objective on the resume highlights skills and abilities which are transferable to all types of work environments. Notice how the Personal Section of the resume emphasizes his ability to adapt easily to new environments—a subtle hint that he is in career change.

Dear Exact Name of Person: (or Dear Sir or Madam if answering a blind ad.)

Can you use an articulate, detail-oriented professional who offers outstanding abilities in the areas of sales program development and management, financial management, and the training and supervision of employees?

You will see by my enclosed resume that I have built a track record of accomplishments with Holiday Inn Management Services where I am currently the Account Director at Yale University in New Haven, CT. During my six years in this position I have reduced labor costs and increased auxiliary sales while overseeing a program with a $900,000 annual operating budget. I oversee two supervisors and a 30-person staff which provides resident dining, catering, conference, and retail dining services on a private college campus.

In addition to my business, inventory control, personnel, and human resources management responsibilities, I also am heavily involved in the development and management of promotional materials and programs. I have refined natural verbal and written communication skills while acting as liaison between corporate headquarters and the university, training and dealing with employees, and handling customer service activities.

I believe that you would find me to be an articulate professional with the ability to learn quickly and apply my organizational skills and common sense.

I hope you will welcome my call soon to arrange a brief meeting at your convenience to discuss your current and future needs and how I might serve them. Thank you in advance for your time.

Sincerely yours.

Callahan Warren

Alternate last paragraph:
I hope you will call or write me soon to suggest a time convenient for us to meet and discuss your current and future needs and how I might serve them. Thank you in advance for your time.

CALLAHAN WARREN

1110½ Hay Street, Fayetteville, NC 28305 • preppub@aol.com • (910) 483-6611

OBJECTIVE

To offer my expertise in reducing costs as well as increasing profits and customer satisfaction while displaying exceptional sales, leadership, and financial management abilities and refining organizational, training, and time management skills.

EXPERIENCE

Built a track record of accomplishments with Holiday Inn Management Services at Yale University, New Haven, CT:

ACCOUNT DIRECTOR. (1993-present). During a six-year period in this role, have reduced total labor costs more than $96,000 while operating a $900,000 program providing this campus with resident dining, catering, conference, and retail dining services.

- Provided outstanding customer satisfaction in all areas of dining services with a staff of two supervisors and approximately 30 employees.
- Increased Operating Profit Contributions (OPC) from $25,000 to $90,000 and auxiliary sales to more than $228,000 over a six-year period by identifying opportunities, developing strategy, and implementing new plans.
- Polished managerial abilities while developing budgets and business plans along with making revisions in procedures which led to increases in sales and production.
- Managed a procurement program for more than 1,000 line items.
- Reconciled profit and loss statements and balance sheet management.
- Supervised accounts payable and receivable, payroll, and weekly financial reports sent to the corporate office while acting as liaison between the corporation and client.
- Assisted the regional sales director in the development of sales proposals by using sales and cost analysis modules.
- Used my communication skills to prepare brochures, calendars, and other promotional materials as well as in the development of a client communication manual.

FOOD SERVICE MANAGER. (1989-93). Gained exposure to a wide range of day-to-day operational activities related to campus dining, catering, and conference food services.

- Applied time management and organizational skills overseeing fiscal areas of operations which included purchasing as well as inventory, labor cost, and cash-handling controls.
- Handled additional activities ranging from vendor specifications, to menu development and implementation, to promotions and marketing, to catering, to sanitation and safety.
- Updated the automated procedures which reduced unit labor costs.
- Implemented a computerized system used to handle associate payroll, accounts payable, accounts receivable, and billing.

MANAGEMENT TRAINEE. (1989). As a food service management trainee, became familiar with customer service, scheduling, and employee training.

STUDENT MANAGER. Holiday Inn Management Services, Davidson University, Augusta, SC (1988). Hired by the corporation while attending the university, was in charge of food-handling controls and supervised 10 part-time employees.

EDUCATION & TRAINING

B.A., Business Administration (minors: Marketing and Finance), Davidson University, SC, 1989. Completed extensive corporate training programs in major areas of emphasis including:

public relations	safety training	human resource management
sales & cost analysis	internal accounting systems	labor productivity I and II
Total Quality Management 1 and II		diversity/sensitivity training
Hazard Analysis Critical Control Points (HACCP)		food handling & food-borne illness

CERTIFICATION

Am a licensed food handler with certification in food-borne illness.

PERSONAL

Fast learner capable of easily adjusting to new environments. Excellent references.

Date

Exact Name of Person
Title or Position
Name of Company
Address (number and street)
Address (city, state, and zip)

Dear Exact Name of Person: (or Sir or Madam if answering a blind ad.)

With the enclosed resume, I would like to formally make you aware of my interest in your organization. As you will see, I have excelled in jobs which required originality and creativity in prospecting for new clients, business savvy and financial prudence in establishing new ventures, as well as relentless follow-through and attention to detail in implementing ambitious goals.

I was recruited for my current job when the company decided that it wanted to set up a new commercial division and needed someone with proven entrepreneurial skills and a make-it-happen style. Under my leadership we have set up a new commercial division which has targeted the healthcare and pharmaceutical industry as a primary customer base in addition to major financial institutions and large corporations. Although I now manage several individuals, I personally prospected for the initial accounts and I discovered that my extensive training and background related to chemicals and microbiology was of great value in interacting with healthcare industry decision makers.

Although I can provide outstanding personal and professional references and am being groomed for further promotion within my company, I have decided that I wish to transfer my skills and knowledge to the healthcare industry. You will notice from my resume that I have been a successful entrepreneur and previously started a company which I sold to a larger industry firm. I succeeded as an entrepreneur largely because of my ability to communicate ideas to others, my strong problem-solving skills, and my naturally outgoing and self-confident nature. I am certain I could excel in the healthcare industry in any role which requires extraordinary sales, marketing, and relationship-building abilities.

If my background interests you, and if you feel there is a suitable position in your organization in which you could make use of my sales and marketing strengths, I hope you will contact me to suggest a time when we might meet to discuss your goals and how I might help you achieve them. Thank you in advance for your consideration and professional courtesies.

Yours sincerely,

Parsival Flanagan

PARSIVAL FLANAGAN

1110½ Hay Street, Fayetteville, NC 28305 • preppub@aol.com • (910) 483-6611

OBJECTIVE To contribute to an organization that can use a dynamic professional who wishes to transfer my exceptionally strong sales and marketing abilities to the pharmaceutical industry.

EXPERIENCE **MANAGER, COMMERCIAL DIVISION.** Drayton Enterprises, Augusta, ME (1995-present). Was aggressively recruited by this company which wanted to establish a new commercial division targeting the healthcare and pharmaceutical industry as a primary client base; provided the leadership in developing the strategic plan for the new division which has annual revenues of more than half a million dollars; now manage several technicians and sales reps.
- Personally prospected for all the initial accounts.
- Utilized my background and extensive training in chemicals and microbiology to facilitate my sales effectiveness in the healthcare and pharmaceutical industry.
- Excelled in building relationships through creative lead generation, astute needs assessment and fulfillment, and strong skills in closing the sale.

FOUNDER/PRESIDENT. Termites Undone, Inc., Richmond, VA (1988-94). Started "from scratch" a company which was bought out by one of the largest pest elimination service companies in the country.
- Succeeded as an entrepreneur and business manager in a highly competitive industry because of my ability to communicate ideas to others, my problem-solving skills, my ability to formulate new ideas based on information obtained from multiple sources, and my outgoing and self-confident nature.
- Handled all financial matters including budgets, profit-and-loss quotas, tax planning, insurance, and purchasing.
- Acquired considerable experience in dealing with government regulatory agencies and in preparing the paperwork necessary to document programs in critical situations.

VICE PRESIDENT OF SALES AND TRAINING. Dana Exterminating Company, Inc., Augusta, GA (1980-88). Was a major force in the company's growth for over eight years; helped establish formal training and hiring policies.
- Began in sales and in my fourth year was promoted to supervisor responsible for 15 individuals, project management, as well as equipment maintenance and troubleshooting.
- In my fifth year was promoted to **Vice President of Sales & Training** responsible for setting/achieving branch goals, defining/implementing training programs, as well as overseeing safety and vehicle/equipment maintenance.

EDUCATION More than two years of college coursework at **Maine University;** courses included biology and social sciences, accounting and economics.
- Corporate sales and technical training sponsored by leading firms.

PERSONAL Business skills include marketing and sales, starting up new business operations, selecting and training employees, controlling inventory, purchasing materials, preparing strategic plans, dealing with regulators, accounting and financial control.

Date

Exact Name of Person
Title or Position
Name of Company
Address (no., street)
Address (city, state, zip)

Dear Exact Name of Person: (or Dear Sir or Madam if answering a blind ad.)

Can you use a resourceful professional with extensive operations and project management experience along with a "track record" of outstanding results in safety, cost reduction, and other areas?

As you will see from my resume, I am currently excelling as a project manager and foreman for a multimillion-dollar company operating all over the east coast. My results have been impressive; I have greatly exceeded my targeted 20% profit margin by actually performing 32% above profit while finishing all jobs within or ahead of schedule and with no accidents.

As Manager of Operations with a major fire prevention company working under contract to GE, IBM, and other industrial giants, I have acquired expert knowledge of OSHA, EPA, and other regulations. I have been certified by OSHA in soil testing and have worked with OSHA officials regarding HAZMAT and MSDS.

I am particularly proud of the contributions I have made in the areas of cost reduction. On numerous occasions I have discovered ways to free up working capital by decreasing inventory carrying costs, automating manual functions, and monitoring everyday activities to find new ways to streamline operations and decrease both overhead and variable costs.

You would find me in person to be a congenial individual who prides myself on my ability to get along well with people at all levels. I can provide excellent references from all previous employers, including from my current company.

I hope you will write or call me soon to suggest a time when we might meet to discuss your current and future goals and how I might help you achieve them. Thank you in advance for your time.

Sincerely yours,

Napoleon Radosevich

NAPOLEON RADOSEVICH

1110½ Hay Street, Fayetteville, NC 28305 • preppub@aol.com • (910) 483-6611

OBJECTIVE	To benefit an organization that can use a skilled operations manager who offers extensive knowledge of OSHA requirements, in-depth experience in project management and cost/inventory control, as well as expertise in recruiting, training, and managing personnel.
EDUCATION	**B.S. degree in Business Administration**, Temple University, Ambler, PA, 1987. • Concentrated in courses in Finance, Management, and Human Resources.
CERTIFICATION	Have been trained and certified by OSHA in soil testing; have worked closely with OSHA and am very familiar with OSHA, EPA, and other safety guidelines.
EXPERIENCE	**FOREMAN & PROJECT MANAGER**. DKS Construction, Roanoke, VA (1994-present). Am being groomed for further promotion by this multimillion-dollar company which operates in states from GA, across to FL, and into VA; manage projects which involve laying utility lines, erecting overhead lines, and installing transformer boxes in commercial/industrial projects such as factories, shopping malls, and large-scale housing developments. • Am considered one of the company's most knowledgeable managers on OSHA. • Work with representatives of all the building trades while essentially operating as a profit center; in the past year, exceeded my goal of producing a 20% profit margin by actually performing 32% above profit. • Finished all jobs on time or early while establishing a perfect safety record of no accidents. **ASSISTANT OPERATIONS MANAGER**. Brooks Brothers, Utica, NY (1991-93). Made impressive contributions to this company which, upon the ratification of NAFTA in 1993, immediately moved its manufacturing facilities to lower-cost Mexico. • For this company which manufactures expensive men's suits, worked side-by-side with the Operations Manager; personally discovered an over- ordering bias and made changes which reduced excess inventory by $150,000 per year. • For more than 500 employees, established production schedules, assured optimum use of production capacity, and coordinated raw materials and labor. • Played a key role in developing a computer program which improved inventory control. **MANAGER OF OPERATIONS**. Caution Equipment, Waterville, NY (1988-91). Shortly after college graduation, excelled in a position which was created for me by this fast-growing company; rapidly automated all office communication and thereby greatly improved overall decision making and the working relationships among sales, personnel, transportation, administrative, and other personnel. • Played a key role in obtaining the first million-dollar sale for this fire prevention company working under contract to IBM, GE, and major wire manufacturers. • Prudently reduced a $1 million excess inventory to a safe $300,000 level. • On my own initiative, established excellent working relationships with OSHA and authored company policy/procedures related to HAZMAT, MSDS, and other areas; assured that company vehicles met DOT standards for carrying Halon. • Monitored policies and procedures in all company areas, from personnel training to safety management, in order to identify new ways to improve efficiency and lower costs. • Directed inventory and warehouse stock control, warehousing, and traffic and shipping. **MANAGER OF PERSONNEL**. Tele-Tector of Montgomery County, Plymouth Meeting, PA (1983-88). Left this 40-person security alarm company where I worked while in high school and college when the owner sold it to Wells Fargo; after beginning in an entry-level job, advanced to handle the development and management of personnel policies and programs
PERSONAL	Offer an ability to use computers to solve management problems. Excellent references.

Date

Exact Name of Person
Title or Position
Name of Company
Address (no., street)
Address (city, state, zip)

Construction Manager

Dear Exact Name:

This manager has found a job
which interests him through an
advertisement in the newspaper,
but he stresses that he wishes his
interest to remain confidential.
Here's a letter which illustrates
how to decide what to put in a
cover letter. This professional
understands that his background in
hospital environments will interest
The Mayo Clinic, so that's what he
highlights in his cover letter.

I would appreciate an opportunity to talk with you soon about how I could contribute to The Mayo Clinic. I am responding to your ad for a Construction Manager with this *confidential* resume and cover letter to express my interest in receiving your consideration for this position.

As you will see from my enclosed resume, I offer approximately 18 years of progressively increasing responsibility in construction management with the specialized knowledge in a hospital environment that you require.

I would like to point out that I am experienced in working within JCAHO (Joint Commission on Accreditation of Healthcare Organizations), DFS (Division of Facility Services), and Interim Life Safety guidelines through my extensive background in construction management in a hospital environment.

Known for my dedication to high quality and compliance with safety standards, I have always been effective in supervising projects and seeing that work is completed on schedule.

I hope you will welcome my call soon to arrange a brief meeting at your convenience to discuss the current and future needs of The Mayo Clinic and how I might serve them. Thank you in advance for your time. I can provide outstanding personal and professional references.

Sincerely yours.

Christopher Oxendine

CHRISTOPHER OXENDINE

1110½ Hay Street, Fayetteville, NC 28305 • preppub@aol.com • (910) 483-6611

OBJECTIVE	To offer a background of 18 years experience in construction including six in construction management and eight in healthcare facility construction projects with proven strengths in inspiring the confidence and trust of others and effective negotiating skills.
TRAINING	Currently enrolled in an AUTO CAD V-12 class, Wake County Technical Community College. • Completed training leading to certification in the following areas: OSHA Construction Safety and Health Mechanical Blueprinting Institute of Government Contracting for Professional Services: ITT Cable Repair
EXPERIENCE	**CONSTRUCTION MANAGER.** Duke University Hospital, Durham, NC (1996-present). Completed construction and renovation projects while taking care of operational aspects including preparing cost estimates, preparing and monitoring schedules for in-house projects, and overseeing quality control to ensure the highest quality workmanship; manage dozens of skilled tradesmen. • Further enhanced my knowledge of JCAHO (Joint Commission on Accreditation for Healthcare Organizations), DFS (Division of Facility Services), and Interim Life Safety. • Evaluated and approved design changes; made recommendations that reduced costs. • Applied communication skills as liaison among administration, staff, and architects as well as while working closely with staff members to coordinate in-house projects. • Resolved complex contractual issues in close cooperation with architects and engineers. *Completed numerous projects for Bechtel Corporation, San Francisco, CA (1990-1996):* **SITE MANAGER.** (1991-93). Oversaw the $19 million project to construct a 187,000-sq. ft. four-story Patient Services Tower (with full mechanical basement) which housed eight operating rooms, intensive care units, fifteen LDRs, three delivery rooms, a coffee shop, pharmacy, and additional support services. • Coordinated field activities of contractors while reviewing contractor quotes and billings. • Handled the resolution of design and coordination conflicts, monitored contract compliance, and provided quality control oversight. • Maintained contact with architects and engineers; completed project documentation. • Prepared and maintained correspondence with the owner, architect, and contractors. • Participated in project scheduling, job progress meetings, and monitored safety. **SITE MANAGER.** (1990-91). Managed a contract to build a $5.5 million two-floor 31,000-sq. ft. vertical expansion of an existing six-floor patient tower complete with an 8,000-sq. ft. penthouse mechanical room; the project also included adding two elevators and renovating four existing elevators to serve the two new floors. **SITE MANAGER.** (1990). Directed the construction of a $3.2 million, 15,000-sq. ft. Central Energy Plant which housed boilers, chillers, cooling towers, pumps, emergency generators, and other major mechanical and electrical equipment capable of servicing the existing South Patient Tower and future Patient Service Tower. **PROJECT SUPERINTENDENT.** Lawrence Kaplan and Associates, Madison, WI (1988-90). Provided managerial support in areas including the following: documentation, review and awarding of subcontracts, supervision of an adequate work force, scheduling, quality control, inspection, monitoring safety compliance, and ensuring contract compliance. • Completed these projects: 27,000-sq. ft. expansion and 3,700-sq. ft. Linear Accelerator addition to a medical office building; 4,200-sq. ft. cat scan and ophthalmology addition.
PERSONAL	Offer computer experience with WordPerfect 6.0 and the Windows operating system.

Exact Name of Person
Title or Position
Name of Company
Address (number and street)
Address (city, state, and zip)

Controller and Finance Manager

Roger Rose lets prospective employers know right away why his most recent job was in North Carolina—he has relocated to Seattle. Then he gets on with the business of the cover letter—letting the prospective employer know about the bottom-line results he has achieved in his previous jobs.

Dear Exact Name of Person: (or Dear Sir or Madam if answering a blind ad.)

I would appreciate an opportunity to talk with you soon about how I could contribute to your organization through my experience in financial management as well as through my skills in the areas of personnel and operations management along with my strong customer service orientation. I have recently relocated to the Seattle area and am exploring employment opportunities with companies that can make use of my management background and financial skills.

You will see from my enclosed resume that I offer an in-depth knowledge of finance and business. My most recent job was as Controller and General Manager of a real estate rental company for approximately eight years. During this time I substantially reduced the company's debt load, virtually eliminated the amount of uncollectibles, and increased occupancy rates to a consistently high 95%. Through my diplomatic but assertive managerial style, I brought this business out of debt and transformed it into a viable operation.

During a successful career in the U.S. Army, I advanced to hold increasingly more responsible managerial positions in the fields of finance, budgeting, and pay administration as well as in personnel administration. I gained skills and refined a natural aptitude for analyzing, controlling, and resolving problems while earning a reputation as a versatile and adaptable professional.

With an associate's degree in Banking and Finance, I could be a valuable asset to an organization that can use a mature individual with the ability to get along with others in supervisory roles.

I hope you will welcome my call soon to arrange a brief meeting at your convenience to discuss your current and future needs and how I might serve them. Thank you in advance for your time.

Sincerely yours,

Roger Rose

Optional sentence that can go as the second sentence in last paragraph:
I would be happy to discuss the details of my salary history with you in person.

ROGER ROSE

Until 12/15/99: 1110½ Hay Street, Fayetteville, NC 28305   (910) 483-6611

After 12/16/99: 538 Pittsfield Avenue, Seattle, WA 95401   (405) 483-6611

OBJECTIVE

To offer a track record of success in managerial roles with organizations requiring knowledge of finance, personnel, and administrative functions along with a reputation for analytical skills and attention to detail as well as a strong customer service orientation.

EXPERIENCE

CONTROLLER & FINANCE MANAGER. Rentals Incorporated, Raleigh, NC (1991-99). Brought about major improvements in several important functional areas while handling multiple roles as a financial manager, partner, and operations manager for a company with 160 rental units; manage two accounting specialists.
- Reduced the organization's debts more than $20,000 in less than a year through the application of my knowledge and experience in business management and finance.
- Almost totally eliminated uncollectibles – reduced them to under 1%.
- Prepared advertising materials which resulted in improved occupancy levels and consistently maintained 95% fill rates on leased units.
- Took charge of all aspects of finance and business administration ranging from maintaining books, to processing all accounting data, to accounts receivable and payable.
- Prepared and managed the budget; reconciled bank accounts.
- Represented the company through heavy contact with the public while showing prospective residents units available for lease or rent.
- Resolved a wide range of customer service as well as budget and fee problems.

GENERAL MANAGER. The Novelty and Games Company, Buies Creek, NC (1988-91). Applied my knowledge of business and finance to build this company from a concept into a viable organization.
- Dealt with all aspects of establishing and successfully operating a small business: prepared and managed budgets, made bank deposits, and reconciled bank accounts as well as maintaining accounts receivable and payable ledgers.
- Controlled inventory from ordering supplies and merchandise to setting prices.

Highlights of earlier experience: Gained and refined knowledge of personnel management and finance/pay activities during a career with the U.S. Army, locations worldwide.
- As the **Manager** of a program studying the need for changes to the personnel structure of the Army, processed information and resolved problems, researched possible changes to determine their impact, and contributed input used in budget preparation.
- As a **Senior Personnel Management Supervisor,** directed up to 40 specialists engaged in processing promotions, reclassifications, transfers, and performance reports.
- As a **Finance Section Manager,** updated personnel's finance records and verified information before entering it into computers; maintained ledgers, cash books, and all related accounting records.
- As the **Chief of Military Pay and Travel,** processed pay activities for personnel in 11 states and four overseas areas.
- As **Manager of a Personnel Section,** processed military personnel and their family members who were going overseas; arranged for transportation to overseas assignments; provided information and briefings on customs, laws, and conditions in overseas areas.

EDUCATION & TRAINING

A.S. degree in **Banking** and **Finance,** Whitefall Technical Community College, Whitefall, TX. Completed numerous courses in finance, management, and personnel administration sponsored by the U.S. Army.

PERSONAL

Am known for my dedication and insistence on seeing any job through to completion. Have a high level of initiative. Enjoy public relations and customer service activities.

Date

Exact Name of Person
Title or Position
Name of Company
Address (number and street)
Address (city, state, and zip)

This professional has more jobs on
his resume than he wishes he had,
but two of the companies he
worked for went out of business.
He uses the cover letter to point
out this fact to potential employers
so they won't feel he's a "job
hopper" who will be "here today,
gone tomorrow" if they hire him.

Dear Exact Name of Person: (or Sir or Madam if answering a blind ad.)

With the enclosed resume, I would like to initiate the process of being considered for employment within your organization.

As you will see from my resume, I hold a bachelor's degree in Business Administration, an associate's degree in Data Processing, and have completed more than 30 hours of Accounting course work. I offer computer programming experience using Cobol, Basic, and RPG, and I am skilled in using popular software including Excel, Lotus, DACEASY, and other programs.

With regard to accounting, I offer experience as a controller, staff accountant, and cost accountant. An extremely loyal individual with a long-term orientation in all my undertakings in life, I want to draw your attention to the fact that there are more jobs on my resume than I am comfortable with. Through no fault of my own, I have been employed by two companies who decided to liquidate their assets or cease business operations. I can provide outstanding references from all my employers, and I can assure you that they would describe me as an industrious and disciplined individual who is very creative in applying my knowledge to improve internal systems and boost profitability.

My permanent home is in Chicago where my wife is employed as a nurse. It is my desire to become a permanent asset to an organization which can benefit from my considerable skills in consulting, management, and accounting. If you can use my experience and knowledge, please contact me to suggest a time when we might meet to discuss your current and future needs and how I might serve them. Thank you in advance for your time.

Sincerely,

Avery O'Farrell

AVERY O'FARRELL

1110½ Hay Street, Fayetteville, NC 28305 • preppub@aol.com • (910) 483-6611

OBJECTIVE
To benefit an organization that can use a detail-oriented professional with a strong bottom-line orientation who offers experience in management accounting and business management.

SKILLS
Computer programming: COBOL, BASIC, and **RPG** languages.
Software: Excel, Lotus, and DACEASY; familiarity with Solomen IV and GAP software.
Accounting: Data processing, payroll, purchasing, cost estimates, tax return preparation, preparation of P&L Statements.

EDUCATION
B.A. degree, **Business Administration,** 1983; and A.A.S., **Data Processing,** 1985; Providence University, Providence, RI.
- Completed 30 hours of course work in **Accounting** at Providence University.

EXPERIENCE
CONTROLLER. IPG Energy, Chicago, IL (1995-1999). Was recruited to supervise accounting functions for a $97 million project which involved maintaining general ledger, accounts receivable, and accounts payable; this firm is now liquidating its assets.
- Reported directly to project manager and CEO.
- Coordinated with the four partners, representatives from lead bank and associate banks, and officials from counties involved in the waste-energy recycling project.

CONTROLLER. Baytree Developers, Chicago, IL (1993-95). Handled all accounting functions associated with operating this two-location, 60-employee business that processed soil and bark products sold primarily to large chain stores, including Lowe's, Food Lion, etc.
- Coordinated and supervised two clerks in the home office and assisted in the day-to-day managing of both processing plants.
- Supervised a variety of accounting procedures including monthly financial statements, bank statement reconciliations, and quarterly payroll tax reports.

STAFF ACCOUNTANT. Sycamore Industries, Chicago, IL (1992-93). Supervised four clerks while preparing monthly financial statements, maintaining general ledger and fixed assets, and working as liaison with corporate accounting office.
- Managed accounts payable and payroll; prepared all monthly, quarterly, and annual sales, fuel, and regulatory tax returns.
- For this construction materials firm with annual revenues in excess of $15 million, prepared various analyses used as management decision-making tools.

BUSINESS MANAGER. Providence Junior College, Providence, RI (1990-91). Prepared reports pertaining to accounts payable and cash disbursements while also maintaining data concerning student accounts receivable.
- Maintained bookstore inventories; made deposits and reconciled bank statements; provided counseling for students regarding financial aid and student loans.

STAFF ACCOUNTANT. Bryson Associates, CPA, Providence, RI (1988-90). Analyzed corporate books for compilations and preparation of financial statements. Prepared individual and corporate tax returns. Participated in field audits.

COST ACCOUNTANT. Anderson Constructors, Providence, RI (1986-88). Prepared job cost reports and assisted with administration of subcontracts.

PERSONAL
Can provide outstanding personal and professional references upon request.

Exact Name
Title or Position
Name of Company
Address (number and street)
Address (city, state, and zip)

**Credit Manager,
Building Supplies**

If you want to job hunt in industries other than the one you're in, keep the Objective on your resume all purpose and versatile. Notice the Personal Section. Sometimes you can show off an accomplishment in the Personal Section which doesn't seem to fit in anywhere else on the resume. It may still be an accomplishment which could make the prospective employer react to you in a positive fashion.

Dear Exact Name of Person: (or Dear Sir or Madam if answering a blind ad.)

With the enclosed resume, I would like to indicate my interest in your organization and my desire to explore employment opportunities.

As you will see from my enclosed resume, as Credit Manager of a large building supply company, I have played a key role in the growth of the company from two stores with sales of less than $15 million to five stores with more than $40 million in sales. I have been in charge of approving all new accounts for all stores, and I have implemented internal controls which have reduced the number of days of sales outstanding by more than 20 days. Although I am held in high regard by my current employer, the business is in the process of merging with a larger regional company, so I am taking this opportunity to explore opportunities with other area firms.

I hope you will welcome my call soon to arrange a brief meeting at your convenience to discuss your current and future needs and how I might serve them. Thank you in advance for your time.

Sincerely yours.

Phillip Harris

Alternate last paragraph:
I hope you will call or write me soon to suggest a time convenient for us to meet and discuss your current and future needs and how I might serve them. Thank you in advance for your time.

PHILLIP HARRIS

1110½ Hay Street, Fayetteville, NC 28305 • preppub@aol.com • (910) 483-6611

OBJECTIVE   To add value to an organization that can use a well-organized manager who is skilled in developing new systems and procedures for profitability enhancement, establishing new accounts and managing existing ones, and administering finances at all levels.

EDUCATION   **Bachelor of Science in Business Administration (B.S.B.A.) degree**, concentration in Finance, Western Tennessee University, 1983.
- Member, Beta Kappa Alpha Banking and Finance Fraternity.
- Was active in intramural softball, basketball, and arm wrestling.
- Worked throughout college in order to finance my college education.

Completed **A.I.B. in Consumer Lending,** Pitt Community College, 1986.

EXPERIENCE   **CREDIT MANAGER.** All Purpose Building Supply, Raleigh, NC (1990-present). Was specially recruited by the company to assume this position which involved establishing a credit department with three employees.
- Played a key role in the growth of the company from two stores with sales of less than $15 million, to five stores with sales of more than $40 million.
- Reduced the number of days of sales outstanding by 20+ days.
- Was in charge of approving all new accounts for five stores.
- Developed and maintained an excellent working relationship with all customers.
- Formulated and implemented key areas of company policy by authoring credit policies; directed activities including account adjustments, skip tracing, liening, and billing.
- Coordinated with the corporate attorney; prepared cash flow projections and provided the controller with financial information for profit-and-loss statements and balance sheets for the company owners.
- Implemented procedures that lowered chargeoffs and increased collection activity while accounts receivables grew from $2 million to $7.5 million.

CONSUMER LOAN OFFICER. East Coast Federal Savings & Loan, Raleigh, NC (1986-90). Was promoted to responsibilities for handling activities in these areas:

commercial lending	consumer lending
collections	credit card approval
credit investigations	marketing of consumer loans

LOAN OFFICER & COLLECTION REPRESENTATIVE. NCNB National Bank of North Carolina, Raleigh, NC (1983-86). After excelling as a Collection Representative, was promoted to Loan Officer, in charge of lending money for consumer purchases and performing credit investigations.
- As a Collection Representative, collected past due accounts, cross-referenced bank records versus automobile dealerships' records, and investigated consumer account payment records while also handling foreclosures, repossessions, insurance claims, and skip tracing of delinquent accounts.
- Performed liaison with banking auditors and legal personnel.
- Gained expertise in all aspects of banking and lending.

SALESMAN/ACCOUNT REPRESENTATIVE. Premier Building Supply, Oakland, TN (1977-83). Worked at this construction industry supply company in the summers and breaks during the years when I was earning my college degree.
- Learned to deal with people while selling building materials, light fixtures, garden supplies, and hardware; graduated into responsibilities for handling major accounts.

PERSONAL   In high school was a member of the National Math Honor Society and the Science Club and set my school's record in the shot put while also excelling in football and wrestling.

Date

Exact Name of Person
Title or Position
Name of Company
Address (number and street)
Address (city, state, and zip)

**Director of Executive Services
and Facility Manager**

What do you do when your
"dream job" suddenly expires?
That's what happened to this mid-
level professional, who had thrived
on the glamour of taking care of
one of America's richest families.
When they sold their estate, she
had to job hunt. Needless to say,
her track record of working only
two places in 20 years is a rare
and positive thing!

Dear Exact Name of Person: (or Sir or Madam if answering a blind ad.)

I would appreciate an opportunity to talk with you about how I could contribute to your organization through my extensive experience in financial management, operations management, events management, and personnel management.

As you will see from my resume, I am currently working as Director of Executive Services and Facilities Manager for the Foxhill Estates, a resort community in The Hamptons, NY, owned for decades by the Rockefeller family which was recently sold to the state of New York for government use. I am assisting in the orderly transition of this property to state ownership. Since 1993, I have shouldered a wide range of management responsibilities including managing a 10-person household staff catering to the Rockefeller family and guests while also overseeing a 25-person staff involved in farming, maintenance, and in the upkeep of facilities which include skeet ranges, tennis courts, swimming pools, riding stables, an 18-hole golf course, and nature trails. I have become an expert in nearly every aspect of hospitality management since we routinely host private parties and corporate events. I have been the property's only on-site person handling accounting procedures as well, and I have excelled in cost control while utilizing accounting software programs to maintain data.

In my previous job with Prestige Oil Company, a diversified business which included car washes, convenience stores, and a large trailer park, I was the "right arm" to the owner and worked faithfully for him from 1980 until 1993, when I joined Foxhill Estates.

I can provide outstanding references, and I can assure you that I have multiple talents and abilities which would permit me to become a valuable member of any organization.

I hope you will welcome my call soon to arrange a brief meeting to discuss your current and future needs and how I might serve them. Thank you in advance for your time.

Sincerely,

Grace Belsky

GRACE BELSKY

1110½ Hay Street, Fayetteville, NC 28305 • preppub@aol.com • (910) 483-6611

OBJECTIVE

To benefit an organization that can use a highly motivated self-starter with expert knowledge of financial accounting and bookkeeping along with proven management skills in organizing private parties and corporate events, managing large-scale property assets and personnel, and coordinating the use of amenities/facilities.

EXPERIENCE

DIRECTOR OF EXECUTIVE SERVICES & FACILITIES MANAGER. Foxhill Estates, Ltd., Hampton, NY (1993-present). Was employed to oversee a 25-person staff of laborers, farmers, mechanics, farmers, and grounds personnel as well as a 10-person household staff comprised of cooks, housekeepers, servers, and other domestic personnel serving the Rockefeller family and their guests.

- Acted as financial agent for all the business and leisure activities, and managed financial relationships among seven partnerships and corporations in the Foxhill Estates Group.
- As the estate's only accountant, utilized Word software for accounting and Excel to maintain accounting information; performed P & L analysis and prepared all documentation for the accounting firm which prepared the taxes while optimizing cash management and handling day-to-day transactions exceeding 300 monthly.
- Coordinated and supervised all details, including intra-state transportation and menu planning, for private parties and corporate events held at the estate.
- Assured proper maintenance of facilities including a skeet shooting range, nature trails, an 18-hole golf course, hunting areas, riding stables, indoor and outdoor swimming pools, as well as tennis and croquet courts.
- Assured impeccable upkeep of five elegant family homes.
- Managed the estate's annual budget, which ranged considerably yearly depending on whether the family allocated funds for capital expenditures and which crops were to be farmed.
- Reported to the General Manager and was frequently in charge of vast property holdings in his absence.
- Was commended for my ability to work without supervision and for my ability to make prudent decisions while using my common sense to solve problems.
- Became skilled in dealing with all sorts of people: day laborers; skilled, white-collar professionals; high-income guests; vendors and suppliers; and co-workers.

OFFICE MANAGER. Prestige Oil Company, Inc., New York, NY (1980-93). Worked continuously for this company and was the owner's "right arm" except for a brief period in 1985-86 when I resigned to care for a terminally ill relative; was rehired by the owner and played a key role in managing and accounting for his diversified business which included the oil company as well as five convenience stores, two car washes, and a trailer park with more than 50 rental units.

- Responsible for all accounting activities, general ledger, accounts payable and receivable, payroll, and all taxes including sales tax, payroll tax, excise taxes, and state and federal gasoline taxes.
- Performed manual and computerized bookkeeping for this company and two other sub-companies; maintained and reconciled six bank accounts.
- Maintained owner's personal checkbook and records and attended to a portion of his personal business.

EDUCATION

Completed numerous professional development courses in financial management, accounting, systems management, and customer service.

PERSONAL

Am a loyal and dedicated employee with outstanding references. Enjoy new challenges and offer versatile financial and public relations knowledge. Excellent references.

Date

Exact Name of Person
Exact Title
Exact Name of Company
Address
City, State, Zip

Dear Exact Name of Person (or Dear Sir or Madam if answering a blind ad):

With the enclosed resume, I would like to make you aware of my abilities as an experienced sales and management professional with exceptional communication and motivational abilities as well as a background in district-level outside sales, retail and industrial management, and staff development.

In my most recent position, I am excelling as a District Sales Manager for Cable Distributing Company, the largest broadline food distributor in the Midwest. During my time there, I have raised gross profit dollars by 72%, total sales dollars by 69%, and increased the customer base in my district by 185%. For these and other accomplishments, I was awarded the President's Club Growth Award for fiscal 1999.

As Co-Manager for a major discount retailer in my previous job, I was in charge of all hard lines areas of a $28 million store, supervising 120 people including 7 department managers. Areas under my direct supervision contributed nearly $10 million dollars annually in sales, and under my management the hard lines area experienced a sales increase of 20% while reducing inventory shrinkage by 70%. In a previous position as a Manager Trainee, I developed spreadsheets to track productivity and quality in key parts and assemblies, and I maintained databases to analyze the effectiveness of "Just-In-Time" processes in assembly areas. I have earned a Bachelor of Science in Economics from Wisconsin University.

If you can use an experienced sales or management professional with exceptional communication and motivational skills, I hope you will contact me to suggest a time when we might meet to discuss your needs. I can assure you in advance that I have an outstanding reputation and would rapidly become an asset to your organization.

Sincerely,

Kyle V. Metge

KYLE V. METGE

1110½ Hay Street, Fayetteville, NC 28305 • preppub@aol.com • (910) 483-6611

OBJECTIVE

To benefit an organization that can use an experienced manager and sales professional with exceptional communication skills as well as experience in district-level outside sales, retail and industrial management, and staff development.

EDUCATION

Bachelor of Arts degree in Economics, Wisconsin University, Milwaukee, WI, 1988.

EXPERIENCE

DISTRICT SALES MANAGER. Cable Distributing, Milwaukee, WI (1994-present). Manage growth of and maintain existing accounts while developing new business in my district for this large broadline food distributor; consistently exceed my personal sales quota while training and managing five junior sales representatives.
- Increased customer base in my district by 185% while maintaining a very high percentage of paid accounts.
- Received President's Club Growth Award for fiscal year 1999.
- Raised gross profit dollars by 72% and total sales by 69% in my district.
- Quickly build a strong rapport with customers, assessing their needs, and assisting them in selecting the products that will best serve their needs.
- Demonstrate exceptional communication skills on a daily basis, presenting new products and services in a clear and persuasive manner.
- Participate in company promotions and regional trade shows.

CO-MANAGER. MarketWorld, Milwaukee, WI (1992-1994). Managed the hard lines area of this $28 million per year retail store; co-responsible for all aspects of store operations.
- Supervised up to 120 people, including seven Department Managers.
- Contributed over one-third of the total sales in a $28 million dollar store, achieving sales of $2 million in the Candy/Food and Electronics departments and $1 million in the Stationery and Appliance departments.
- The store doubled its net income for fiscal 1993.
- Maintained a sales increase for the hard lines area of more than 20% while reducing inventory shrinkage by 70%.
- Coordinated the ordering of merchandise in basic and seasonal areas.
- Utilized the perpetual inventory system and other inventory controls to ensure a strong in-stock position on fast-moving items.
- Served as third-shift manager in charge of all shipping and receiving.

MANAGER TRAINEE. Murphyville Furniture Industries, Milwaukee, WI (1989-1992). Cross-trained in all aspects of furniture production in this busy, high-volume facility.
- Assisted the production manager in producing detailed sketches of parts and assemblies, to increase accuracy and productivity.
- Developed spreadsheets to track productivity and quality in key parts and assemblies.
- Utilized data and spreadsheets to improve quality of key components, including table tops, doors, frames, drawers, moldings, etc.
- Maintained data to analyze effectiveness of and compliance with "Just- In-Time" process in assembly areas.

PERSONAL

Excellent personal and professional references are available upon request.

Date

Exact Name of Person
Title or Position
Name of Company
Address (No., street)
Address (city, state, zip)

Freight Manager,
Fortune 500 Company

Although he is "held in high
regard" by his current employer,
as he states in his cover letter, Mr.
Palacios heard through the
grapevine that his company was
going to downsize and he didn't
want to be caught without
options. Developing options is
what his resume and cover letter
are designed to do.

Dear Exact Name of Person: (or Dear Sir or Madam if answering a blind ad.)

I would appreciate an opportunity to talk with you soon about how I could contribute to your organization through my experience in all aspects of traffic and transportation management. I offer extensive knowledge of LTL, TL, Intermodal, rate negotiations, pool shipments, and cost analysis to determine the most economical method of shipping.

As you will see from my resume, I am currently site freight coordinator for a Fortune 500 company, and I have continuously found new ways to reduce costs and improve efficiency while managing all inbound and outbound shipping. On my own initiative, I have recovered $10,000 in claims annually while saving the company at least 40% of a $10 million LTL budget. In addition to continuous cost cutting, I have installed a new bar code system in the finished goods shipping area and have installed a new wrapping system.

In previous jobs supervising terminal operations, I opened up new terminals, closed down existing operations which were unprofitable, and gained hands-on experience in increasing efficiency in every terminal area.

With a reputation as a savvy negotiator, I can provide excellent personal and professional references. I am held in high regard by my current employer.

I hope you will call or write me soon to suggest a time convenient for us to meet and discuss your current and future needs and how I might serve them. Thank you in advance for you time.

Sincerely yours,

Pedro Palacios

Alternate last paragraph:
I hope you will welcome my call soon to arrange a brief meeting at your convenience to discuss your current and future needs and how I might serve them. Thank you in advance for your time.

PEDRO PALACIOS

1110½ Hay Street, Fayetteville, NC 28305 • preppub@aol.com • (910) 483-6611

OBJECTIVE   To contribute to an organization that can use a skilled traffic management professional who offers a proven ability to reduce costs, install new systems, optimize scheduling, negotiate rates, anticipate difficulties, solve problems, and keep customers happy.

EXPERIENCE   **SITE FREIGHT COORDINATOR**. DuPont Corporation, Wilmington, DE (1989-present). For this Fortune 500 company, have continuously found new ways to cut costs and improve service while managing all inbound transportation as well as outbound shipping totaling in excess of one million dollars in finished goods daily; supervise ten people.
- Saved the company at least 40% of a $10 million LTL budget by resourcefully combining my technical knowledge with my creative cost-cutting skills.
- Recovered $10,000 annually in claims; prepare all cargo claims documents for corporate office and oversee all procedures for proper claims documentation.
- Installed a bar code system in Finished Goods Shipping, and also installed a new wrapping system.
- Reduced overtime by 90% while simultaneously cross-training some employees and improving overall morale.
- Became familiar with Total Quality Processes while analyzing transit times to ensure consistent and timely Just-In-Time delivery schedules.
- Am a member of the B & D corporate committee for North American rate negotiations; negotiate rates with various carriers on special moves.
- Justify capital appropriation requests for funding special projects; audit all freight bills and process them for payment.
- Prepare all documents for export shipments to Canada; also advise about the shipment of hazardous materials and maintain proper documentation placards and labels.
- Coordinate all site printing of product information and warranty cards.
- Am responsible for site switcher and equipment such as leased trailers.
- Have earned a reputation as a savvy negotiator with an ability to predict future variables that will affect traffic costs.

SUPERVISOR. International Freightways, Inc., Atlanta, GA (1986-88). Supervised up to 12 drivers while managing second-shift operations and controlling inbound and outbound freight at this terminal operation.
- Increased efficiency in every operational area; improved the load factor, reduced dock hours, and ensured more timely deliveries.

INVENTORY SPECIALIST. La-Z-Boy East, Inc., Florence, SC (1984-86). Learned the assembly process of this name-brand furniture manufacturer while managing replenishment of subassemblies for daily production.

Highlights of other experience:
- As Terminal Manager for Spartan Express, opened a new terminal in South Carolina; determined the pricing structure, handled sales, and then managed this new operation which enjoyed rapid growth.
- Gained experience in closing down a terminal determined to be in a poor location.
- As Operations Manager for a break bulk operation, supervised up to 12 people in a dock center while managing the sorting/segregating of shipments from origin to destination.

EDUCATION   Studied business management and liberal arts, Ohio State and LaSalle University. Completed extensive executive development courses in the field of transportation and traffic management sponsored by University of Toledo and Texas Technical University

PERSONAL   Can provide outstanding personal and professional references. Will relocate.

Date

Mr. John Bailey
Quality Shipping
4250 Jonestown Road SE
Atlanta, GA 30315

Freight Terminal Manager

If you want to compare the resumes of two similar professionals, compare this resume with the resume of Pedro Palacios on the preceding pages. Mr. Velasquez emphasizes that he has worked for the same company for the past 14 years.

Dear Mr. Bailey:

I would appreciate an opportunity to talk with you soon about how I could benefit Quality Shipping as a Branch Terminal Manager/Account Manager through my strong background in the transportation industry.

Known for my expertise in increasing sales and revenue while reducing costs, you will see by my enclosed resume that I have in-depth experience gained while working for the regional carrier McDonald Transportation. In my 14 years with this company I advanced to management roles after beginning in a ground-floor position as a Driver and Freight Handler. I am also a skilled accounts representative and enjoy the challenge of selling transportation services. I have become very adept at selling transportation services based mostly on quality and service rather than on price.

Throughout my career with McDonald Transportation, I consistently made changes which resulted in increased sales and revenue while reducing costs and eliminating unnecessary expenses. For instance, in my most recent position as Branch Terminal Manager at the Raleigh, NC, terminal I was credited with bringing about a 35% increase in sales and revenue, a 15% reduction in operating costs, and an increase in on-time rates from 89% to a near-perfect 98%.

Selected to attend corporate training courses in quality management, sales, and front-line supervisory techniques, I was appointed to Quality Improvement Teams beginning in 1991 and was elected as team chairman for 1995.

I am certain that you would find in me a talented manager who communicates effectively with others at all levels and is experienced in making sound decisions under pressure. With an excellent reputation within the transportation industry, I am a flexible and versatile individual who would consider serving your needs in a variety of capacities and functional areas. I can provide very strong references.

I hope you will welcome my call soon to arrange a brief meeting at your convenience to discuss your current and future needs and how I might serve them. Thank you in advance for your time.

Sincerely yours.

William Velasquez

WILLIAM VELASQUEZ

1110½ Hay Street, Fayetteville, NC 28305 • preppub@aol.com • (910) 483-6611

OBJECTIVE

To offer my reputation as a thoroughly knowledgeable professional with special abilities related to terminal operations, sales, quality management, and customer service gained while advancing to increasingly higher managerial levels within the trucking industry.

QUALITY MANAGEMENT

Appointed to Quality Improvement Teams in Georgia, North Carolina, and South Carolina (1991-96), was elected as chairman in 1995. Believe in total quality results, top to bottom.

EXPERIENCE

Built a track record of promotion while becoming known for my expertise in increasing sales and reducing operational costs with McDonald Transportation, an interstate trucking company operating predominately in the southeastern U.S.:

BRANCH TERMINAL MANAGER. Raleigh, NC (1996-present). Continued to find ways to increase revenue and efficiency while managing all aspects of daily terminal operations ranging from staffing and training, to managing a sales territory, to supervising the terminal's account manager.
- Displayed a talent for introducing changes which increased annual sales/revenue 35%.
- Brought about a 15% reduction in operating costs while increasing on-time delivery rates to an almost-perfect 98% rate from the previous 89%.

TERMINAL MANAGER. Greensboro, NC (1994-96). Reduced operating costs 10% over a two-year period while directing total terminal operations including staffing and training employees in every section of the business; supervised two account managers.
- Increased annual sales and revenue 30% each year.

ACCOUNT MANAGER and **BRANCH TERMINAL MANAGER.** Baxley, GA (1992-94). Wore "two hats" as a combination Account Manager and Branch Terminal Manager; earned rapid promotion because of my success in sales and in hiring/supervising 15 people.
- During only nine months in this job, made improvements resulting in a 30% growth in sales and revenue as well as an 18% decrease in operating costs.

SALES REPRESENTATIVE. Miami, FL (1991-92). Refined sales and customer service skills as the account manager for approximately 50% of the customer base for a company which provides sales and service within 80-100 miles of each local terminal.
- Maintained a strong repeat customer base while bringing about a 41% increase in sales,

DISPATCHER/OPERATIONS MANAGER. Orlando, FL (1988-91). Learned to remain in control under pressure and constant deadlines while scheduling deliveries and pick ups and dispatching trucks throughout the area.
- Applied my problem-solving skills by decreasing the number of missed pick ups 70%, thereby increasing customer satisfaction and boosting the bottom line.

SHIPPING SUPERVISOR. Orlando, FL (1987-88). Supervised ten dock workers; established truck routes; ensured shipments were on time with no errors or damage.
- Improved procedures so that the number of damage claims was greatly reduced while also reorganizing routes so that work loads increased and costs decreased.

TRAINING

Was selected to attend numerous corporate-sponsored professional development programs and seminars related to these and other areas:

Front-line supervisory practices	Sales and closing techniques
Breaking down work processes	Making quality improvements

PERSONAL

Offer an outstanding reputation within the transportation industry and can provide excellent references. Am skilled in competing based on quality and service, not just on price.

Date

Mr. Tom Fineagan
Greystone Funeral Home
3512 Buloxi Boulevard
New Orleans, LA 87503

Dear Mr. Fineagan:

I would appreciate an opportunity to talk with you about how I could contribute to your organization through my extensive experience in the death care industry.

At 43 years of age, I have been in the funeral service industry for more than 25 years and offer expertise in every facet of the business, including pre-need sales and arrangement, funeral direction, as well as embalming and embalming management. I have utilized my business degree well in our industry; through the years I have devised and implemented numerous techniques and systems which have improved efficiency and profitability while maintaining quality service and absolute customer satisfaction. I have applied my business background while managing and maintaining $1.5 million worth of property through a family trust and over the past eight years increased annual income more than 100%.

Considered an expert in embalming and restorative procedures, I have enjoyed sharing my knowledge with the many young students whom I have trained over the years. I am also known as a leading citizen in my community and have established an excellent personal and professional reputation, a fact which has generated much business through the years. I genuinely enjoy working with the public, and I am skilled at earning the trust and confidence of people from all races, religions, and backgrounds.

If you need a truly versatile professional who is skilled at every functional area related to mortuary science and funeral direction, I hope you will contact me to suggest a time when we might meet to discuss your needs and how I might serve them. Thank you for your time.

Sincerely,

Frank Davidson

FRANK DAVIDSON

1110½ Hay Street, Fayetteville, NC 28305 • preppub@aol.com • (910) 483-6611

OBJECTIVE To contribute to an organization that can use a versatile and knowledgeable professional who is experienced in all aspects of the death care industry including pre-need sales and arrangement, funeral direction, as well as embalming and embalming management.

EDUCATION Received **Diploma in Mortuary Science**, Cincinnati College, Cincinnati, OH, 1975. Associate's **Degree in Business**, MaComber College, MaComber, LA, 1972.

LICENSE Am a **Licensed Funeral Director**; became a Florida Funeral Service Licensee in 1975 and am required to obtain five hours of continuing professional education annually. Am National Board Certified.

AFFILIATIONS Have been active in my community; following are highlights of my involvements:
- Member, Nursing Home Advisory Board
- Member, Parks and Recreation Board
- Member, Administrative Board, Wilson United Methodist Church
- Master of Masonic Lodge, Shriner
- Past member, West Ft. Lauderdale Rotary Club

EXPERIENCE **FUNERAL DIRECTOR** and **EMBALMER**. Wesleyan Funeral Service Crematory, Ft. Lauderdale, FL (1995-present). Use my extensive experience in funeral directing and embalming to enhance the overall profitability and efficiency of funerals; have introduced several new techniques which simplified funeral arrangements.
- Apply my expert knowledge of the laws and requirements related to funeral home administration and State Board licensing.
- Refined the skills of junior personnel by sharing with them the many secrets and shortcuts in embalming and restorative work which I have learned in my 20 years of experience.
- Have a reputation as an outstanding communicator who easily establishes rapport with people from every race and background, and am very knowledgeable with regard to discussing and tailoring funeral needs to specific religious beliefs.
- Gained experience with cremation; learned how to operate a crematory.

FUNERAL DIRECTOR and **EMBALMER**. Best Funeral Home, Ft. Lauderdale, FL (1981-94). Excelled in handling the full range of activities involved in the selling, conducting, and pre-need arranging of funerals.
- Was responsible for the overall preparation of bodies, and became known for my expertise in embalming and restorative procedures.
- Played a key role in supervising the maintenance of the extensive building and grounds.
- Took pleasure in training many students working at this funeral home through the years.
- Wrote the policy training manual related to OSHA, EPA, and other similar standards and regulations.
- Helped design and plan a new preparation room as well as numerous improvements to the physical plant and grounds.
- Maintained outstanding relationships with law enforcement officials, the media, and with a wide variety of community, state, and local organizations and officials.
- Promoted a strong relationship between the death care industry and the public.

ASSISTANT MANAGER. Piedmont Funeral Home, Lexington, NC (1975-80). Excelled in my first job in the funeral industry; moved up through the ranks to assume responsibilities in all phases of funeral home operations including shift leader and assistant manager.

PERSONAL Can provide outstanding personal and professional references. Genuinely enjoy working with the public. Am a talented organizer, motivator, communicator, and manager.

Date

Mr. David Geer
East West Partners
190 Finley Golf Club Road
Chapel Hill, NC 27514

Golf Professional

Sports professionals need resumes, just like people in other fields. This accomplished professional is seeking a particular position at a prestigious club, so the cover letter is tailored specifically to that club. With minor alterations, he could transform this special letter into an all-purpose letter which he could use as "fish bait" with many other clubs.

Dear Mr. Geer:

With the enclosed resume, I am formally indicating my interest in the Head Golf Professional position at The Country Club of North Carolina.

In my current job as the Head Golf Professional at The Foxfire Resort and Country Club in Pinehurst, NC, I have improved every aspect of the golf program at this esteemed country club. Although I am quite happy in my current situation and am appreciated for the significant improvements I have made in every area of the golf program, it has always been my goal to become associated one day with a prestigious club such as The Country Club of North Carolina. I am aware of the high-profile clientele you serve, and I feel certain I could add value to your operation and enhance the superior climate for which you already are known.

At Foxfire Resort and Country Club, I have resourcefully found new ways to save money every year while making sure customers are satisfied with all "the little things" that can drive members crazy if they're not perfect! By those "little things" I include things such as the variety and quality of golf shop inventory, the tournament program, golf instruction, golf cart operation and bag storage, driving range administration, as well as the operation of starters and rangers. I have taken golf instruction to a new level and, while supervising seven employees, I have continually developed the instructional abilities of my assistants.

I have completed PGA Business School I, II, and III, have served on the PGA Oral Interview Committee, and was invited by fellow PGA Professionals to act as instructor for the Georgia Junior Golf League. In my previous job, I gained extensive experience in organizing and managing an extensive tournament schedule including The Southern Amateur Tournament, National Amputee Tournament, and the U.S. Senior Golf Association Tournament.

You would find me in person to be a congenial individual who prides myself on my ability to relate well to anyone. I believe strongly in the ability of golf to teach and refine virtues including honesty, fairness, courtesy, responsibility, and discipline.

I hope you will write or call me to suggest a time when we might meet in confidence to discuss your needs. I can provide outstanding references.

Sincerely yours,

Charles Gebhardt

CHARLES GEBHARDT

1110½ Hay Street, Fayetteville, NC 28305 • preppub@aol.com • (910) 483-6611

OBJECTIVE

To benefit an organization that can use a respected golf professional who offers experience in financial management, proven skills in teaching and training, as well as an intense commitment to the highest standards of excellence in both personal and professional areas.

EXPERIENCE

HEAD GOLF PROFESSIONAL. Foxfire Resort and Country Club, Pinehurst, NC (1995-present). Have earned a reputation as an enthusiastic and hard-working professional who has improved every aspect of the golf program at this prestigious country club.

- **Golf shop sales and service**: Improved customer service, accounting practices, and the quality of merchandise; boosted sales from $155,000 to $177,000 in my first year, to $223,000 in my second year, and to more than $230,000 in the third year.
- **Financial administration**: Resourcefully found new ways to decrease expenses while improving services; proposed a 1993 budget that is $21,000 less than the 1992 budget and have already reduced expenses by $6,000 in 1994.
- **Tournament program**: Hosted the 1994 North Carolina Amateur Tournament and generally increased the club's level of interest in competition.
- **Golf instruction**: Continually developed the instructional abilities of my assistants and improved the golf game of every student I taught.
- **Starters and rangers**: Improved course scheduling, developed new approaches to helping members find games, and ensured a reasonable pace on busy days.
- **Junior Golf Program**: Exposed juniors to the great virtues golf can teach — honesty, fairness, courtesy, responsibility, determination, and discipline.
- **Golf cart operation and bag storage**: Improved maintenance, repairs, and customer satisfaction with all aspects of these operations.
- **Driving range**: Developed an attractive range membership plan.
- **Employee supervision**: Supervised seven employees; am known for my fairness.

ASSISTANT GOLF PROFESSIONAL. The Country Club of South Carolina, Myrtle Beach, SC (1989-95). Supervised nine bag storage and cart operation personnel while managing accounts receivable/payable, inventory control, and merchandising.

- Organized and managed an extensive tournament schedule which included The Southern Amateur Tournament, National Amputee Tournament, and U.S. Senior Golf Tournament.

FIRST ASSISTANT PROFESSIONAL. Atlanta Country Club, Atlanta, GA (1986-89). Managed part-time cart staff and pro shop staff; planned budgets for cart staff and operation costs for the driving range; and handled accounts receivable/payable, inventory control, and merchandise selection; organized Men's and Ladies' Clinics as well as a Junior Golf Camp.

FIRST ASSISTANT PROFESSIONAL. Foxfire Resort and Country Club, Pinehurst, NC (1984-86). Began as Second Assistant Professional in 1984 and was promoted to First Assistant Professional in less than a year; learned the "nuts and bolts" of program management.

EDUCATION

Completed **PGA Business School I, II, and III**, Nashville, TN, and Atlanta, GA, 1984, 1985, and 1992.
Completed workshops focused on business planning for the golf professional, techniques for outclassing the competition, improving the appearance of the club scoreboard, food and beverage principles, wage and hour laws, and computer software.

HONORS

Invited by fellow PGA Professionals to be an instructor, Georgia Junior Golf League, 1987. Appointed member, PGA Oral Interview Committee, 1988.

PERSONAL

Enjoy hunting, fishing, and spending time with my family when not at work. Am known as a powerful motivator and communicator who knows how to develop people to their fullest .

Date

Exact Name of Person
Title or Position
Name of Company
Address (number and street)
Address (city, state, and zip)

Head Buyer, Consumer Products Distribution

What do you think would motivate a young single professional to quit his good job and move to another city? You guessed it—a woman. He has an excellent track record to show off to prospective employers in Atlanta: He's worked for only one company since graduating from college, and he has been promoted to increasing responsibilities.

Dear Exact Name of Person: (or Sir or Madam if answering a blind ad.)

With the enclosed resume, I would like to initiate the process of being considered for employment within your organization. Because of family ties, I am in the process of relocating to the Atlanta area by a target date of December 20. Although I already have an Atlanta address which is shown on my resume, it is my mother's home and I would prefer your contacting me at my current telephone number if you wish to talk with me prior to December 20th.

As you will see from my resume, since graduating from the University of Florida in 1993, I have excelled in a track record of rapid promotion with a corporation headquartered in Miami which distributes thousands of products to convenience stores and grocery chains all over the southern states. I began as an Assistant Branch Manager and Head Buyer, was cross-trained as a Sales Representative, and have been promoted to my current position in which I manage the selling process related to 3,500 different products. In that capacity, I am entrusted with making responsibilities for nearly $10-15 million annually in expenditures, and I maintain excellent working relationships with more than 200 vendors of name-brand consumer products sold through chain and convenience stores.

In my job, rapid change is a daily reality, and I have become accustomed to working in an environment in which I must make rapid decisions while weighing factors including forecasted consumer demand, distribution patterns, inventory turnover patterns, and vendor capacity and character. I have earned a reputation as a persuasive communicator and savvy negotiator with an aggressive bottom-line orientation.

If you can use my versatile experience in sales, purchasing, distribution, and operations management, I hope you will contact me to suggest a time when we might meet to discuss your needs and how I might serve them. I can provide excellent personal and professional references at the appropriate time, and I can assure you in advance that I am a hard worker who is accustomed to being measured according to ambitious goals for profitability in a highly competitive marketplace.

Yours sincerely,

Nathan Fleishman

NATHAN FLEISHMAN

Until 12/15/99: 1110½ Hay Street, Fayetteville, NC 28305   (910) 483-6611

After 12/20/99: 538 Pittsfield Avenue, Atlanta, GA 78401   (805) 483-6611

OBJECTIVE

To benefit an organization that can use a resourceful manager with proven skills in managing the selling process while prudently overseeing inventory carrying costs and maintaining excellent relationships with vendors.

EDUCATION

B.S. in Business Administration, University of Florida, Gainesville, FL, 1993.
- Was the Rodney G. Herman Scholarship award recipient.
- Extensive professional training in sales, purchasing, and customer service.

EXPERIENCE

Since graduating from the University of Florida, have excelled in a track record of rapid promotion with Florida Distributors:

HEAD BUYER. Gainesville, FL. (1996-present). For a company which buys up to $25 million annually in consumer products which are then distributed to the consumer through chain and convenience stores, I personally handle more than half of the buying.
- Maintain effective working relationships with more than 200 vendors including Hershey, Nabisco Foods, Quaker, and other vendors of name-brand juices, candy, health and beauty aids, and groceries.
- Perform extensive liaison with sales representatives; coordinate contests and promotions for sales representatives and customers.
- Attend national trade shows and buying conventions.
- Played a key role in my branch's being named "Branch of the Year" in 1999.
- Am responsible for prudently managing the selling process and making astute buying decisions related to 3500 products in a highly competitive market in which rapid turnover is critical.

HEAD BUYER. Tampa, FL (1995-96). Reported directly to the Vice President while handling the buying of more than $10 million annually.
- Established and maintained excellent working relationships with 150 vendors while purchasing juices, candy, health and beauty aids, and other consumer products.
- Was commended for my excellent decision-making ability in forecasting inventory needs and purchasing products on a timely basis at lowest cost; made weekly buying decisions.
- Maintained a close working relationship with 12 warehouse managers.
- Conducted semi-annual inventory of the Tampa location.
- Maintained strict accountability; entered receiving documents into computer to update inventory status daily and reconciled all invoices monthly; monitored inventory turnover.
- Learned to resourcefully troubleshoot a wide variety of inventory problems.

BUYER & ASSISTANT BRANCH MANAGER. Hope Mills, NC (1994-96).
Became skilled in buying groceries and tobacco products while also functioning as **Sales Representative.**

AFFILIATIONS

Member, Executive Development Division, national group of young executives
Member, Alpha Nu Delta, a professional business fraternity

COMPUTERS

Lotus, Microsoft Excel, Microsoft Word, Harvard Graphics, WordPerfect.

PERSONAL

Can provide outstanding references. Known for reliability and integrity.

Exact Name of Person
Title or Position
Name of Company
Address (number and street)
Address (city, state, and zip)

Home Health Care Manager

You will see a steady progression of advancement in the resume of this home health care professional. Her industry is expanding, and she is using this resume and cover letter as "fishing bait" to catch the best job.

Dear Exact Name of Person: (or Dear Sir or Madam if answering a blind ad.)

With the enclosed resume, I would like to indicate my interest in your organization and my desire to explore employment opportunities.

As you will see from my enclosed resume, I am an experienced home health care manager currently excelling as Regional Director of 12 branch offices with 35 administrative personnel reporting to me. Although I am held in high regard by my current employer and can provide excellent references at the appropriate time, I am attracted to your company because of its #1 ranking in the home health care industry.

I hope you will welcome my call soon to arrange a brief meeting at your convenience to discuss your current and future needs and how I might serve them. Thank you in advance for your time.

Sincerely yours.

Terri Alligood

Alternate last paragraph:

I hope you will call or write me soon to suggest a time convenient for us to meet and discuss your current and future needs and how I might serve them. Thank you in advance for your time.

TERRI ALLIGOOD

1110½ Hay Street, Fayetteville, NC 28305 • preppub@aol.com • (910) 483-6611

OBJECTIVE   To offer my strong background in health care management to an organization that can use a mature professional known for leadership and self motivation as well as analytical and problem-solving abilities which enhance my practical nursing and patient care skills.

EXPERIENCE   *Advanced in administrative roles with Comprehensive Home Health Care, Atlanta, GA:*
REGIONAL DIRECTOR. (1993-present). Oversee operational areas including patient management, regulatory affairs, corporate planning and development, and financial management of 12 branch offices and a work station; manage 35 people in 12 locations.
- Coordinated each office's accounts receivable issues and concerns while working with the accounts receivable supervisor.
- Assisted in the development of and then managed Quality Assurance and Risk Management programs as well as policy and programs in all operating areas.
- Ensured compliance with applicable federal, state, and local laws, regulations, and rules.

ASSISTANT ADMINISTRATOR and **DIRECTOR OF PROFESSIONAL SERVICES (DPS).** (1990-93). Continued to function as DPS after earning a promotion to assist the administrator in overseeing activities in each branch office and ensuring that staff members received adequate training and supervision.

DIRECTOR OF PROFESSIONAL SERVICES. (1986-90). Held responsibility for managing both clinical and operational activities in the Augusta branch office.

HOME HEALTH NURSE and **HOSPITAL COORDINATOR.** (1984-86). Provided home health care to patients while keeping primary care staff informed of the disposition of their patients when they received hospital care; received updates from hospital staff on our patients and developed contacts with their physicians.

STAFF REGISTERED NURSE. Numerous locations in SC. Ensured that general medical and surgical patients received total nursing care; assessed physical and mental health and recorded information on patient charts; implemented treatment plans.

EDUCATION   Bachelor of Science in Nursing degree, Orion State University, Orion, MT, 1995; 3.9 GPA.
Associate's degree in Nursing, Sandhills Community College, Carthage, NC, 1981; with honors.

LICENSES   Received Home Health Nurse certification from the American Nurses' Credentialing Center, October 1995.
Licensed Registered Nurse in Georgia, certification number 123245.
Licensed Registered Nurse in South Carolina, license number 34578.

AFFILIATIONS   American Nurse's Association, 1992-99
Georgia Association for Home Care Intermediary Relations Committee, 1995-99
Georgia Association for Home Care Ethics Subcommittee, 1997-98
Georgia Association for Home Care Provider Services Committee, 1996-99

AWARDS   Award for Academic Excellence in Nursing, May 1999
Award for Academic Excellence, April 1995
Georgia "Great 100 Nurses," October 1998
Hanni Schultz Memorial Award for Academic Excellence, May 1992

PERSONAL   Am results oriented. Have an enthusiastic, caring manner which makes others comfortable. Feel that I offer a well-rounded background of clinical and managerial skills.

Exact Name of Person
Title or Position
Name of Company
Address (number and street)
Address (city, state, and ZIP)

**Human Resources Director,
Military Officer Background**

This mid-level manager is well into
his second career in the human
resources field. He was in the
personnel field prior to going into
the Army, and now he is retiring
from the military at 42 years of
age and seeking to re-enter
the personnel field.

Dear Exact Name of Person: (or Dear Sir or Madam if answering a blind ad.)

With the enclosed resume, I would like to indicate my interest in your organization and my desire to explore employment opportunities.

As you will see from my enclosed resume, in my current job as Human Resources Director, I have established training programs described as "the best ever seen." In prior human resources positions with firms in the construction and telecommunications industries, I established new offices, developed innovative personnel policies and programs, and handled all activities related to large-scale hiring, termination, and relocation. In a job as a Division Chief, I gained expert skills related to re-engineering and restructuring as the organization went through dramatic downsizing.

I hope you will welcome my call soon to arrange a brief meeting at your convenience to discuss your current and future needs and how I might serve them. Thank you in advance for your time.

Sincerely yours.

Neil Daniel

Alternate last paragraph:
I hope you will call or write me soon to suggest a time convenient for us to meet and discuss your current and future needs and how I might serve them. Thank you in advance for your time.

NEIL DANIEL

1110½ Hay Street, Fayetteville, NC 28305 • preppub@aol.com • (910) 483-6611

OBJECTIVE	I want to contribute to an organization that can use a dynamic and highly motivated leader who offers strong communication skills along with experience in human resources administration, sales and marketing, as well as budgeting and finance.
EXPERIENCE	*While being promoted to the rank of Colonel, have excelled in the following track record of achievement, U.S. Army, Ft. Sam Houston, TX:*

HUMAN RESOURCES DIRECTOR. (1996-present). Was promoted to direct and coordinate the administrative, supply, and training support for all U.S. Army Reserve, National Guard, and Reserve Officer Training Corps (ROTC) individuals and organizations that use Ft. Sam Houston as a training site; manage a program which trains 60,000 people.
- Plan and administer a budget of $1.6 million annually.
- In a formal performance evaluation, was praised for "masterfully creating the best cohesive training program in the Army."
- Was credited with "making Ft. Sam Houston the model" for training operations, and have been cited as producing the "best training programs ever seen."
- Developed and implemented resource and efficiency objectives related to restructuring and "right-sizing;" was the author and implementer of initiatives which resulted in the re-engineering of a headquarters of more than 60 people into a more efficient 10-person staff which provided superior customer service.

DIVISION CHIEF. (1991-96). Based on my outstanding performance in the job below, was handpicked for a position coordinating training activities of up to 46,000 people in 11 states.
- Routinely interfaced with people at all organizational levels, from top-level Washington and Pentagon officials to trainees at all skill levels.
- Became recognized as a foremost authority on organizational re-engineering.
- After developing and implementing aggressive and innovative programs, subsequently reduced troubleshooting cycle time by 50%.

BRANCH CHIEF. (1989-91). While I was an officer in the Reserves, became a valuable consultant to the U.S. Special Operations Command at a time when it was forming a new organization to manage all Special Operations; in 1989, the U.S. Army Special Operations Command created a new full-time position especially for me so that I could take charge full-time of strategic planning and implementation.
- Directed a staff of nine professionals while preparing detailed plans and budgets to redesign, consolidate, or eliminate more than 100 subordinate organizations.
- Contributed vital input to congressional legislation which authorized creation of a new organization with more than 25,000 personnel.
- Rapidly earned respect for my expertise in designing/redesigning organizations in order to achieve maximum productivity and optimize strategic effectiveness.

HUMAN RESOURCES DIRECTOR. James Construction Co., Jonestown, SC (1981-89). Developed and implemented formal personnel and human resources policies for a 20-year-old company with 500 employees and $80 million in annual sales.

PERSONNEL MANAGER. International Telephone & Telegraph (ITT), Greensboro, NC (1978-81). Determined manpower needs and oversaw personnel staffing/administration for a $600 million start-up project involving 2,500 employees.
- Established offices in London, Bangkok, Tel Aviv, and New York.
- Handled grievances, layoffs, transfers, terminations, and recruitment.

EDUCATION	M.B.A. degree, Webster University, Pope AFB campus. B.S. degree, Business Administration, University of North Carolina, Chapel Hill, NC.

Exact Name of Person
Title or Position
Name of Company
Address (no., street)
Address (city, state, zip)

**Manufacturing
Department Manager**

Want to know why Mr. Williamson
puts his Education section so far
down on his resume? It's because
he doesn't have "the right degree"
for the manufacturing environment
he's in, and he doesn't want the
employer to notice—until the end
of his resume—that he has a
political science degree.

Dear Exact Name of Person: (or Dear Sir or Madam if answering a blind ad.)

I would appreciate an opportunity to talk with you soon about how I could contribute to your organization through my manufacturing background as well as my proven management and supervisory skills.

As you will see from my resume, in 1992 I began as a Product Manager with Raytheon and then progressed into positions as a Department Manager of increasing larger and more complex operations. I have become well known for my personal initiative. In my current job, I have directed a pilot project which has increased production in a key area of manufacturing by 6%. I pride myself on my ability to develop and implement time-saving and cost-efficient programs and procedures.

I hope you will welcome my call soon to arrange a brief meeting at your convenience to discuss your current and future needs and how I might serve them. Thank you in advance for your time.

Sincerely yours,

Richard Williamson

Alternate last paragraph:
I hope you will call or write me soon to suggest a time convenient for us to meet and discuss your current and future needs and how I might serve them. Thank you in advance for your time.

RICHARD WILLIAMSON

1110½ Hay Street, Fayetteville, NC 28305 • preppub@aol.com • (910) 483-6611

OBJECTIVE

To benefit an organization that can use a manager with a strong manufacturing background and excellent leadership skills as well as the ability to develop and implement time-saving and cost-efficient programs and procedures.

EXPERIENCE

At Raytheon Textiles, have advanced in the following "track record" of increasing responsibility with this large manufacturer:

1998-present: **DEPARTMENT MANAGER II.** Reston, VA. Due to my success in managing the Spinning and Winding department, was entrusted with the supervision of an additional department (Carding).
- Directly manage seven supervisors and 140 employees producing 250,000 pounds of finished product per week.
- Develop and manage a quarterly supply budget of $120,000 as well as an $80,000 quarterly projects budget; total budgetary responsibility is $800,000 per year.
- Direct a pilot project which has increased spinning frame production by 6%.
- Responsible for the maintenance of $7 million in manufacturing equipment.
- Coordinated a technical trial involving several departments which resulted in detection of a critical processing defect; correction of the problem would greatly improve quality and runnability.

1997-98: **DEPARTMENT MANAGER II.** Reston, VA. Promoted to this position; managed the Spinning/Winding department.
- Developed a program and coordinated efforts with the Engineering Department which resulted in an annual energy savings of $60,000.
- Implemented procedures that resulted in a 3% capacity increase.

1994-97: **DEPARTMENT MANAGER I.** Merriweather, GA. Promoted to this position from a Product Manager/Supervisor position at the SC plant; managed the Spinning/Winding department.
- Managed four supervisors and 80 employees.
- Developed new programs for producing tencel and high-twist yarn.
- Achieved and maintained 16% improvement in S&E labor cost.

1992-94: **PRODUCT MANAGER, SUPERVISOR.** Mayfield, SC. Performed texturing process during shift assignment.
- Produced two-thirds of the written documentation for implementing I.S.O. procedures including all of the Manufacturing and Quality Control sections; our facility was the first Burlington plant to achieve I.S.O. 9002 certification.

With the United States Marine Corps, achieved the rank of Captain and proudly served in the Persian Gulf War:
OFFICER. U.S.M.C. Cherry Point, NC (1988-1992).
- As a HAWK missile Platoon Commander, managed 70 personnel and $45 million worth of advanced equipment.
- Effectively presented a new training program involving senior agencies that was adopted in preparation for Operation Desert Storm.
- Received numerous prestigious awards and medals for exemplary service.

EDUCATION

Bachelor of Arts degree in Political Science, South Carolina State University, 1988.
Numerous professional development courses related to manufacturing, leadership, and management as well as military training.

PERSONAL

Have excellent communication skills. Excellent references available.

Exact Name of Person
Title or Position
Name of Company
Address (no., street)
Address (city, state, zip)

Manufacturing Production Manager

Employers are looking for employees whom other employers want to hire or hold onto. Mr. Nunez states in a straightforward way that he is considered to be "on the fast track" and is being groomed for rapid promotion within his company, but he and his wife have a desire to relocate to South Carolina for family reasons. Remember that employers are nosy—they'll wonder why you want to move, so tell them!

Dear Exact Name of Person: (or Dear Sir or Madam if answering a blind ad.)

I would appreciate an opportunity to talk with you soon about how I could contribute to your organization through my strong management and communication skills as well as my leadership ability and organizational know-how.

As you will see from my resume, in 1992 I began in a management trainee program with Raytheon Industries and advanced into a supervisory position as Production Manager in less time than any management trainee in my plant. Although I am considered within Raytheon to be on the "fast track" and am being groomed for rapid promotion into corporate management, I have a great desire to put down roots in the South Carolina area, where both my wife and I are from. As you will also see from my resume, I graduated from The Citadel and was elected to serve on the Honor Court in my senior year.

While working at Raytheon, I have had an opportunity to demonstrate my supervisory ability and have managed people in various jobs within the plant. I am widely respected for my knack for solving stubborn technical problems, and I have recently improved the speed and efficiency of a particular yarn for a major customer through taking a new approach to an old problem.

You would find me in person to be a dedicated and hard-working individual who prides myself on giving my best effort to my employer. I believe I could become a valuable asset to your organization, and it would be my desire to make a difference to your strategic posture and operating efficiency. I can provide outstanding personal and professional references upon request.

I hope you will welcome my call soon to arrange a brief meeting at your convenience to discuss your current and future needs and how I might serve them. Thank you in advance for your time.

Sincerely yours,

Rick Nunez

RICK NUNEZ

1110½ Hay Street, Fayetteville, NC 28305 • preppub@aol.com • (910) 483-6611

OBJECTIVE	To contribute to an organization that can use a resourceful young professional who offers a proven ability to troubleshoot and solve problems in industrial environments along with exceptionally strong communication skills, leadership ability, and organizational know-how.
EDUCATION	B.A. degree in **Economics and Business**, The Citadel, 1992. • Was elected by my peers in my senior year to serve on the **Honor Court**, the judicial body which administers the Honor System.
EXECUTIVE TRAINING	During 1993 and 1994, completed several months of technical and professional training sponsored by Raytheon Industries and North Carolina State University in these areas:

Spun yarn manufacturing	Industrial engineering
Production management	Quantitative analysis
Employee supervision	Systematic decision making

COMPUTERS	Am proficient in the use of WordPerfect, Lotus 1-2-3, Word, and Excel. Am thoroughly knowledgeable of Uster Sliverdata, an on-line production and quality monitoring system in spinning production.
EXPERIENCE	**PRODUCTION MANAGER.** Raytheon Industries, Virginia Beach, VA (1992-present). Was specially recruited for this management position by Raytheon Industries, and am being groomed for rapid promotion to key corporate management positions; while excelling in Raytheon's rigorous management trainee program, advanced to a supervisory position more rapidly than any trainee in my plant. • Through the formal training program, have gained knowledge about every phase of the manufacturing process. • Acquired "hands-on" experience in a variety of supervisory jobs throughout the plant as the regular and off-shift manager of operational areas ranging from raw material coordination to finished product distribution. • Supervised between 10 and 35 employees in nearly every aspect of plant operation. • On my own initiative, combined what I learned in formal training with my natural creativity in devising a way of improving speed and efficiency of a particular yarn for a major customer. • Have been commended for my ability to rapidly master complex technical concepts and for my ability to apply my training in solving stubborn production problems. • Have become not only well versed in the details of production management but also knowledgeable about the "big picture" of the textile industry and sister industries in the global market.

SUPPLY MANAGER & MILITARY OFFICER. U.S. Army, Ft. Lee, VA (1992). After graduating from The Citadel, was commissioned as a second lieutenant, and then completed a six-month course pertaining to these areas:

supply management	service operations management
subsistence ordering	petroleum supply management

• Became knowledgeable about the "nuts and bolts" of the supply process, from the procurement process to the disposal of environmentally hazardous materials.

TECHNICAL ASSISTANT. Ivy Hill Golf Club, Forest, VA (Summers, 1989-92). Learned supervisory skills at an early age while supervising three adults performing maintenance.

PERSONAL	Have been told that I am on Raytheon's "fast track" and have a bright future in the company. Feel confident in my ability to transfer my management skills, creative problem-solving ability, and technical training to any industry. Excellent references.

Date

Exact Name of Person
Title or Position
Name of Company
Address (no., street)
Address (city, state, zip)

Medical Marketing Manager

It is often difficult for professional people immigrating to the U.S. to find employment quickly and at the level they are accustomed to. A great resume and cover letter can play a key role in opening doors for people whose experience has been in other countries.

Dear Exact Name of Person: (or Dear Sir or Madam if answering a blind ad.)

I would appreciate an opportunity to talk with you soon about how I could contribute to your organization through my extensive experience in medical sales and marketing, medical billing, and nutritional consulting.

Fluent in English and Spanish, I hold an undergraduate degree in Nutrition and Dietetics **cum laude**, and I have worked as a full-time Nutritionist and Marketing Consultant for both the Beech-Nut and Quaker Oats Companies. In those jobs, I visited hospitals, doctors, health centers, and supermarkets to promote products and conduct special marketing events. I am a skilled public speaker and have coordinated numerous conferences and publicity activities.

I have also excelled in sales and sales management positions with a major pharmaceutical company. I began with the company in 1987 as a Medical Marketing Representative and progressed rapidly into sales management responsibilities which involved training up to eight medical sales professionals. With my naturally outgoing personality and extensive background in the sciences and nutrition, I became one of the company's most valuable employees and most visible spokespersons.

You will see from my resume that I am a hard worker. While excelling in my full-time positions mentioned above, I worked part-time during the evenings and on the weekends for nearly ten years handling all medical billing for a six-doctor medical practice. I had a fully equipped office in my home, and I am very experienced in utilizing WordPerfect and medical billing software including Medifast.

You would find me to be a personable and well-educated individual who relates well to people and who adapts easily to new organizational environments. I can provide excellent personal and professional references.

I hope you will call me soon to suggest a time when we might meet to discuss your current and future needs and how I might serve them. Thank you for your time.

Sincerely yours,

Soraya Zahran, LDN

SORAYA ZAHRAN, LDN

1110½ Hay Street, Fayetteville, NC 28305 • preppub@aol.com • (910) 483-6611

OBJECTIVE	To contribute to an organization that can use an experienced young professional who offers an education as a dietitian along with experience in medical marketing and administration.
EDUCATION	Bachelor of Science in Nutrition and Dietetics, **cum laude**, University of Puerto Rico, 1984. Completed graduate-level internship in Dietetics, 1984-85.
EXPERIENCE	**NUTRITIONIST & MARKETING MANAGER.** Quaker Oats Company, Puerto Rico (1990-99). As the company's internal nutritionist, coordinated visits to hospitals and health centers in order to present lectures on nutrition, dietetics, and other subjects; explained the benefits of Quaker products in the outpatient setting.

- Trained sales professionals and suppliers regarding product knowledge.
- Marketed Quaker products through visits to doctors' and nutritionists' offices.
- Coordinated and participated in conventions in order to promote products.
- Trained and supervised outside publicists in developing marketing materials.

MEDICAL MARKETING MANAGER. Sterling Products, Intl., Puerto Rico (1987-90). For a major pharmaceutical company, marketed medical and pharmaceutical products to public and private hospitals; began with the company as a Medical Sales Representative and then progressed into sales management; supervised eight sales representatives.

- Became one of the company's most productive sales professionals as well as a highly visible and trusted spokesperson respected for my extensive expertise related to over-the-counter drugs.
- Developed special events at medical conventions to promote the company's products; coordinated all special publicity and promotional activities.
- Trained company as well as customer personnel on new products.
- Visited prospective new clients to present products; was known as a skillful negotiator with the ability to close the sale.
- Visited doctors, hospitals, and pharmacies to promote the company's products.

NUTRITIONIST & MARKETING MANAGER. Beech-Nut Nutrition Corporation, Puerto Rico (1986-87). As a Nutritionist, visited hospitals, health centers, doctors' offices, and supermarkets in order to explain the advantages of Beech-Nut products.

- Promoted products for babies and infants and expectant mothers; designed special promotions with supermarkets and stores which generated extensive sales.
- Marketed products and trained sales/marketing sales professionals for the company in both Puerto Rico and the Dominican Republic.

CHIEF OF DIETETIC SERVICES. Hospital Gubern, Puerto Rico (1985-86). Supervised a department with 12 employees; oversaw the training and scheduling of all employees.

- Performed nutritional assessments of hospital patients; provided dietary instructions to patients being discharged.
- Purchased nutritional products and food; integrated products into the hospital menu.

COMPUTERS, LANGUAGES	Extremely computer literate; skilled in using WordPerfect and Medifast for medical billing. Fluent in both English and Spanish.
PERSONAL	Have a U.S. Social Security Number. Extremely self-motivated individual. Adapt easily.

Date

Mrs. Janet Smith
Search Committee
Rape Crisis Center
Address
Houston, TX 89034

Non-Profit Executive Director

This letter makes it clear that the approach is confidential and the interest in Houston's Rape Crisis Center is expressed in confidence.

Dear Mrs. Smith:

I am sending you the enclosed resume which you requested, and I would like to formally indicate my interest in the position as Executive Director of the Rape Crisis Center in Houston. I offer extensive experience in managing crisis counseling and intervention, and working with women in crisis is something that interests me very much.

You will see from my resume that I have excelled in key roles in state government which placed me in charge of administering social services programs for the disadvantaged. Those administrative roles allowed me to gain great insight into the mindset of the poor and disadvantaged, and I feel that many of the women who utilize the services of the Rape Crisis Center in Houston are economically and socially disadvantaged.

Although I can provide excellent references at the appropriate time, I would appreciate your holding my interest in the position in confidence until we have an opportunity to talk in person. I am held in high regard in my current position and have an excellent relationship with my board of directors, and I would not want my colleagues to learn of my interest in the Rape Crisis Center at this time.

If you can use dynamic administrator who offers a reputation for maximizing the efficiency of every dollar, I hope you will contact me to suggest a time when we might talk in person. I am very much aware of the fine work performed by the Rape Crisis Center in Houston, and I would enjoy discussing the possibility of becoming a part of this important and vibrant mission in our society.

Yours sincerely,

Kathleen Dow

KATHLEEN DOW

1110½ Hay Street, Fayetteville, NC 28305 • preppub@aol.com • (910) 483-6611

OBJECTIVE
To offer a track record of distinguished performance as a dedicated, innovative professional with proven analytical, motivational, and planning skills along with a reputation for excellence in program development and non-profit management.

EXPERIENCE
EXECUTIVE DIRECTOR, PERSONAL CRISIS CENTER. Wimberley, TX (1995-present). Manage two full-time professional staff employees and one part-time bookkeeping employee while overseeing the entire business operation and the Crisis Center which provides 24-hour-a-day telephone crisis intervention/support and information/referral services.
- *"Within the last year and a half, have taken the Crisis Center from a quiet to a high-profile service organization within the community,"* as stated by a Board Member.
- Have improved and reorganized internal management; developed mission statement and strategic plan; agency became a member of the Chamber of Commerce.
- Introduced creative fund-raising strategies, grant acquisitions, and provided the leadership needed to take the organization from a deficit to a positive balance.

DIRECTOR, TEXAS DIVISION OF SOCIAL SERVICES. Houston, TX (1987-95). Supervised the administration of 100 county social services departments through a staff of 1,150 employees and a billion-dollar-plus budget. Developed changes which allowed the 100 county departments to operate more efficiently and productively.
- Provided guidance for a wide range of programs including child protective, adult, child support enforcement, food stamp, foster care and adoption, and employment programs.
- Guided the JOBS (Job Opportunities and Basic Skills) program to recognition as one of the country's most outstanding models under the 1988 Federal Family Support Act.
- Was the first to secure funding from the General Assembly for the state's child protective services program.
- Prepared documentation which convinced a private foundation to provide funding used for a massive reorganization of the entire child welfare system: devoted 18 months to planning which resulted in Texas becoming one of eight states to receive this assistance which totaled $3.3 million in the program's first year.
- Developed a program which saved more than $200 million over five fiscal years through a unique initiative to reduce erroneous benefit payments.

REGIONAL DIRECTOR, TEXAS DEPARTMENT OF HUMAN RESOURCES. Houston, TX (1983-87). Was recruited and handpicked for the state director's position on the basis of my performance in this capacity. Provided a 33-person staff and a 17-county region with leadership in child welfare, public assistance, child support and other related programs.
- Managed a child welfare program recognized as the best in the four regions.

EDUCATION
Master of Social Work (MSW) degree, The University of Texas at Houston, TX.
Public Management Program (PMP), The State of Texas Office of State Personnel.
B.S., Secondary Education, University of North Carolina, Chapel Hill, NC

HONORS
- Was appointed to The Presidential Commission on Childhood and Youth Deaths.
- Received a U.S. Department of Human Resources Unit Award for Distinguished Service for superb efforts in implementing a unique cooperative federal, state, and local initiative to reduce erroneous benefit payments: saved nearly $200 million over five fiscal years.
- Was honored with the APWA Leadership Award in recognition of outstanding leadership on behalf of program simplification and coordination.
- Received the Social Security Administration Commissioners' Award for delivering high quality disability benefits and service to the citizens of Texas.

PERSONAL
Possess strong mediation skills and the ability to remain diplomatic yet get my point across.

Date

Merck, Sharp & Dohm
P.O. Box 56
Dayton, OH 34587

Dear Sir or Madam:

With the enclosed resume, I would like to make you aware of the considerable skills and sales abilities I could put to work for you in the position as Pharmaceutical Sales Consultant which you recently advertised.

As you will see from my resume, I am currently excelling in a job which requires a dynamic recruiter, manager, and motivator. As Area Executive Director for the American Diabetes Association, I manage more than 170 volunteers in seven counties. Since taking over the position in 1996, I have nearly tripled the number of volunteers while increasing income by 170%. I have developed a strong network of contacts throughout those seven counties while working with hospitals, health departments, and other health agencies to communicate the mission of ADA.

In a part-time job for two years while earning my college degree in Marketing at Weylon University (where I was on scholarship and a member of the Honors Program), I excelled in my first sales job while working as a Sales Associate at Payless Shoe Source.

You would find me in person to be a poised individual with outstanding leadership ability and a high level of personal initiative. I am known for creativity and resourcefulness, and I am also respected for my attention to detail and follow-through. I would welcome the opportunity to work with a fine company that challenges its employees to adopt an attitude of "what if?"

Thanks for your time and consideration.

Sincerely,

Maryls Henry

MARLYS HENRY

1110½ Hay Street, Fayetteville, NC 28305 • preppub@aol.com • (910) 483-6611

OBJECTIVE	To benefit an organization that can use a resourceful and dynamic hard worker with proven sales and marketing abilities, outstanding motivational and time management skills, as well as the personal initiative and highly motivated nature necessary to succeed in unique and challenging assignments that require persistence and creativity.
EDUCATION	B.S. in Marketing, Weylon University, Richmond, VA, 1994.

* Received a four-year academic scholarship based on my SAT/ACT scores.
* Member, Honors Program, for four years.
* Major GPA 3.57/4.0; was on the dean's list three semesters.
* Named to Student Advisory Board, Honors Program, Weylon University, 1993.
* Received President's Youth Service Award.

COMPUTERS   Microsoft Office, WordPerfect, WordPro, Lotus Smart Suite, LotusNotes

EXPERIENCE   **EXECUTIVE DIRECTOR, SOUTHEASTERN REGION.** American Diabetes Association (ADA), Southeastern Ohio (1997-present). Have utilized my sales, marketing, recruiting, and motivational skills to make significant contributions to this organization while managing 170 volunteers in 7 counties.

* Under my strong leadership, income has increased 179% in the last fiscal year.
* In one county alone, boosted annual receipts from $186 in 1997 to $50,000 in 1998.
* Recruit, train, manage, and motivate volunteers, and have succeeded in nearly tripling the number of volunteers to our current total of 170 individuals.
* Work with hospitals, health departments, and other health agencies to communicate the mission of the ADA; have developed a network of contacts within the medical community.
* Plan, organize, and manage fund-raising including annual Diabetes Campaign.
* Have developed and maintained partnerships with appropriate organizations; for example, developed a partnership between the American Diabetes Association and the Ohio Regional Medical Center to facilitate services for diabetes patients.

MEMBER ACCOUNTS COORDINATOR. Lifestyle & Fitness Association, Dayton, OH (1995-97). Created, organized, and implemented marketing and promotional campaigns and events; presented corporate membership plan to various companies, maintained all accounting records, supervised receptionists and enrollment process, handled member billing and inquiries, assisted in developing departmental procedures.

* Prepared daily deposits, trained staff, ordered/displayed items for sale in pro shop.
* Structured and implemented a computer system to implement sales transactions, member reports, and recurring charges.

CUSTOMER SERVICE REPRESENTATIVE. Quality Fuel Gas Company, Richmond, VA (1994). Assisted with administering Low Income Rate Assistance Program (LIRA). Contacted eligible customers and informed them of program requirements and benefits. Utilized computer software to enter data.

HEAD ADMINISTRATIVE COORDINATOR. Honors Program, Weylon University, Richmond, VA (1991-93). Worked as part of a three-member team to coordinate tutoring and mentoring services provided by the Honors Program.

SALES ASSOCIATE. Payless Shoe Source, Richmond, VA (1991-93). As a college student, trained new staff, maintained the store, and provided customer service.

PERSONAL   Outstanding personal and professional references available on request. Active member of the community with affiliations which include the Chamber of Commerce.

Exact Name of Person
Title or Position
Name of Company
Address (no., street)
Address (city, state, zip)

Nutrition Products and Services Manager

This letter is directed to an employment agency which has placed an advertisement in the newspaper. Since Ms. Wagner is relocating from the east coast to the west coast, she will utilize all available methods of contacting prospective employers.

Dear Exact Name of Person: (or Dear Sir or Madam if answering a blind ad.)

I am writing in response to your ad in the *Los Angeles Times*. I am planning to relocate to the Los Angeles area and am sending you a copy of my resume so that you can assist me in my search for a challenging and rewarding position in this area.

As you will see from my resume, since early in 1988 I have been successful in a management position with the nationally known Nutrition for Life organization. Despite the fact that this corporation has declared bankruptcy and more than 800 locations have had to close, I have been able to not only keep my Raleigh, NC, locations open but have increased sales. In 1999, I edged out some tough competition to earn the respected "Manager of the Year Award" from among approximately 1,600 other professionals.

My degree is in Psychology and Sociology and I offer additional experience as a Social Worker. After demonstrating that I could handle a case load of 120-150 clients and consistently complete my cases ahead of schedule, I was promoted to Eligibility Specialist in the Department of Social Services.

I have managed a staff of up to 25 and all aspects of operations in a facility which reached the $900,000 level in annual sales and serviced as many as 300 clients a week.

I am an enthusiastic, energetic, and well-organized professional. I offer a talent for getting the most from employees and finding effective ways to keep things running smoothly and productively—even under very unsettled circumstances.

I hope you will welcome my call soon to discuss how you might be able to help me in my job search in your area. Thank you in advance for your time.

Sincerely yours,

Veronica Wagner

VERONICA WAGNER

1110½ Hay Street, Fayetteville, NC 28305 • preppub@aol.com • (910) 483-6611

OBJECTIVE   To offer my superior communication and motivational skills to an organization that can use an experienced management professional who has demonstrated a bottom-line orientation and a talent for selling concepts and services through an enthusiastic and energetic style.

EXPERIENCE   **GENERAL MANAGER** and **CUSTOMER SERVICE MANAGER**. The Matthews Group (Nutrition for Life), Raleigh and Goldsboro, NC (1988-present). Continue to set sales records and steadily increase the customer base despite the fact that the parent corporation declared bankruptcy in 1993 and more than 800 locations nationwide were forced to close.
- Singled out as **"Manager of the Year for 1999"** from among 1,600 qualified professionals nationwide, displayed knowledge of every aspect of Nutrition for Life operations.
- Increased sales by more than 50% during reorganization following a corporate takeover.
- Handled a wide range of functional activities ranging from setting sales and service goals, to developing business plans, to recruiting/training/supervising employees.
- Oversaw daily operational areas including financial management, inventory control, and customer follow up procedures.
- Handpicked for my effectiveness in running the Raleigh site, was selected to open the Goldsboro location and hold the position of interim area manager.
- During a two-month period prior to opening the Goldsboro center, hired and trained personnel and set up their operation.
- Applied my knowledge of marketing techniques while developing campaigns which used successful clients in radio ads and placed "lead boxes" throughout the city.
- Supervised up to 25 employees in a facility which saw from 250 to 300 clients a week and made $900,000 in its peak years before corporate reorganization.
- Maintained a $500,000 to $600,000 level with approximately 140 clients a week and about 12 employees in 1994.
- Through personal attention and rapport with clients, built a strong customer base which continues to generate about four new clients a week.

ELIGIBILITY SPECIALIST. Department of Social Services, Raleigh, NC (1986-87). Through my ability to communicate effectively with others and quickly establish rapport, was effective in working closely with agency clients to assess their needs and using established guidelines to determine their eligibility for various types of aid.
- Was promoted after managing a case load of from 120 to 150 clients and displaying my ability to organize and deal with a heavy schedule by always completing my cases on schedule and pitching in to help other social workers with theirs.
- Investigated approximately 60 cases a month through a combination of office and home visits to obtain information to determine eligibility for aid.

EDUCATION   B.S., Psychology and Sociology, University of Wisconsin, River Falls, WI, 1984.
- Earned recognition in "Who's Who Among American College Students" on the recommendation of Sociology Department faculty members.
- Maintained a 3.8 GPA and was one of the top two students in my graduating class.
- Received "Special Honors" and "Highest Academic Honors" upon my graduation.
- Founded and then served as president of the university's Sociology Club; planned and coordinated a wide range of campus activities for the Student Activities Committee.
- Completed independent study in Europe on the use of alternative medicines.

COMPUTERS   Experienced with all Microsoft products including Word, Excel, and Access.

PERSONAL   Am an energetic and enthusiastic individual with a flair for handling human, material, and fiscal resources. Contribute to my community in assisting the homeless and disadvantaged.

Date

Mr. Jack Smith
Personnel Officer
City of San Francisco
San Francisco, CA 98764

Deputy Police Chief

This law enforcement professional
is seeking advancement into
management ranks.

Dear Mr. Smith:

Enclosed please find a copy of my resume. I would appreciate your consideration for the position of Senior Deputy Sheriff with the San Francisco Police Department. My management skills have been tested and refined in my current position, and I would consider it an honor to be part of the management team of the respected San Francisco Police Department.

As you will see from my resume, I amply meet the qualifications for this position based on my experience with the Wake County Sheriff's Department in Raleigh, NC. My background includes almost three years in investigation, collection and interpretation of fingerprints, photography, and other technical police work.

I completed the Basic Law Enforcement Training Program in 1993 after earning an A.A.S. degree in Criminal Justice-Protective Services Technology. As detailed on my enclosed resume, I have also received specialized training in such specific areas as crime scene preservation, infectious control and handling of hazardous materials, reporting procedures, and law enforcement photography.

With a reputation as a thorough, detail-oriented young professional, I feel that I offer the training and experience your department needs to fill this important position. I hope you will call or write me soon to suggest a time convenient for us to meet and discuss your current and future needs and how I might serve them. Thank you in advance for your time.

Sincerely yours,

Christopher Love

CHRISTOPHER LOVE

1110½ Hay Street, Fayetteville, NC 28305 • preppub@aol.com • (910) 483-6611

OBJECTIVE	To offer a reputation as a confident, articulate, and detail-oriented law enforcement professional with special emphasis in the areas of crime scene investigation and the technical aspects of police work.
EXPERIENCE	**DEPUTY SHERIFF** and **CRIME SCENE TECHNICIAN.** The Wake County Sheriff's Department, Raleigh, NC (1993-present). Rapidly earned a reputation as a self-motivated professional who could be counted on to ensure that crime scene evidence was thoroughly collected, investigated, and documented according to regulations and so that the chain of custody remained intact.

- Have a 100% conviction rate for the few occasions when my cases have gone to trial and have proven myself a reliable and credible witness — however, the bulk of my cases are settled by plea bargains and never go to trial.
- Received a Letter of Commendation for singlehandedly locating and detaining two suspects upon responding to an attempted armed robbery.
- Responded to the full range of crimes: burglary, felony larceny, recovered stolen vehicles, armed robbery, sexual assaults, and child abuse as well as shootings, stabbings, homicides, officer-involved shootings, suicides, and auto or fire fatalities.
- Provided support by processing crime scenes for all of the separate police departments in Wake County and handled a wide range of duties including the following:
  - *processed* the scene to *collect and preserve* latent prints
  - *photographed* the scene for evidence which could not be removed
  - *prepared* sketches and diagrams
  - *collected* items of evidence to be submitted to the SBI lab for processing
  - *prepared* evidence for use in court and *testified* when required
- Earned special praise from Wake Medical Center personnel as one of several deputies who fingerprinted and photographed large numbers of children "with patience and calm" despite long lines at a community EMS awareness program.
- Was promoted to Corporal early in 1997.

EDUCATION	Completed the 500-hour **Basic Law Enforcement Training (BLET) Program** leading to certification, Raleigh, NC, 1993.

- Excelled in studies which included weapons, self-defense, civil law, and criminal law.

Earned an **Associate of Applied Science (A.A.S.) degree in Criminal Justice-Protective Services Technology**, Wake County Technical Community College (WCTCC), NC, 1990.
- Maintained a 3.5 GPA.

Completed WCTCC and department-sponsored specialized training related to crime scene preservation, juvenile laws, dealing with victims and witnesses, domestic violence, patrol techniques and OSHA standards, reporting procedures, involuntary commitment, use of force, pursuit driving, infectious control and the handling of hazardous materials.
Completed Polaroid-sponsored training in law enforcement photography.

TECHNICAL EXPERTISE	Through training and experience, offer special skills and knowledge of the following:

- Am experienced with 35mm and instant cameras.
- Use different powders and chemicals to develop latent fingerprints: graphic powder, magnetic powder, "super-glue," and iodine fuming.
- Am experienced in using plaster casting to make tire and shoe impressions.
- Offer state certification with the .45 caliber and .380 caliber Sig Sauer pistols.
- Am thoroughly familiar with the proper techniques used in the collection and preservation of physical evidence and in maintaining the chain of custody.
- Have gained experience with autopsy and post-mortem examination procedures.
- Offer basic computer knowledge with Word, WordPerfect, Harvard Graphics, and Windows.

Date

Exact Name of Person
Title or Position
Name of Company
Address (number and street)
Address (city, state, and zip)

Dear Exact Name of Person: (or Sir or Madam if answering a blind ad.)

I would appreciate an opportunity to talk with you soon about how I could contribute to your organization through my versatile experience as an engineer in product engineering, product marketing, and project management.

As you will see from my resume, I have excelled in a track record of accomplishment with General Electric since graduating with my B.S. degree in Industrial Engineering.

I started my employment with the company as a Design Engineer and earned an Engineering Recognition Award in 1993. I have developed multiple control designs for use in several industries. I became a Product Marketing Manager in 1994 and received a prestigious award in 1995 for Excellence in Marketing. As a Product Marketing Manager, I played a key role in producing a gross sales increase of $22.6 million over a two-year period.

In 1996 I was specially selected to act as a Product Engineering Manager and relocated to Paducah, KY where I have handled a wide range of tasks related to the strategic and tactical transfer of products from an assembly plant in Bowling Green to a Custom OEM assembly plant in Paducah. I have set up the engineering department, standardized product production of $20 million in sales, communicated with outside sales professionals and customers during the phase-in process, and created documentation related to the manufacture and assembly of products. While supervising a team of nine design engineers and two draftspeople in developing new products and planning production methods, we have added $3.4 million in revenue through recent product development programs.

I am approaching your company because I believe my versatile experience in project management, product development, marketing analysis and sales, and engineering design could be of value to you. I can provide outstanding personal and professional references at the appropriate time. If you can use a superior performer with a strong bottom-line orientation and an ability to think strategically, I hope you will contact me to suggest a time when we might meet to discuss your needs and how I might help you achieve them. Thank you in advance for your time.

Sincerely,

Holman Chesterfield

HOLMAN CHESTERFIELD

1110½ Hay Street, Fayetteville, NC 28305 • preppub@aol.com • (910) 483-6611

OBJECTIVE   To benefit an organization that can use an engineer with a reputation as a creative problem solver along with experience in project management, electrical and mechanical product design, product marketing, quality assurance, documentation/auditing, and profitability management.

EDUCATION   Bachelor of Science in Industrial Engineering, Kentucky University, Bowling Green, KY, 1987. Completed training programs sponsored by General Electric:

Demand Flow Workshop	Interpersonal Skills	Communication Skills
Value Added Services	Microsoft Office	ISO 9001
Market Analysis	Quality Audits	Customer Coordination

EXPERIENCE   *Since earning my B.S., have worked for General Electric:*

1996-present: PRODUCT ENGINEERING MANAGER. Paducah, KY. Was transferred from the Virginia Beach location to handle a wide range of tasks related to the strategic and tactical transfer of products from an assembly plant in Bowling Green to a Custom OEM assembly plant in Paducah.

- **Project Management:** Was tasked to develop the phase-in operation plan for a new plant, which involved the detailed plan for product phase-in as well as the transfer of equipment from other sites; this plan determined the timetable for a $6 million inventory transfer and the employment of 185 production personnel.
- **Start-up Management:** Set up the engineering department of a customer OEM assembly plant; standardized product production of $20 million in sales.
- **Product Development and Employee Supervision:** Supervised a team of nine design engineers and two draftspeople in developing new products meeting customer requirements and in planning product production methods. **Recent product development programs have added $3.4 million in revenue.**
- **Training Development:** Developed the training course for new production employees.
- **Customer Communication and Liaison:** Coordinated a product phase-in which involved two manufacturing plants, 7 product lines, and thousands of product variations.
- **Documentation:** Created documentation required to manufacture and assemble products including mechanical and electrical drawings, assembly instructions, bill of materials, and agency approvals; developed warranty return policies and procedures and automated order entry procedures.
- **Quality Assurance:** Quality assurance initiatives, procedures, and practices we established have increased first-time yield rates from 76% to 92%.

1994-96: PRODUCT MARKETING MANAGER: Virginia Beach, VA. Increased assigned product sales volume by 40% while boosting overall net profit by 2%, and was responsible for a gross sales increase of $22.6 million over this period.

- **Marketing Award:** Received a prestigious *1995 Award for Excellence in Marketing.*
- **Market Analysis and Sales:** Identified target industries for sales penetration, then oversaw field sales personnel's activities in gaining new accounts.
- **Profitability Management:** Monitored profit margin of products; established pricing levels.
- **Forecasting:** Forecast items for production including supplying part number information.

1986-94: DESIGN ENGINEER. Virginia Beach, VA. Formulated product plans for sales presentation, support manufacturing disciplines, and product design.

- **Engineering Award:** Received a special *Engineering Recognition Award in 1993.*
- **Creativity:** Developed multiple control designs for use in several industries.
- **Accreditation:** Assisted in ISO 9001 accreditation as audit interface with ISO (DNV).

PERSONAL   Excellent references. Proficient with AUTOCAD and other software and have installed software on numerous department computers. Excellent organizational skills.

Exact Name of Person
Title or Position
Name of Company
Address (no., street)
Address (city, state, zip)

Restaurant Manager

This mid-level manager is happy with his industry; he is simply seeking a new challenge in the restaurant business.

Dear Exact Name of Person: (or Dear Sir or Madam if answering a blind ad.)

I would appreciate an opportunity to meet with you confidentially to discuss the possibility of my joining your organization. As you will see from my resume, I have excelled in a variety of roles within the Family Steak & Seafood Corporation, and I have the highest regard for our management team and for my associates. Although I am essentially happy in my current organizational home, I am interested in learning more about your company's strategic direction, because I feel I could contribute to your goals and add value to your company.

While working with Family Steak & Seafood Corporation for the past eight years, I have had an opportunity to acquire skills in every functional area of restaurant operations. Most recently I played a key role in opening a restaurant which has become the highest-volume unit in the chain's history. While overseeing every aspect of operation in this 235-person restaurant, I have instilled in employees an attitude of "attention to detail" which has produced an exceptionally strong commitment to quality standards.

With a reputation as a dynamic motivator and trainer, I have been commended for my ability to hire, train, develop, and motivate some of the industry's finest human resources. I believe strongly that it is the quality of your people and the way you train them that is the key to success in our highly competitive industry. You will see from my resume that I have won numerous awards and honors, including awards for closing down strong competitors.

You would find me in person to be a gregarious and outgoing fellow who offers a proven ability to relate well to customers and to employees at all levels. I have won numerous awards for my exceptional results in the areas of training, profit, sales, and operations.

I hope you will welcome my call soon to arrange a brief meeting at your convenience to discuss your current and future needs and how I might serve them. Thank you in advance for your time.

Sincerely yours,

Belinda Oliver

BELINDA OLIVER

1110½ Hay Street, Fayetteville, NC 28305 • preppub@aol.com • (910) 483-6611

OBJECTIVE To benefit an organization that can use a dynamic and resourceful general manager who offers expertise in restaurant operations including experience in starting up new units, overseeing multiple locations, and troubleshooting problems in existing establishments.

ACHIEVEMENTS & DISTINCTIONS

- Started up a restaurant that is the highest-volume restaurant in the chain's history.
- **Top Training Manager** award; have been recognized for my expertise in training employees and developing human resources considered the best in the industry.
- **Top Ten Award**; through my management skills, transformed an average operation into a restaurant in the "top 10%" of the company's units in sales/profits.
- Two **Notch in the Gun** awards for closing down two competitors.
- **ServSafe**; received this award from the National Restaurant Association for my impeccable sanitation and health practices.

EXPERIENCE *For the past eight years, worked at Family Steak & Seafood Restaurant, the largest restaurant chain in the Carolinas; earned a reputation as a dynamic motivator, skilled trainer, creative organizer, and innovative manager.*

RESTAURANT MANAGER. Family Steak & Seafood Corporation, Charleston, SC (1997-present). Relocated to Charleston after completing an extensive executive development training session in the operation of metropolitan units; then opened a restaurant which has become the chain's highest-volume unit.

- *Employee training and supervision*: Oversee hiring, training, and scheduling of the restaurant's 235 employees; reduced labor costs 6% within three months after opening.
- *Inventory control*: Cost-effectively manage the purchasing, receipt, and utilization of an inventory of perishable and non-perishable items.
- *Finances*: Prepare profit-and-loss statements; oversee payroll administration.
- *Quality control*: Have instilled in employees an attitude of "attention to detail" that has produced a strong commitment to quality standards.
- *Sales and profitability*: Have exceeded every monthly record established for sales since opening in May, 1994.

PARTNER/MANAGER. Family Steak & Seafood Corporation, Wilmington, NC (1987-97). Excelled in a variety of roles because of my versatile management skills.

- *Operations management*: Increased sales in off-season by 35% over a six-year period; learned that persistence and hard work are the keys to achieving sales goals in the restaurant industry.
- *Competitive spirit*: Despite the disadvantage of having to compete with limited seating space, closed down two competitors and increased sales by 26%.
- *Training and development*: Trained district managers, partner managers, franchise service consultants, and assistant managers.
- *Area supervision*: Functioned as a Temporary Area Supervisor and helped selling units with a variety of problems when the district supervisor was overloaded.
- *Coordination*: Became skilled in every aspect of unit operations management including sales/profit control, hiring/training, scheduling, and food cost control/ordering.

ASSISTANT MANAGER. Family Steak & Seafood Corporation, Roanoke Rapids, NC (1986-87). Was commended for my creative approach to community involvement and acquired expertise in guest services while training employees and controlling food/labor costs.

EDUCATION Business Administration studies, North Carolina State University, Raleigh, NC, 1982-85. Completed extensive executive/management training, Family Steak & Seafood, 1986-99.

PERSONAL Expertise in setting up menu matrices, completing sanitation paperwork, handling purchasing.

Exact Name of Person
Title or Position
Name of Company
Address (number and street)
Address (city, state, and zip)

Retail Department Manager

Although this mid-level manager
has advanced in the retail industry,
she is making a career change so
that she can utilize the degree in
business administration with a
concentration in finance which she
earned in her spare time.

Dear Exact Name of Person: (or Dear Sir or Madam if answering a blind ad.)

I would appreciate an opportunity to talk with you soon about how I could contribute to your organization through my education in finance as well as through my reputation as a hard-working, knowledgeable, and dedicated professional.

As you will see from my enclosed resume, I received my Bachelor of Business Administration (B.B.A.) degree with a concentration in Finance from The University of Georgia in 1996. I personally financed my college education by working full time. I am especially proud that I accomplished this while simultaneously advancing in demanding management positions with one of the world's best known discount retailers.

Although I have built a track record of accomplishments and have held supervisory positions since the age of 20 with this national retailer, I am ready for a career change which will allow more opportunity to apply my education in finance.

If you can use a self-confident and self-motivated individual who is persistent and assertive, I hope you will give me a call to suggest a time when we might meet to discuss your needs and how I might help you. Thank you in advance for your time.

Sincerely,

Frances Thorliefson

Alternate last paragraph:
I hope you will call or write me soon to suggest a time convenient for us to meet and discuss your current and future needs and how I might serve them. Thank you in advance for your time.

FRANCES THORLIEFSON

1110½ Hay Street, Fayetteville, NC 28305 • preppub@aol.com • (910) 483-6611

OBJECTIVE
To offer my education in finance and financial planning to an organization that can benefit from my ability to prioritize multiple tasks and activities, effectively manage human and material resources, and produce bottom-line results.

EDUCATION & TRAINING
Bachelor of Business Administration (B.B.A.) degree in **Finance**, The University of Georgia, Atlanta, GA, 1996.
- Refined time management and organizational skills while financing my education through full-time employment and commuting to attend college.

Take advantage of every opportunity to attend corporate-sponsored training programs and have completed courses in union conflict prevention and resolution, violence in the workplace, stress management, and distribution procedures.

EXPERIENCE
Am earning advancement in managerial and supervisory positions with national retail giant Mart King:

DEPARTMENT MANAGER. Acworth, GA (1997-present). Selected to assist in setting up and organizing this department in a new area distribution center, have built and now supervise a 30-person workforce which processes incoming shipments and breaks them down for shipment to retail locations in the area.
- Hired, trained, and then cross-trained personnel for this new facility.
- Oversaw personnel management actions including writing performance evaluations and commendations as well as monitoring the quality and productivity level of each employee.
- Became familiar with the operations of other department in order to be able to communicate and share ideas which impact productivity.

PERSONNEL COORDINATOR. Huntsville, AL (1996-97). Processed payroll actions and managed personnel files for a distribution center with 800 employees while gaining knowledge of the corporation's personnel policies and procedures.
- Applied my financial know-how while completing equipment and report audits.
- Designed procedures implemented by a new order filling department.
- Displayed strong oral communication skills while orienting new employees.

ASSISTANT SUPERVISOR. Huntsville, AL (1990-96). Helped the Breakpack Department Supervisor train, supervise, and evaluate employees while overseeing daily activities and ensuring that procedures were carried out safely and accurately and on time.
- Refined supervisory and managerial skills while developing a reputation as a well-organized and detail-oriented young professional with a talent for getting the most out of others.
- Was selected for a six-month assignment as **Billing and Data Processing Supervisor** in recognition of my skills and education in this area.

FREIGHT HANDLING SUPPORT SPECIALIST. Huntsville, AL (1989-90). Handled actions including processing damaged freight and adjusting stock levels to ensure space was available for incoming freight.
- Provided support which allowed order fillers to be accurate and productive.
- Was promoted after only three months as an **Order Filler,** a job which gave me the opportunity to learn the value of team work and dedication.

SPECIAL SKILLS
Troubleshoot and utilize corporate-specific Real-Time Solutions software as well as billing, payroll, and data processing systems; familiar with Microsoft Excel, Word, and PowerPoint.

PERSONAL
Offer familiarity with German and Spanish. Enjoy challenges; am persistent and determined to overcome obstacles. Have a talent for helping others. Excellent references.

Exact Name of Person
Title or Position
Name of Company
Address (number and street)
Address (city, state, and ZIP)

Sales District Manager, Magazine Distribution

A round of mergers and acquisitions in the magazine distribution business—with the potential of layoffs—has caused this manager to prepare his resume so that he can change fields if he finds himself "downsized."

Dear Exact Name of Person: (or Dear Sir or Madam if answering a blind ad.)

Can you use a top-notch sales professional who offers exceptional communication and marketing skills which have resulted in increasing territory profitability?

Currently the District Sales Manager for the New York City-based McAllister News Company, Inc., since 1993 I have consistently increased sales and currently handle a territory with $2 million in sales annually. While selling and distributing magazines to wholesalers throughout both North and South Carolina, I have used my analytical skills and "industry instincts" to determine trends and make changes which increased sales. Because the publishing/wholesaling business is in such a state of flux, with larger companies buying up the smaller ones, I have become accustomed to the need for flexibility and resourcefulness.

As you will see from my enclosed resume, I am a versatile professional who can easily adapt to selling different types of products or services. I am highly effective in developing new sources and expanding a territory for increased sales and profits. Known for my warm sense of humor, I can provide outstanding references.

I hope you will welcome my call soon to arrange a brief meeting at your convenience to discuss your current and future needs and how I might serve them. Thank you in advance for your time.

Sincerely yours.

Preston Blum

Alternate last paragraph:
I hope you will call or write me soon to suggest a time convenient for us to meet and discuss your current and future needs and how I might serve them. Thank you in advance for your time.

PRESTON BLUM

1110½ Hay Street, Fayetteville, NC 28305 • preppub@aol.com • (910) 483-6611

OBJECTIVE	To offer my top-quality communication and marketing skills to an organization that can use an accomplished sales professional with sales management experience who offers a track record of increasing territory profitability.
EXPERIENCE	**DISTRICT SALES MANAGER**. McAllister News Company, Inc., Charleston, SC (1993-present). Sell and distribute magazines to wholesalers in North and South Carolina while consistently increasing sales in this territory which has a volume of over $2 million annually.

- Analyze sales information from retail chains; create strategic plans and continuously monitor/modify distribution efforts to maximize sales.
- Have increased sales by at least 5% every year at a time when the industry was experiencing much turbulence, with larger wholesalers buying smaller ones with the result that buyer names and faces were constantly changing.
- Am extremely knowledgeable of the channels of distribution and industry structure related to magazine/book publishing and wholesaling; am highly respected for the strong negotiating and customer service skills I use to compete for shelf space in this competitive industry with tight margins.

SALES REPRESENTATIVE. Southeastern Concrete, Tampa, FL (1988-93).
Demonstrated my ability to rapidly excel in the sale of industrial products; while selling concrete, checked building permits for leads and contacted contractors, concrete finishers, and other members of the building public to arrange delivery of the product.

SALES REPRESENTATIVE. Systel Business Equipment Company, Raleigh, NC (1986-87). Cold-called businesses and non-profit organizations to evaluate the need for copier equipment and deliver proposals for services.
- Was honored as *"Salesman of the Month"* for six out of 12 months.
- Negotiated selling prices, lease agreements, and maintenance contracts.
- Maintained accurate records of customers' equipment in order to be able to offer them upgraded equipment.

CREW LEADER/TRUCK DRIVER. Trucking Movers, Durham, NC (1983-85).
Negotiated contract and insurance agreements for moving household and personal property.

GENERAL MANAGER. Shear Salon, Tampa, FL (1978-81). Started "from scratch" and then managed a hair salon business; became skilled in purchasing supplies and in obtaining the best prices for materials through resourceful buying and skillful negotiating.
- Managed all operational areas of this thriving business including bookkeeping, payroll, merchandising, and hiring/training.

Highlights of other experience: Excelled in the highly technical field of electronics maintenance while proudly serving with the U.S. Navy.

EDUCATION	Earned an **A.A. degree in English**, Tampa Community College, Tampa, FL, 1981.

- Graduated *with honors*.

PERSONAL	Have earned the respect of both my peers and upper-level management for my outstanding sales and marketing skills. Enjoy developing territories and providing top-quality service. Am known for my warm sense of humor. Excellent references.

Date

Exact Name
Exact Title
Exact Name of Company
Exact Address
City, State, Zip

Dear Exact Name:

With the enclosed resume, I would like to introduce myself and the substantial sales and marketing background I could put to work for you.

As you will see, I offer a proven track record of outstanding results in producing a profit, improving the profit margin, developing new accounts, increasing market share, satisfying customers, and expanding territories. In my current position, I have developed a new territory while training and managing an eight-person sales staff. I am contributing significantly to the company's bottom line through my results in delivering a 40% profit margin. Prior to being recruited for my current position, I was part of a four-person team which boosted sales 15% at a plant in Toronto.

I am known for my ability to creatively and resourcefully apply my considerable knowledge, and I am always on the lookout for new ways to refine my own selling techniques. I am confident of my ability to produce a highly motivated team of sales professionals.

If you can use my talents and knowledge, please contact me and I will make myself available for a meeting with you to discuss your needs and how I might help you. I can provide outstanding personal and professional references.

Sincerely,

Rodney Lewis

RODNEY LEWIS

1110½ Hay Street, Fayetteville, NC 28305 • preppub@aol.com • (910) 483-6611

OBJECTIVE

To become a valuable member of an organization that can use an outgoing and highly motivated sales professional who offers a proven ability to produce a profit, improve the profit margin, develop new accounts, satisfy customers, as well as motivate employees.

EDUCATION

Received Bachelor of Arts degree in **Psychology**, University of Miami, Miami, FL, 1986. Have excelled in numerous sales and sales management training programs sponsored by major industrial suppliers.
- Pride myself on my ability to creatively and aggressively apply any and all sales training.
- Have especially benefited from advanced training related to product marketing, cold calling and other sales skills, and techniques for increasing sales, profits, and motivation.

EXPERIENCE

SALES MANAGER. TrueTest Supply Network, Macon, GA (1995-present). Was recruited by key marketing officials in the parent company for this job which has involved developing a new territory as well as hiring and supervising an eight-person sales staff.
- In addition to my management responsibilities, am actively involved in sales; call on colleges, major retailers, hospitals, military accounts, and large industrial facilities.
- Sell virtually any product needed for the daily operations; provide products ranging from cleaning supplies to televisions, VCRs, refrigerators, nuts and bolts, and light bulbs.
- Have trained and organized the eight-person sales team so that it is now a sales machine known for outstanding product knowledge, customer service, and resourcefulness.
- Taught my sales peers how to improve profit in each sale by at least 5%.
- Have learned how to "work smart" in order to increase sales and sales calls by 32%.
- Trained sales personnel to establish aggressive goals and then helped them learn the practical tools which would help them achieve those goals.
- Am contributing significantly to the company's bottom line through my ability to deliver a 40% profit margin.

SALES MANAGER. Braxton & Co., Chicago, IL and Toronto, Canada (1993-95). Was recruited to join a four-person sales team responsible for increasing by 5% the sales of a plant in Toronto which was affiliated with a company with total annual sales of $368 million.
- Greatly exceeded management expectations and our targeted goals; increased sales by 15% instead of the projected 5%.
- Re-trained sales personnel in Canada in all aspects of their jobs; significantly improved their ability to prospect for new commercial and retail accounts and refined their ability to close the sale.
- Personally established numerous new commercial accounts and dramatically expanded the territory which the company had been servicing.

SALES CONSULTANT & SALES REPRESENTATIVE. Dallas, TX (1986-93). Worked for one of the country's leading sales/marketing consulting firms; acted as a management consultant under contract with numerous companies that wanted expert help in expanding their territories, boosting sales, and improving profitability. Called on and established new retail and commercial accounts.

PERSONAL

Am skilled at dealing with people and earning their confidence. Hard working, dependable, honest. Am always seeking new opportunities to improve my sales presentation skills. Known for my ability to creatively apply the knowledge I already have. Will relocate.

Exact Name of Person
Title or Position
Name of Company
Address (number and street)
Address (city, state, and zip)

Sales Manager,
Automobile Dealership

A desire to move up to a
General Manager position is
the motivation behind this
resume and cover letter.

Dear Exact Name of Person: (or Sir or Madam if answering a blind ad.)

With the enclosed resume, I would like to make you aware of my desire to become General Manager of a BMW Automobile Dealership.

As you will see from my enclosed resume, I have excelled in a track record of accomplishment with BMW of Columbia, MD. I am proud of the results I achieved as Sales Manager, Finance & Insurance Manager, Used Car Manager, and General Sales Manager. My exceptionally strong leadership skills have been refined in the highly competitive environment of the automobile sales business, and I offer a reputation as a powerful leader and motivator with the ability to inspire people to perform to their highest levels of competence. You will notice on my resume that I have used my outstanding personal reputation and ability to influence others to take action in high-visibility community leadership roles when a trusted leader was needed to take on a tough job and mobilize people to accomplish difficult tasks.

I am willing to relocate according to company needs in order to accomplish my goal of becoming General Manager of a dealership. I can assure you in advance that I am confident in my ability to take a good dealership and make it great or to transform a troubled operation into a well-oiled machine. My skills as a motivator and team builder are highly respected, and I can provide outstanding references throughout the industry.

Please favorably consider my desire to take the next logical step in my career of becoming a General Manager and suggest a time when we might meet to discuss your goals and how I might help you achieve them. I will look forward to your response.

Yours sincerely,

William Cislak

WILLIAM CISLAK

1110½ Hay Street, Fayetteville, NC 28305 • preppub@aol.com • (910) 483-6611

OBJECTIVE

To benefit an organization that can use a General Manager with exceptional motivational and communication skills who offers a strong background as a sales trainer and a track record of excellence as a general sales manager, used car manager, and finance manager.

EDUCATION

Bachelor of Arts degree in Philosophy, University of Florida, Gainesville, FL, 1975.
Associate of Arts in General Education, Florida Community College, Jacksonville, FL, 1973.

COMMUNITY LEADERSHIP

Offer a reputation as a highly respected local leader who believes in helping my community:
1991-92: Appointed President, Columbia Middle School Athletic Booster Club; organized the club from scratch, served as its first president, and created revenue-generating plans.
1989-92: President, Columbia Sports Association. Took control of a small athletic association comprised of 8 teams totaling 120 people and, in three years, transformed it into a 43-team organization with more than 700 people affiliated. Established new programs for children including flag football and persuaded city government to better equip playing fields.

EXPERIENCE

With BMW of Columbia, MD, have advanced in the following "track record:"
1997-present: **GENERAL SALES MANAGER.** Advanced to this position after excelling as Used Car Manager and Sales Manager, was tasked with the additional responsibility of overseeing the operation of the entire sales department; continued to serve as Used Car Manager.
- Supervise up to 14 employees, including Automotive Sales Representatives, Finance Managers, and Sales Managers.
- Serve as director of employee training for all departments; track completion of training courses required by BMW and ensure that all employees receive proper instruction.
- Achieved and consistently maintain a Customer Service Index of #1 among all Automotive Group dealerships.
- New car sales consistently exceed National, South Area, and Territory averages.

1994-present: **USED CAR MANAGER.** Promoted from a Sales Man position; responsible for managing all operational aspects of the Used Car department.
- Monitor used car inventory, ensuring that the dealership doesn't become overstocked, controlling the number of overaged units, and ordering program vehicles to meet the dealership's needs.
- Perform appraisals of vehicles being traded in based on condition, black book value, and existing unsold inventory of the same or similar used vehicles.
- Due to my initiative, net profit for the used car department increased by 47%, and is currently returning a net-to-gross profit ratio greater than 29%; the used car department is consistently ranked in the top four among all BMW dealerships.

1985-1994: **SALES MANAGER and FINANCE & INSURANCE MANAGER.** Hired by BMW of Columbia to serve as Sales Manager of the existing sales team; also acted as a backup Finance and Insurance Manager.
- Supervised a staff of Automotive Sales Representatives; set daily, weekly, and monthly sales goals and motivated them to achieve or exceed those goals.
- As Finance Manager, maximized the dealership's profit by selling and promoting the sale of aftermarket products such as extended warranties and credit life insurance.

Other experience: **DIRECTOR OF TRAINING & INSURANCE SALES REPRESENTATIVE.** Nationwide Insurance, Columbia, MD (1975-1985). Supervised training of all new and existing Nationwide agents for all of Maryland, teaching sales techniques, products, and services.

PERSONAL

Excellent personal and professional references on request. Outstanding reputation.

Date

Exact Name of Person
Title or Position
Name of Company
Address (number and street)
Address (city, state, and zip)

Dear Sir or Madam:

**Sales Manager,
Regional Operations**

Although it's usually best not to communicate your preferences in an initial cover letter, this professional will not consider opportunities which are not located in middle Tennessee or north Georgia, where he and his wife want to live and retire. He intends to "screen out" offers based on that main criterion.

Can you use an experienced sales professional with a history of success in training others and setting sales records while applying my knowledge of inventory control and record keeping in the process of establishing new accounts and building repeat business? I would especially enjoy discussing with you how I might serve your needs in the east/middle Tennessee or north Georgia areas. My extended family is located in those parts of the country, and I have many contacts and acquaintances throughout that region.

Since 1981, I have been a record-setting representative for Greystone, Inc., in Pinehurst, NC. After winning recognition as the top producer for 1998, 1997, 1995, and 1993, I have reached the $1.5 million in annual sales level for fiscal 1999. I regularly service approximately 160 accounts in an area which covers Raleigh-Cary, Pinehurst, and Southern Pines, and which extends as far west as Albemarle.

Prior experience includes dealing with both the general public and building contractors with Lowe's, selling heating and air-conditioning supplies and equipment, and managing outside sales for another refrigeration supply business. I am skilled at conducting sales meetings and coordinating awards programs.

I hope you will welcome my call soon to arrange a brief meeting at your convenience to discuss your current and future needs and how I might serve them. Thank you in advance for your time.

Sincerely yours,

Claude Ingersoll

CLAUDE INGERSOLL

1110½ Hay Street, Fayetteville, NC 28305 • preppub@aol.com • (910) 483-6611

OBJECTIVE

To contribute to an organization that is in need of an experienced sales professional who offers knowledge related to sales management, inventory control, report preparation, and training others.

EXPERIENCE

REGIONAL SALES MANAGER. Greystone, Inc., Pinehurst, NC (1981-present). Consistently among the region's top producers, achieved a sales volume of over $1.5 million for fiscal year 1999 for this home-comfort products company; train and coach two junior sales representatives.

- Was honored as the region's top sales professional in 1998, 1997, 1995, and 1993.
- Excelled in earning the respect and trust of professionals in the building and electrical industries through my skills in every phase of making contact, demonstrating products, and closing the sale.
- Demonstrated excellent planning skills by researching a company's needs and requirements prior to my initial call.
- Serviced approximately 160 accounts in an area ranging from Albemarle, to Sanford, to Cary and Raleigh, to Fayetteville, to Southern Pines and Pinehurst.
- Used my abilities as a communicator and my product knowledge to conduct sales meetings where employees learned effective techniques for selling the company's product line.
- Spend a great deal of my time calling on the end users of my company's products to ensure their satisfaction with our products.
- Became involved in the design and installation of display systems while selling to lighting showrooms, electrical wholesales, building supply stores, and plumbing wholesalers.

Highlights of prior experience in the sales field, Raleigh, NC:

Lowe's. Further developed my salesmanship abilities and knowledge of customer relations while dealing with both building contractors and the general public.

- Gained experience in stocking, inventory control, and computer operations.

Merritt-Holland. Sold heating and air conditioning equipment to customers throughout the eastern part of North Carolina.

- Was selected to oversee the details of coordinating special awards such as trips for high-volume sales personnel.
- Managed a wide range of advertising programs including newspaper, radio, and yellow pages advertising.
- Applied my organizational skills to arrange and coordinate dealer sales meetings.

Longley Supply Co.. Established a sales territory which included Lumberton, Hamlet, and Laurinburg as well as Raleigh; sold heating and air-conditioning equipment and supplies.

- Handled the details of arranging and then hosting dealer conventions.

W.L. Smith Refrigeration Supply. As the Outside Sales Manager, was in charge of pricing and inventory control for five stores.

- Conducted regular monthly inventories and rotated stock between the stores.

EDUCATION & TRAINING

Attended courses in professional sales techniques, stress management, and positive self-suggestion as well as a 10-week Dale Carnegie course in human relations.
Studied heating and air conditioning at Fayetteville Technical Community College, NC.

PERSONAL

Am a results-oriented professional. Offer a high degree of expertise in the qualities that add up to "salesmanship." Am skilled in establishing and maintaining effective relations.

  Date

                        Exact Name of Person
                        Exact Title
                        Exact Name of Company
                        Address
                        City, State, Zip

**Senior Merchandise
Manager, Retailing**
                        Dear Exact Name of Person (or Dear Sir or Madam if answering a blind ad):

This mid-level manager is involved
in an aggressive career change
from retailing into "who-knows-
what." Here's a tip for those of
you trying to change careers:
Instead of abandoning everything
you know for an entirely new field,
try to find a niche within your
industry. In Mr. Acampora's case,
he is trying to get out of the
weekend hours required by
retailing. What he will do first in
his job hunt is approach vendors
with whom he worked with a
view to representing their lines.
This kind of job will keep him in
retail without retail hours. (The
reason he wants out of retail hours
is that he is trying to finish his MBA
before he hits 40 years old.)
                        With the enclosed resume, I would like to make you aware of my interest in
                        becoming associated with your fine product line in a sales role. Although I have
                        excelled in retail management for the past 13 years with Macy's, I have decided that I
                        wish to change careers and embark on a career in sales. I am particularly interested
                        in your product line and would like to explore suitable opportunities with you.

                        From 1989 until a few weeks ago, I excelled in a track record of advancement
                        with the Macy's organization, where I started as a management trainee and advanced
                        into a senior management position in charge of 25 individuals. After earning my
                        undergraduate degree in Business Administration with a minor in Economics, I was
                        attracted to the Macy's organization because of its tradition of regarding its managers
                        as profit centers and treating them essentially as entrepreneurs.

                        Although I was excelling in my job and held in high regard, I made the decision
                        to resign from Macy's in late 1998 for two reasons: first, I wanted to spend a few weeks
                        caring full-time for my widowed mother, who had undergone a serious operation, and
                        second, I had decided that I wished to pursue a career in sales. I left on excellent terms
                        and can provide outstanding personal and professional references within the Macy's
                        organization including from my immediate supervisor, Bob Kleinstein, who would
                        gladly welcome me back at any time.

                        While performing my buying function at Macy's, I became aware of your fine
                        products and I would enjoy discussing with you the possibility of my representing your
                        products to retailers such as Macy's.

                        I am single and would cheerfully travel as your needs require. If you feel that my
                        skills and background might be of interest to you, I hope you will contact me to
                        suggest a time when we might meet in person to discuss your needs.

                                                                    Sincerely yours,

                                                                    Nells Acampora

NELLS ACAMPORA

1110½ Hay Street, Fayetteville, NC 28305 • preppub@aol.com • (910) 483-6611

OBJECTIVE	To benefit an organization that can use an experienced manager who offers a background in managing budgets and performing financial analysis, buying and controlling inventory, supervising personnel, and handling public relations.
EDUCATION	**Bachelor of Arts, Business Administration major with a minor in Economics**, Newark College, Newark, NJ, 1987. Pursuing MBA from Davidson University, Davidson, NJ. Have completed extensive management training sponsored by Macy's.
EXPERIENCE	Excelled in a track record of promotion at Macy's Department Store in Newark, NJ; recently resigned from Macy's in order to devote my full time to caring for my widowed mother in the aftermath of a serious operation, and to seek a career outside retailing. • Resigned under excellent conditions; can provide an outstanding reference from Bob Kleinstein, my immediate supervisor, and from numerous other Macy's executives.

1995-99: SENIOR MERCHANDISE MANAGER. Was promoted to manage 25 sales associates while controlling a $5 million inventory; this position placed me in charge of this large-volume Children's Department; also managed the Home and Infant Departments.
- Interviewed and hired new sales associates.
- Consistently increased department sales by a minimum of 5% annually.
- In the Macy's environment, the Senior Merchandise Manager is in an essentially entrepreneurial role and, unlike in most department stores, the Senior Manager undertakes the buying function; performed extensive liaison with suppliers and manufacturers who acted as vendors to Macy's.
- Prepared business plans four times a year; reviewed goals monthly.
- While performing in the role of Senior Manager/General Manager, have been extensively involved in leadership and public relations roles in the community; worked with the YMCA to coordinate a "Kid of the Year" event.

1994: PROJECT MANAGER. Because of my reputation as an excellent communicator and public speaker, was selected to take on a special project related to implementing a new Designer Implementation Program; as coordinator of this program, traveled extensively to talk with store managers.
- Was commended for my ability to articulate the concepts of this new program in ways managers could understand.

1993: MANAGER. Men's Clothing and Men's Accessories.
1992: MANAGER. Infant Department.
1991: MANAGER. Housewares Department.
1989-91: MANAGEMENT TRAINEE. Was attracted by Macy's outstanding management training program and by the opportunity as a manager to function in an essentially entrepreneurial role with broad decision-making abilities after advancing into management.

MERCHANDISE MANAGER. Penney's, Newark, NJ (1985-89). Worked part-time at Penney's for two years while completing my college degree which I earned in 1987.
- Received the Manager's Award for achievement in hourly productivity.

PERSONAL	Am seeking a career outside retailing primarily so I can attend classes two nights a week in pursuit of my MBA. Work well under pressure and am known for attention to detail. Proficient with Word. Single; will travel extensively. Excellent references.

Mr. Vincent Nair
Human Resource Manager
Billows & Klein Recruiters
5881 North Delaware Street.
Miami, Florida 39023

Dear Mr. Nair:

With the enclosed resume, I would like to introduce myself and make you aware of the considerable experience in purchasing, contracting, property management, finance, and operations management which I could put to work for you. I am currently in the process of relocating to the Florida area where my extended family lives, and I would appreciate an opportunity to talk personally with you about how I could contribute to your organization.

With my current employer, I have been promoted to Senior Purchasing Manager. I am responsible for the property management of more than 5,000 houses and apartments, including a fleet of 72 service vans. I also prepare and resourcefully utilize a budget of more than $1.6 million annually for repair parts, outside services, support equipment, and materials. On my own initiative, I have totally streamlined the bidding process. In consultation with the System Manager, I implemented a new computer program to track bids, thereby transforming a previously disorganized manual process into an efficient computerized system. Additionally, I streamlined purchasing procedures while taking over a job which had previously been done by two people. Using available software, I have also established accounting and budgeting programs for a small business.

In all my previous jobs, I have been recognized—sometimes with cash bonuses—for developing new systems which improved efficiency and customer service. For example, while working for the U.S. Embassy in Miami, I created a computerized method of financial reporting which greatly enhanced the budgeting and fiscal accountability functions. In another job as a Purchasing Agent, I exceeded expected standards while handling critical functions including making decisions on the most advantageous sources, assisting in bidding solicitations, and evaluating quotations for price discounts and reference materials.

I have never been in a job where I did not find creative and resourceful ways to cut costs, improve bottom-line results, and strengthen relationships with customers.

I hope you will call or write me soon to suggest a time convenient for us to meet and discuss your needs and how I might serve them. Thank you for your time.

Sincerely,

Robert Rountree

ROBERT ROUNTREE

Until 12/15/99: 1110½ Hay Street, Fayetteville, NC 28305   (910) 483-6611
After 12/16/99: 538 Pittsfield Avenue, Orlando, FL 58401   (805) 483-6611

OBJECTIVE	To contribute to an organization that can use a resourceful purchasing manager who is skilled in contract negotiation, operations management, and personnel administration.
EDUCATION	Completed one year of master's degree work in Urban Management, Texas State University, Mercerville, TX, 1995-96. Earned B.S. in Health Education, University of Washington, Washington, DC, 1991. Received A.A. in General Education, Miami Dale Community College, Miami, FL, 1986. Completed executive development and non-degree-granting training programs in: Cost Accounting Managerial Accounting Procurement Computer Operations Inventory Control Budget Administration
COMPUTERS	Lotus 1-2-3, dBase IV, WordPerfect, Managing Your Money, Windows 95, others
EXPERIENCE	**SENIOR PURCHASING MANAGER.** Briley & Co., Ft. Hood, TX (1994-present). Have acquired a broad understanding of government contracting procedures while achieving an excellent track record of promotion in the finance and purchasing field. • Was originally employed as a Purchasing Agent in 1994 to replace two buyers; have been promoted to Senior Purchasing Manager in charge of five associates. • Am responsible for an annual budget of approximately $2.1 million of which $1.6 million is used by me to purchase repair parts, outside services, support equipment, and materials. • Responsible for property management: within a $150,000 monthly budget oversee maintenance and repairs performed on 5,000 housing units and a fleet of 72 vans. • In a formal letter of appreciation, was commended for saving at least $400,000 annually by combining my extensive purchasing knowledge with my creative problem-solving skills. • On my own initiative, streamlined the bidding process; developed a new system for obtaining price quotes from potential vendors and worked with the System Manager in developing a computer program to track quotes: this transformed the manual quotation to an efficient new process which reduced the time necessary to prepare quotes. • Established excellent working relationships with vendors all over the country, and am known for my ability to quickly find difficult-to-obtain parts for critical needs. • Knowledgeable of government contracting and new product testing. **CONSULTANT & VICE PRESIDENT OF FINANCE.** Branson Enterprises, Miami, FL (1991-94). Played a key role in helping the owner build a new business; established budgeting and accounting systems. Negotiated the details of the company's largest contract. **PURCHASING MANAGER.** Contracting Division of the U.S. Air Force, Washington, DC (1989-91). Handled critical functions including making decisions on the most advantageous sources, assisting in bidding solicitations and acceptance, and evaluating quotations for price discounts as well as delivery/transportation costs. Developed outstanding relationships and received a Laudatory Best Operation performance appraisal with cash bonus. **PROCUREMENT OFFICER.** The American Embassy in Miami (1986-89). Began working for the Embassy as a Warehouse Manager and, holding a **Top Secret** security clearance, excelled in managing warehouse operations and in relocating warehouse contents to new facilities. • Because of my problem-solving ability, was promoted to Procurement Officer; took over a disorganized operation and created a computerized method of reporting Local Operational Funds (LOF) which enhanced efficiency of the budgeting and fiscal functions.
PERSONAL	Outstanding personal and professional references. Will cheerfully travel/relocate.

Reference: Job #GA-TSZ
TRAVELSPAN Human Resources
400 Fortune Parkway, NW
Atlanta, GA 30339

Senior Travel Agent

Sometimes employers are drawn to potential employees who are single and able to relocate. This travel agent now working in a small town is interested in joining the best-known travel agency in the country.

Dear Sir or Madam:

With the enclosed resume describing my considerable expertise in the travel industry, I am responding to your recent advertisement for a Sales Manager in your Atlanta office. I am single and willing to relocate, and I find the Atlanta location particularly appealing.

As you will see from my resume, I am currently excelling as Senior Travel Agent with a travel agency in Colorado. I offer advanced computer skills and am my office's "internal expert" on all matters of software and hardware technology, including troubleshooting hardware malfunctions. I have completed Datas II, Worldspan, and Advanced Professional Sabre courses and am very interested in teaching Worldspan software. I am also my agency's expert on advanced ticketing applications including ticket exchanges, coupon redemption, and group airline ticketing.

With a commitment to continuous professional training, I am always seeking ways to improve my knowledge in my spare time. I hold an A.A. degree in Liberal Arts.

Although I am equipped to book travel worldwide, I offer particularly strong knowledge related to most major U.S. cities, the Caribbean, Great Britain, Italy, Greece, and Bermuda. I have traveled extensively myself and am a former resident of St. Croix.

I can provide outstanding references from my current employer as well as from both corporate and leisure clientele. A hard worker who thrives on new challenges and who rapidly masters new concepts, I feel certain I could excel as a Sales Manager in your Atlanta office. I, of course, know of your company's fine reputation, and I would be honored to be associated with a company respected for its industry leadership and commitment to customer service.

I hope I will have the pleasure of meeting with you in person to discuss my strong qualifications for and interest in the position you advertised. I look forward to hearing from you soon to suggest a time when we can talk about your needs and my ability to meet them. Thank you in advance for your time.

Sincerely yours,

Frances Rothstein

FRANCES ROTHSTEIN

1110½ Hay Street, Fayetteville, NC 28305 • preppub@aol.com • (910) 483-6611

OBJECTIVE To offer my experience to an organization that can benefit from my knowledge of domestic and international travel planning related to leisure travel, corporate accounts, and tour packages as well as my expertise related to travel industry computer technology.

LEADERSHIP Am highly respected within the community in which I work, and serve as Chairwoman of the Board of Directors, Scottish Pilot Club of San Angelo.

EXPERIENCE **SENIOR TRAVEL AGENT.** Travelers, Inc., San Angelo, CO (1990-present).
Have become the top sales agent while gaining broad exposure in all aspects of the travel industry; have earned a reputation as a knowledgeable professional and serve a large repeat clientele because of my courteous service orientation and attention to detail.
- **Management:** Provide oversight and technical leadership to four other junior travel agents.
- **Advanced Computer Skills:** Am the office's "internal expert" on computer software and hardware, and am the individual who teaches software enhancements to office personnel while also troubleshooting hardware malfunctions; have excelled in the following courses:
  > **Datas II**, Atlanta
  > **Worldspan**, Atlanta
  > **Advanced Professional Sabre**, Dallas
- **Areas of Expertise:** Am equipped to book travel worldwide, but offer particularly strong knowledge of most major U.S. cities as well as the Caribbean, Bermuda, Great Britain, Greece, Italy, and most major cruise lines; am a former resident of St. Croix, US Virgin Islands.
- **Commitment to Continuous Professional Training:** In my spare time, am working on the Disney College of Knowledge Diploma; have attended several CLIA workshops, and have also attended two "See the Ships" seminars and Carnival Cruise Lines seminars in Miami; currently enrolled in a Microsoft Office course at Richmond Community College.
- **Advanced Ticketing Applications:** Am in charge of advanced ticketing applications from ticket exchanges, coupon redemption, and group airline ticketing.

Highlights of other experience: Polished public relations and office operations skills in earlier jobs including:
- **OFFICE MANAGER:** For a dentist office with four partners, was in charge of accounts receivable and billing; filed insurance claims and formulated payment plans.
- **DEPARTMENT SECRETARY:** Earned promotion based on my accomplishments and professionalism, Wake Forest University, Winston-Salem, NC.
- **ART INSTRUCTOR:** Taught art under ESEA Title I summer school program.
- **VOLUNTEER:** Volunteer within the public school system.

EDUCATION & TRAINING Hold an **A.A., Liberal Arts,** Mount Vernon College, Washington, DC.
Studied computer applications, Titusville Community College, Titusville, CA.
Excelled in a word processing course, Northern Virginia Community College, Manassas, VA.

PERSONAL Enthusiastic quick learner and self starter. Accustomed to producing ongoing reports according to established schedule. Am single and willing to relocate. Excellent references.

Exact Name of Person
Title or Position
Name of Company
Address (number and street)
Address (city, state, and zip)

**Stockbroker
and Financial Consultant**

Having a wife who is interested
in moving back to her
hometown to be near her aging
parents is what has prompted
this high achiever to seek
employment in a new area.

Dear Exact Name of Person: (or Dear Sir or Madam if answering a blind ad.)

With the enclosed resume, I would like to make you aware of my interest in exploring suitable opportunities within your organization which can utilize my proven sales abilities, entrepreneurial spirit, as well as my background as a Stockbroker and Investment Counselor.

Although I am excelling in my current position with a South Carolina Bank and am being groomed for further rapid promotion, I am exploring opportunities in your area. I can provide outstanding references from my current employer at the appropriate time.

As you will see from my resume, in my current position as a Stockbroker and Investment Counselor I am responsible for 22 branch locations in nine counties and am involved in meeting with clients and potential clients to develop investment plans and strategies. I have consistently generated $800,000 a year in revenues and have been ranked for the past four years in the top four of the top sales producers at my bank. Although I came to the bank armed with my Series 6 and 63 licenses, I have recently earned my Series 7 license while excelling in my full-time job. In my prior position, I excelled as a Securities and Insurance Broker with a securities firm where I rapidly became respected for my creativity, technical knowledge, and dynamic marketing style. I am highly computer literate and am skilled at using various software programs to create graphics, charts, illustrations, and printouts.

You would find me in person to be a congenial individual who can be counted on to produce outstanding results in the most competitive situations. If you can use a dedicated professional who can provide outstanding personal and professional references, I hope you will write or call me to suggest a time when we might meet to discuss your needs and goals and how I might meet them. I can assure you that I could rapidly become a vital and contributing member of your team.

Sincerely,

Richard David Beers

RICHARD DAVID BEERS

1110½ Hay Street, Fayetteville, NC 28305 • preppub@aol.com • (910) 483-6611

OBJECTIVE

To benefit an organization that can use a hard-working and aggressive young professional with unlimited initiative and resourcefulness, strong communication and organizational skills, as well as proven sales and marketing abilities.

FINANCIAL LICENSES

Hold Series 7, 6 & 63 Securities Licenses, licensed by the NASD and the SEC.
Obtained a Life & Health Insurance License.
- Studied for and obtained these licenses while excelling in full-time jobs.

EDUCATION

B.A. degree in Sociology, New Haven University, New Haven, CT, 1987.
Excelled in Ranger School, the 72-day "stress-test" management school designed to test the mental and physical limits of the military's most talented leaders.

COMPUTERS

Familiar with software including Word, WordPerfect 5.1, Microsoft Works, and Windows 3.1. Skilled in formulating different investment strategies using software programs to create graphs, charts, and printouts; adept at developing illustrations for mutual funds and annuities.

EXPERIENCE

STOCKBROKER & FINANCIAL CONSULTANT. Nation's Bank Investment Services, Florence, SC (1996-present). Responsible for 22 branch locations in nine counties, am involved in meeting with clients and potential clients to develop investment plans and strategies; train key individuals at the 22 branches to recognize qualified customers through profiling and by helping these customers develop financial plans.
- Have consistently generated $800,000 per year in revenue through my ability to set high goals and then persistently following through with well executed plans.
- Studied for and obtained my Series 7 license while excelling in this full-time job.
- Ranked in the top four of the bank's top sales performers for four straight years.
- Have become skilled at analyzing customer needs and developing financial plans.

SECURITIES & INSURANCE BROKER. Dale Securities, Inc., Florence, SC (1993-96). Rapidly became respected for my creativity, technical knowledge, and dynamic marketing style while developing portfolios/plans for private pensions, retirement, and investments for individuals, family entities, and organizations.
- Became known for my skill in creating packages with products including tax-sheltered mutual funds and annuities, 401(k) plans, as well as variable universal life insurance.
- In the belief that "a picture is worth a thousand words," used my computer software knowledge to create printout "pictures" for investment strategy proposals.
- Acquired valuable insights into the tax advantages available for different types of investors, depending on risk aversion and overall goals in financial planning.
- Gained expert knowledge regarding laws governing mutual funds and annuities.
- Learned how to talk about financial planning and investment concepts with all types of people, from the savvy businessperson to the person with no technical knowledge of finance.

PRINCIPLES OF MANAGEMENT INSTRUCTOR. U.S. Army, Ft. Bragg, NC (1990-93). At the Army's largest U.S. military base, was specially selected as an instructor in the Non-Commissioned Officer's Course, a seven-week management training program.

GENERAL MANAGER. U.S. Army, Ft. Bragg, NC (1988-90). As a squad leader in the famed 82nd Airborne Division, excelled in leading a six-person Scout Squad—an organization which had to remain continuously ready to relocate worldwide in order to respond to international crises, terrorism, conflict, or disasters; controlled an inventory valued at $125,000.
- Designed and supervised the implementation of training programs.

PERSONAL

Am an extremely positive and cheerful person who adapts easily to new situations.

Date

Jason Robart
General Manager
Western of Missouri
Columbus, OH 53408

Dear Mr. Robart:

   With the enclosed resume, I would like to make you aware of my interest in the job of Sales Manager in the Columbus, OH area. As you know, we had the pleasure of working together when you were Events Coordinator. I can also provide an outstanding reference from Nathan Johnson. I believe you are already aware of my track record of outstanding performance as well as my demonstrated abilities related to operations management, sales management, customer service, and inventory control.

   As you know, I have excelled as Store Manager in Kansas City. I began with Western as a Parts Clerk and gained expertise in that aspect of the business. I believe you are aware that I have excelled in my positions at Western while also working a full-time job as a Military Policeman. As an MP, I worked in jobs which included Investigator and United Nations Body Guard.

   It is my desire to continue working to advance the profitability and growth of Western, and I wanted to formally ask you to consider me for the job of Sales Manager. I offer proven sales abilities and have trained employees at the Kansas City store in effective sales techniques. I believe solid product knowledge is a key to effectiveness in sales, and I certainly offer expert understanding of bikes and motorcycles. I am proud of the fact that I have hired and developed employees in the Kansas City store whom I have trained to utilize strong selling skills.

   Let me know if you need any information other than what I have provided. I would enjoy the opportunity to talk with you by phone or in person about this position, and I feel certain I would further contribute to the company in that capacity. I send best wishes.

                                        Sincerely,

                                        Grif Wadleigh

GRIF WADLEIGH

1110½ Hay Street, Fayetteville, NC 28305 • preppub@aol.com • (910) 483-6611

OBJECTIVE	To contribute to the Western company through my track record of outstanding performance which has demonstrated my abilities related to operations management, sales management, customer service, and inventory control.
EDUCATION	Completed numerous military training courses including Military Police School, Airborne School, as well as leadership and management training.
	Graduated from Carter High School, Oakland, CA 1989.
	Completed extensive on-the-job training with the Western company related to store operations, sales management, computerized inventory control, events management, personnel hiring and supervision, and service management.
EXPERIENCE	**Have progressed in the following track record of advancement with Western:**
	1997-1998: STORE MANAGER. Western, Kansas City, MO. Was promoted to manage the Kansas City store after excelling as a Parts Clerk; was responsible for interviewing, hiring, and managing new employees.
	• Oversaw all areas of operation including the servicing of wreck estimates.
	• Am known for my exceptional sales abilities, and have trained new employees in the most effective techniques of bike sales.
	• Scheduled and coordinated special events including rallies, parties, and charity events; these events have greatly improved the store's visibility in the community.
	1994-95: PARTS CLERK. Gained expert knowledge of Western's inventory while selling parts and accessories, using various catalogues to research the products of numerous parts distributors, and ordering parts for special orders.
	• Learned to expertly handle the job as a Service Writer; became known for my persistence in locating sources for hard-to-find, custom, and high-performance parts.
	• Advised customers on what repairs were needed on their bikes and motorcycles and coordinated the arrangements for scheduling and making the repairs.
	Military experience: Served my country with distinction in the following positions while simultaneously working at Western in my spare time:
	MILITARY POLICEMAN. U.S. Army, Ft. Nelson, MO (1995-98). Worked mostly at night as a Military Policeman and Team Leader.
	• Developed an attitude of maintaining constant vigilance and attention-to-detail while controlling access in and out of a Top Secret compound.
	• Played a vital role in rewriting a key Standard Operating Procedure.
	1994-95: INVESTIGATOR. U.S. Army, Ft. Nelson, MO. Was specially selected for a special assignment to work as an Investigator with the Sheriff's Department.
	1993-94: MILITARY POLICEMAN. U.S. Army, Ft. Nelson, MO. Maintained the peace and wrote traffic tickets while patrolling the Ft. Nelson military reservation.
	1990-92: UNITED NATIONS BODY GUARD. U.S. Army. Worked in civilian clothes while acting as a Body Guard for United Nations personnel and driving security escort missions for Swiss and Swedish officers.
	• Was frequently commended for my poise when interacting with VIPs.
PERSONAL	Hobbies include western activities and golfing. In my limited spare time, volunteer to help Little League players. Will relocate.

Date

Exact Name of Person
Title or Position
Address (number and street)
Address (city, state, and zip)

Store Manager, Food Industry

After a track record of promotion within the grocery store management field, this mid-level manager is seeking a career change. She would like to be involved in work in which she can apply her education in human resources management. Her practical problem is that she must match the compensation level of nearly $60,000 which she is making now, and it's not easy to "start over" and make that kind of money in a new field. (Employers usually pay us the most money to do what we already know how to do!)

Dear Exact Name of Person: (or Dear Sir or Madam if answering a blind ad)

I would appreciate an opportunity to talk with you soon about how I could contribute to your organization through a combination of education and experience in the field of human resources management, well-developed training and personnel development skills, and excellent time management and planning abilities.

As you will see from my enclosed resume, I have been highly successful in all operational areas of store and customer service management with the Giant Foods grocery store chain. I am a highly respected management professional and winner of numerous awards for my expertise in developing employees, reducing shrinkage, increasing productivity and customer satisfaction, and boosting bottom-line profitability. Although I am held in high regard by my employer and can provide outstanding references at the appropriate time, I have decided that I would like to transfer my human resources knowledge and management skills to another industry.

With a B.S.B.A. degree concentrating in Human Resources Management from University of Kentucky, I possess an educational background which complements my 13-plus years of practical management experience. I have always enjoyed the challenge of training and guiding the professional development of others. I have trained dozens of Giant Foods' managers and have produced highly effective professionals who are now some of Giant Foods' best managers. In company opinion polls conducted annually of employees, I am always described by employees as a fair yet firm supervisor who treats all people with respect. I believe attitude is one of the most important indicators of an employee's future success in a job, but I also believe that effective supervisory skills can shape attitudes, stimulate productivity, and minimize turnover.

When we meet in person, you will see that I am a flexible, mature, and reliable professional with a highly self-motivated nature, enthusiasm, and in-depth management experience which could be useful assets in your organization.

I hope you will call or write me soon to arrange a brief meeting to discuss your current and future needs and how I might serve them. Thank you in advance for your time.

Sincerely,

Lynne Schaper

LYNNE SCHAPER

1110½ Hay Street, Fayetteville, NC 28305 • preppub@aol.com • (910) 483-6611

OBJECTIVE To offer my positive, results-oriented leadership style to an organization that can use my education and experience in human resources management as well as my excellent time management, personnel development, and planning skills.

EDUCATION B.S. in Business Administration with a concentration in Human Resources Management, University of Kentucky, Lexington, KY, 1986.

COMPUTERS Utilize IBM and Digital computers on a daily basis; operate highly specialized systems which are linked to the national home office

EXPERIENCE *Have become known for special talents in developing and training top-quality personnel as well as for my ability to increase bottom-line profits and strengthen employee satisfaction and productivity with the 1,200-store Giant Foods grocery chain:*
STORE MANAGER. Salisbury, KY (1995-present). Increased profit levels 25% in this $11.5 million a year store by applying my versatile knowledge of all operational areas to make significant changes in this 100-employee store.
- Increased sales by an impressive 20% overall.
- Provided hands-on training for seven people who moved into management role; guided all stages of their training and professional development.

STORE MANAGER. Graham, KY (1992-95). Increased store profits 12% and led this $8.5 million store through a major renovation and expansion project through my expertise in the areas which included control of wage costs, better utilization of available labor, reduction of shrinkage, and more efficient control of inventory.
- Helped train managers from other districts.
- Managed the pilot project which introduced a new front-end accounting program that reduced labor hours and simplified many computer tasks.

STORE MANAGER. Crayfield, KY (1989-92). Gained a reputation as an effective manager of human, material, and fiscal resources in a store with $7 million in annual sales.
- Was cited for my accomplishments which included increasing bottom line profits 30% and exceeding production standards for 24 consecutive months.

CUSTOMER SERVICE MANAGER. Mertonville, KY (1987-89). Based at a rural store, was selected to travel to stores which were having problems and assist them in putting better cash controls in place and in solving their customer service problems.
- Displayed an ability to re-train personnel so they could become better employees; personally trained and developed four customer service managers for 15 area stores.

CUSTOMER SERVICE MANAGER. Bentonville, KY (1984-87). Originally hired as a Cashier for this store located adjacent to a university campus, was soon promoted and cited for my abilities related to reducing cash losses and employee theft as well as my skill in providing helpful and courteous one-on-one service.
- Trained three customer service managers in the region's best store in cash control.

PERSONAL Possess a fair but firm management style. Offer a reputation as one who can be counted on to make my expectations clear. Consistently receive excellent ratings in opinion surveys.

Date

Exact Name of Person
Title or Position
Name of Company
Address (number and street)
Address (city, state, and zip)

Store Manager,
Retail Accounting Manager

A desire to finish her degree is
what has prompted this
experienced retail manager to look
for employment outside retailing.

Dear Exact Name of Person: (or Dear Sir or Madam if answering a blind ad.)

With the enclosed resume, I would like to indicate my interest in your organization and my desire to explore employment opportunities.

As you will see from my enclosed resume, I am an experienced manager of people, assets, and financial resources. In my current position I am managing the store which is the Top Volume Store in sales in the region. Although I am excelling in my current position and am held in high regard by upper management, I am interested in transferring my considerable management skills to another industry.

I hope you will welcome my call soon to arrange a brief meeting at your convenience to discuss your current and future needs and how I might serve them. Thank you in advance for your time.

Sincerely yours.

Gerry Reeves

Alternate last paragraph:
I hope you will call or write me soon to suggest a time convenient for us to meet and discuss your current and future needs and how I might serve them. Thank you in advance for your time.

GERRY REEVES

1110½ Hay Street, Fayetteville, NC 28305 • preppub@aol.com • (910) 483-6611

OBJECTIVE
To benefit an organization that can use a persuasive and dynamic professional who combines outstanding sales and marketing abilities, management experience, and a proven ability to make sound decisions and achieve ambitious bottom-line goals.

EDUCATION
Completing Bachelor's degree in my spare time at night; completed three years (98 credit hours) of course work from Baptist College, Austin, TX with a concentration in Marketing. Have excelled in numerous management and executive development training programs.

EXPERIENCE
STORE MANAGER. Toys "R" Us, Denton, TX (1996-present). Manage up to 50 employees while controlling a $625,000 inventory level and maintaining tight operational control of a $2 million store.
- Am managing the store which is considered the Top Volume Store in sales in the entire region.
- Have hired, trained, and developed several managers who have gone on to become key management professionals for the Toys "R" Us chain.
- Increased profit margin from 37% to 39.2% in a one-year period while also increasing profit by $15,000 year-to-date through effective cost-cutting measures on store-controlled expenses without jeopardizing overall store productivity.
- Although I am highly regarded in my current position and enjoy the fast pace of this bustling retail environment, I am seeking an equally challenging position which will fully energize my leadership and energy while permitting me to complete, in my spare time, the year of studies remaining for my college degree.

MANAGER. Fashion Coordinators, San Antonio, TX (1996). Was recruited by this company to take over its multi-unit operations; raised sales at the Dellwood Park Mall location 80% over the previous year's figures in my first month supervising that location, and then played a key role in closing the Centerfield Mall location.
- At the Centerfield mall location, inventoried equipment, supplies, and client records and selected team members to be transferred.
- Was successful in raising sales average from $120-130 per client to $190-200 per client consistently per pay period.
- Sought new acquisitions in client base to increase business, and serviced existing clients with a standard of excellence in customer service; was effective in statistical management, including sales average, client survey scores, and payroll management.

SENIOR STORE MANAGER. The Paladium, San Antonio, TX (1992-96). Worked alone with no direct supervision on implementing company guidelines and goals among three stores generating $2.3 million in sales.
- Promoted to Senior Store Manager after consistently exceeding expectations in all aspects of managing overall operations
- Set sales goal and payroll allocations with given budget among the three stores.
- Kept shortage levels consistently under goal, and brought a high-shortage store down from a 3.8% shortage to .96% in a six-month period.
- Was the Liaison between corporate and six stores in Texas through 4th Quarter.

CO-MANAGER. New York Fashions & Accessories, Houston, TX (1990-92). Supervised the daily operations of a store with annual sales exceeding $1.5 million after being promoted from Assistant Manager to Co-Manager in a 10-month period; responsible for productivity of a 13-member sales team, and led by example with personal sales always exceeding given goals.
- Organized and presented merchandise to create a unique fashion image tailored by watching customer trends.
- Utilized available fixtures and equipment for optional usage.

Exact Name of Person
Title or Position
Name of Company
Address (no., street)
Address (city, state, zip)

Tennis Professional

This highly regarded tennis pro is happy with his current situation, but he is curious about "what's out there." He is approaching a select number of clubs in the towns where he and his family might want to live.

Dear Exact Name of Person: (or Dear Sir or Madam if answering a blind ad.)

I would appreciate an opportunity to talk with you soon about how I could contribute to your organization through my outstanding personal reputation and technical expertise as a Director/ Head Tennis Pro.

Although I am highly regarded in my current job as Head Pro for the New World Country Club, where I have been since 1993, I am attracted to your organization because of its fine reputation and feel I have much to offer you. As you will see from my resume, I have excelled as a Tennis Pro at Van Der Meer Tennis University, Tennis Coach at a tennis academy, and Head Pro at a sports center and country club before coming to New World Country Club as Head Pro. In 1994 I became one of only four people in North Carolina certified as a USPTR National Tester, and I have conducted USPTR coaches' workshops for persons wanting to be certified or to upgrade their certification.

So much of what I could offer an already-outstanding program such as yours is my creativity, I believe, since I know you have an excellent staff. I believe that the main way to keep the membership involved and the tennis professionals motivated is by developing new programs, and I have combined my tennis skills and creativity in developing highly successful programs for adults and juniors while also utilizing my public relations and media skills to develop new community awareness of and involvement in tennis.

I would appreciate your keeping my interest in your club confidential at this point, but if you have any idea that you could use a talented tennis pro who could take your program to new levels of excellence, I would appreciate your contacting me.

Sincerely yours,

Clifton Newman

Alternate last paragraph:

I hope you will welcome my call soon to arrange a brief meeting at your convenience to discuss your current and future needs and how I might serve them. Thank you in advance for your time.

CLIFTON NEWMAN

1110½ Hay Street, Fayetteville, NC 28305 • preppub@aol.com • (910) 483-6611

OBJECTIVE

I want to contribute to an organization that can use a well-trained tennis professional who offers expert teaching and motivational skills along with the proven ability to develop, manage, and promote new programs.

CERTIFICATION

Am a USPTR **National Tester**, one of only four in North Carolina.
Am certified by the Professional Tennis Registry of the U.S.A. as a **Tennis Professional**, the highest of three ratings.

EXPERIENCE

HEAD TENNIS PRO. New World Country Club, Charlotte, NC (1993-present). At this 2,700-member club, dramatically increased tennis participation; manage classes, tournaments, maintenance, and a full-service pro shop, while supervising a staff of four and administering a $65,000 facility budget.
- Was awarded a Local Excellence Training (LET) Program, which has trained youngsters from throughout North Carolina.
- Ran two successful USTA tournaments (KCC Junior Invitational and KCC Men's Invitational), which drew players from all over the southeast.
- Developed the Adult Team Tennis Interclub Program, the most successful adult program at KCC to date; formed three USTA adult league teams.
- Have participated in the Teams Across America Program sponsored by USPTA.
- Have developed several community programs to boost tennis popularity, including work with school programs (Super Saturdays — a kindergarten through third-grade program).
- Have conducted USPTR coaches' workshops for persons wanting to be certified or to upgrade their certification.
- Participated in an internship program with students from an area college.
- Led over 75 players of all ages to compete in their first tournaments.

TENNIS PROFESSIONAL. Pine Valley Country Club, Pine Valley, NC (1991-93). Increased participation in the club's juniors' program to an all-time high.
- Conceived and developed an academy which trained over 80 young tennis players.
- Managed a juniors' tournament which included nationally ranked players.

TENNIS COACH. James Johnson Tennis Academy, Atlanta, GA (1989-91). Taught daily classes and weekend clinics for junior, college, and pro-tour tennis players; traveled to ATP and WTA tours as a professional coach; while traveling the National Junior Circuit, worked with top juniors including the #1 ranked John Smith.

HEAD TENNIS PRO. The Sports Center, Atlanta, GA (1986-89). While managing the total tennis program at this 1,000-person club, developed a juniors' program with 30 participants, many of whom were ranked in the state; was USTA Schools' Program Coordinator.

TENNIS PRO. Van Der Meer Tennis University, Hilton Head, SC (1986). Had the opportunity to work with world-class players at this famous tennis university/resort.

EDUCATION

Achieved USTA Sport Science Level I certification and Sport Science Level II training.
Attended several Elite Coaches training programs conducted by the USTA and USPTR.
Attended numerous professional workshops at the Annual Tennis Symposium, 1988-present.
Awarded a scholarship to **Van Der Meer Tennis University**, Sweet Briar College, VA, 1985.

PROFESSIONAL AFFILIATIONS

Am a member of the following professional organizations/associations:
United States Professional Tennis Registry (USPTR), United States Professional Tennis Association (USPTA), U.S. Tennis Association (USTA), North Carolina Association of Tennis Professionals, and Prince Pro Team.

Date

April Stanfield
Stephens & Rothchild, Inc.
P.O. Box 3098
Houston, TX 89023

Dear Ms. Stanfield:

**Territory Manager,
Food Service Industry**

In this resume, you will see the background of a professional who is in his second career. In his first career, he worked for nearly 20 years as a funeral director. Then he transferred his "people" skills and sales ability into a sales position. Having established an excellent reputation in his second career, he has prepared this resume in response to a food industry company that is attempting to recruit him away from his current employer.

With the enclosed resume, I would like to formally indicate my interest in discussing the Food Broker positions available with your company. Although I am excelling in my job with Delby Food Service and can provide excellent references at the appropriate time, I would appreciate your treating my enquiry in confidence at this time.

As you will see from my resume, in 1996 I made a career change and became a Territory Manager with Delby Food Service. I rapidly became successful. In my first assignment I took over an existing territory and, with no prior food service experience, boosted sales 25% in my first month. Since then I have played a key role in helping my district to its #1 ranking among the corporation's 62 districts with sales in our district of $160 million. Although I am now living in Dallas, I have cheerfully adapted to varying territorial assignments as company needs have required, and I have established and maintained relationships with restaurants as well as day care and health care organizations all over Texas. I believe much of my success derives from the fact that I truly feel I am "in partnership" with my accounts.

In my previous experience, I was a funeral director, which is itself a "people business." With a reputation as an outstanding communicator and negotiator, I became skilled at establishing rapport with people from every race and background, and I maintained effective relationships with law enforcement officials, the media, as well as a variety of state, local, and federal officials. I genuinely enjoy working with people.

If my skills and experience interest you, please contact me to suggest a time when we might talk in more detail about your needs. I am single and can relocate as your needs require. Thank you in advance for your time, and I send belated wishes for a Happy New Year.

Yours sincerely,

Gary Rosenko

GARY ROSENKO

1110½ Hay Street, Fayetteville, NC 28305 • preppub@aol.com • (910) 483-6611

OBJECTIVE	I want to contribute to the success of an organization that can use a versatile and knowledgeable professional who offers highly refined skills in sales and customer service.
EXPERIENCE	**TERRITORY MANAGER.** Delby Food Service, Crowley, TX (1996-present). Was recruited in 1996 for a position with the largest food service company in the U.S., and have rapidly become successful; in my first assignment, took over an existing territory and, with no prior food service experience, boosted sales $25% in my first month. • Have played a key role in helping my district to its #1 ranking among 62 corporate districts with overall district sales of $160 million. • Establish and nurture accounts with restaurants, health care, and day care organizations. • Have cheerfully adapted to varying territorial assignments within the company as corporate needs have required; established and maintained excellent relationships in counties all over Texas. • Am skilled at all aspects of my job including collecting delinquent accounts, establishing and maintaining rapport, and increasing profitability of existing accounts. • Believe that success in sales comes from establishing a "partnership" with my accounts. **FUNERAL DIRECTOR.** Dallas Funeral Service Crematory, Dallas, TX (1995-96). Used my extensive experience in funeral directing to enhance profitability and efficiency of funerals; introduced several new techniques which simplified funeral arrangements. • Applied my knowledge of laws related to funeral home administration/licensing. • Gained a reputation as an outstanding communicator who easily establishes rapport with people from every race and background, and became very knowledgeable with regard to discussing and tailoring funeral needs to specific religious beliefs. **FUNERAL DIRECTOR.** Jason G. Smith Funeral Home, Dallas, TX (1981-94). Excelled in handling the full range of activities involved in the selling, conducting, and pre-need arranging of funerals. • Wrote the policy training manual related to OSHA, EPA, and other similar regulations. • Maintained outstanding relationships with law enforcement officials, the media, and with a wide variety of community, state, and local organizations and officials. • Was respected for my excellent skills in managing people and resources while routinely coordinating numerous simultaneous projects under tight deadlines.
EDUCATION	Associate's **Degree in Business**, Texas Central College, Dallas, TX, 1972. Received **Diploma in Mortuary Science**, Brazelton, IN, 1975.
LICENSE	**Licensed Funeral Director**; became a Texas Funeral Service Licensee in 1975.
AFFILIATIONS	Have been active in my community; following are highlights of my involvements and affiliations: • Former Member, Nursing Home Advisory Board and Parks and Recreation Board • Past member, Administrative Board, Master of Masonic Lodge, Shriner
PERSONAL	Outstanding personal and professional references. Genuinely enjoy working with the public.

Date

Director of Personnel
City of Chesterfield
Grayson Hall, Suite 123
Chesterfield, VT 98231

Warehouse Manager

Sometimes even experienced professionals find themselves lacking in the kind of experience they need for specific jobs. Here you see a warehouse professional trying to become a firefighter.

Dear Sir or Madam:

With the enclosed resume, I would like to formally initiate the process of becoming considered for a job as a Fireman within your organization.

As you will see when you read my resume, I have excelled in every job I have ever taken on. Currently I am a member of the management team for one of the area's largest and oldest furniture stores, and I have become skilled at problem solving and decision making. I began with the company in a part-time job, was hired full-time after one week, and have been promoted to increasing responsibilities because of my proven ability to make sound decisions under pressure.

While serving my country in the U.S. Army, I was promoted ahead of my peers to a job as Telecommunications Center Operator and earned numerous commendations for my management ability and technical skills. I was praised on numerous occasions for my ability to "think on my feet" and to remain calm and make prudent decisions under stressful circumstances. I was entrusted with a Secret NAC security clearance.

Throughout my life, I have been known as a highly motivated self starter with a strong drive to excel in all I do. Even in high school, I was on the All-Star baseball team and was elected Captain of the football team in my senior year.

I am sending you my resume because it is my strong desire to make a career in the firefighting field, and I am willing to start in an entry-level position and prove myself. I am always seeking new ways in which to improve my skills and increase my knowledge; for example, I am learning Spanish in my spare time because I feel Spanish language skills will be an asset in any field with our growing Hispanic population. I can assure you that I would bring that same level of self motivation to firefighting as a career field, and I hope you will give me an opportunity to show you in person that I am a dependable young individual who could become a valuable part of your organization.

I hope you will contact me to suggest a time when we might meet to discuss your needs and how I might serve them. I can provide outstanding personal and professional references. Thank you in advance for whatever consideration and time you can give me in my goal of becoming a professional firefighter.

Sincerely,

Jorge Perez

JORGE PEREZ

1110½ Hay Street, Fayetteville, NC 28305 • preppub@aol.com • (910) 483-6611

OBJECTIVE

To contribute to an organization that can use a hard-working young professional in excellent physical condition who offers a proven ability to make prudent decisions under stressful conditions and within tight deadlines.

LANGUAGES

Working knowledge of Spanish and German; am highly motivated to better myself and master new skills, and am learning Spanish in my spare time.

EDUCATION

College: Completed two years of college course work concentrated in History and Liberal Arts, University of Maryland.

Military: Excelled in more than a year of college-level training sponsored by the U.S. Army related to electronics and telecommunications, safety and quality control, and management.

High School: Graduated from Jamestown High School, Jamestown, RI, 1989.
- Was an **All-Star** Baseball player, **Captain** of the Football team in my senior year and a starter on the football team all three years of high school.

First Aid: Obtained First Aid and CPR Certification through ROTC training.

EXPERIENCE

WAREHOUSE MANAGER. Fancy Furniture, Chesterfield, VT (1995-present). Began in a part-time position and was offered full-time employment after one week; worked in the warehouse and learned the "nuts and bolts" of warehouse operations while working my way up from warehouse worker to driver's helper; was selected as Assistant Warehouse Manager after eight months.
- Supervise, train, and evaluate seven warehouse employees while also filling in for absent employees as needed; operate 24-foot truck and forklift.
- Oversee security of a furniture inventory worth half a million dollars.
- Have become skilled in problem solving and decision making while handling public relations and solving customer complaints; am now entrusted with the authority to make numerous management decisions independently.
- Have refined my planning and organizational skills while earning a reputation as a prudent decision maker who thinks well on my feet and who excels in maximizing efficiency and productivity.

INDEPENDENT CONTRACT REPAIRMAN. Bath and Kitchen Fixtures, Chesterfield, VT (1994-95). Increased new business accounts by 30% through my outstanding sales and customer service skills.
- Traveled from store to store that sold bath and kitchen fixtures and provided personal demonstrations and testimonials of my repair work; accounts skyrocketed through my personal selling skills.

TELECOMMUNICATIONS CENTER OPERATOR. U.S. Army, Ft. Bliss, TX (1989-91). Learned valuable work habits and acquired a disciplined approach to work while becoming promoted ahead of my peers to Telecommunications Center Operator; earned numerous commendations for my excellent coordinating and management skills.
- Held a Secret NAC security clearance.

PERSONAL

Outstanding personal and professional references. Strong work ethic.

PART FOUR
SELF-EMPLOYED MANAGERS AND ENTREPRENEURS

Self-employed managers and entrepreneurs find themselves in a job hunt for a variety of reasons. Some entrepreneurs sell the company they founded and, if they do, they may find themselves in a non-compete agreement for a period of time, which usually means that they have to change fields or relocate if they want to work. Sometimes an entrepreneur is forced to close his business. Other entrepreneurs find themselves "stuck" in a business which is too small to keep them interested for a long time. Most entrepreneurs find themselves lured from time to time by a new entrepreneurial challenge.

The "hidden" problem or disadvantage of the entrepreneur in a job hunt

When an entrepreneur goes into the job market, she is usually greeted with mixed feelings. On the distrustful and negative side, there is often the perception on the part of prospective employers that the entrepreneur is not really interested in working for other people and isn't accustomed to having a boss. On the positive side, there is respect for the creativity and industry of anyone who can start a business "from scratch" and keep it running, and many large companies advertise that they are seeking "entrepreneurial instincts" when they advertise for certain positions.

The advantage of the entrepreneur in a job hunt

One advantage the entrepreneur has in a job hunt is that she has lots of achievements and accomplishments to put on the resume! Another advantage entrepreneurs have is that they are usually outgoing individuals accustomed to dealing with people, so they are often comfortable talking to people in a job hunt.

Job titles of the entrepreneur

Even though the entrepreneur usually owned the company he worked for, it's often wise to forego words like "owner" in job titles and choose words that describe the functional area of involvement such as "General Manager" or "Sales Manager." This will tend to (1) make the entrepreneur look more like other people in the job hunt and (2) decrease the emphasis on the ownership of the business. Prospective employers are looking for people who "need" to work, and they would turn away from a prospective employee who appeared to have made a lot of money in his own business and didn't need to work.

The entrepreneur is well-suited to the direct approach. Since the direct approach implies a process of imagining where you want to live and what types of companies you'd like to work for, the creative entrepreneur is instinctively in tune with the notion of directly approaching employers using a resume and cover letter. The idea of being persistent and following up on resumes which she sends out is "second nature" to the entrepreneur.

Exact Name
Exact Title
Company Name
Address
City, state zip

**Cleaning Service
General Manager**

Establishing a company "from scratch" and managing it was just a means to an end for this hard-working individual who used the business she founded as a way of paying for her education. Now she is able to pursue the career in social services which she has always dreamed about!

Dear Sir or Madam:

I would appreciate an opportunity to talk with you soon about how I could contribute to your organization through my formal education in social work as well as my versatile experience in social services, business management, office operations, and transportation management.

As you will see from my resume, I recently completed the B.A. in Social Work degree which I started several years ago and was unable to complete quickly because my husband was being relocated worldwide as a military professional. I am especially proud that, through my persistence and determination, I was able to complete my degree in 1999 even while managing a successful and fast-growing small business which I started "from scratch" and directed until recently, when we relocated to Washington.

In a previous job in the human services/social work field prior to receiving my degree, I worked as an Eligibility Specialist for the County of San Bernardino and was involved in interviewing clients and assessing their needs. I gained a reputation as a caring counselor and respected co-worker, and I was encouraged to apply for a social work position in the county if we were ever again residing in San Bernardino.

From my work experience in the Air Force and in office environments, I am accustomed to dealing graciously with the public while working under tight deadlines and solving difficult problems. I offer a naturally compassionate personality along with an ability to handle large volumes of work efficiently and accurately. I can provide outstanding personal and professional references.

I hope you will welcome my call soon to arrange a brief meeting at your convenience to discuss your current and future needs and how I might serve them. Thank you in advance for your time, and I will look forward to meeting you.

Sincerely yours,

Marlene Routhier

MARLENE ROUTHIER

1110½ Hay Street, Fayetteville, NC 28305 • preppub@aol.com • (910) 483-6611

OBJECTIVE I want to contribute to an organization that can use a cheerful hard worker who offers an education related to social work and human services along with experience which includes proudly serving my country in the U.S. Air Force.

EDUCATION **Bachelor of Arts (B.A.) degree in Social Work**, California State Polytechnic University, Pomona, CA, 1999; worked at night to finish this degree while managing a business during the day.

Studied Social Work at Northwestern State University, Natchitoches, LA, 1980-82 and 1988.

Excelled in supervisory and management training sponsored by the U.S. Air Force, 1982-87.

EXPERIENCE **GENERAL MANAGER.** Marlene's Cleaning Service, Pomona, CA (1995-99). On my own initiative and with only a fifty-dollar initial investment, set up "from scratch" a business which provided cleaning services for residential and commercial property; hired and supervised clerical and cleaning personnel while personally establishing the company's 18 major accounts.

- Only two months after starting the business, generated monthly cash flow of $1700 and personally handled the finances including accounts receivable/payable, financial reporting, tax preparation, and collections.
- Was frequently commended for my gracious style of dealing with people.

ELIGIBILITY WORKER. County of San Bernardino, San Bernardino, CA (1992-95). Performed assessments of clients to determine eligibility for medical assistance in the form of Medicaid.

- Became acquainted with the vast interlocking network of social services organizations, and referred clients to those agencies and organizations as appropriate.
- Assisted clients in preparing budgets and strengthened their ability to manage their finances.
- Earned a reputation as a compassionate counselor and effective motivator while treating people from all walks of life with dignity and respect.
- Became skilled in handling a heavy case load and large volumes of paperwork.

OFFICE MANAGER'S ASSISTANT. M.T.S. Insurance Service, Brea, CA (1990-92). Worked as the "right arm" of a busy office manager in a fast-paced insurance office, and excelled in activities ranging from word processing, to invoicing, to customer service.

DATA ENTRY OPERATOR. The Broadway, Los Angeles, CA (1988-90). Operated a computer in order to input data provided by sales associates; worked with customers in establishing delivery dates, and verified financial/accounting transactions.

PASSENGER & HOUSEHOLD GOODS SPECIALIST. U.S. Air Force, McGuire AFB, NJ (1982-87). While serving my country in the Air Force, specialized in managing the transportation of people and property all over the globe.

- Developed expertise in working with commercial airlines and shipping operations.
- Expertly processed every kind of paperwork related to making reservations for domestic and international travel, issuing tickets, coordinating shipments of personal goods, and preparing monthly reports and bills of lading.
- Learned to solve problems creatively and resourcefully in the process of locating "lost" people and property worldwide.
- Received two prestigious medals for exceptional performance and exemplary service.

COMPUTERS Have used Word and WordPerfect for word processing; can rapidly master new software.

PERSONAL Am a patient, calm person who can handle a heavy work load and not get stressed out by tight deadlines. Have been told many times that I am a gifted counselor and communicator. Can provide outstanding personal and professional references upon request.

Date

Exact Name
Exact Title
Company Name
Address
City, state zip

**Company President
and Sales Manager**

Employers are *very* inquisitive about
why an entrepreneur wants to
make a change. This accomplished
individual uses his cover letter to
emphasize that he has worked in a
big company as well as in the
small company which he founded,
and he makes it clear that he now
wishes to be involved in sales.
(Employers are looking for people
who know what they want to do;
entrepreneurs are usually definite
in their preferences about what
they want to do next.)

Dear Sir or Madam:

With the enclosed resume, I would like to introduce you to the sales expertise, leadership ability, and management skills which I could put to work for your organization.

I am in the process of selling a company which I built "from scratch" and which, through my strong sales and management skills, I have grown into a profitable and respected small company in only two years. Although I have been successful in this entrepreneurial venture, I have decided that I wish to devote most of my energies to sales rather than to the day-to-day management details of a small business.

As you will see from my resume, I also offer a track record of proven results in managing a large company. In my first job after leaving the University of North Carolina at Chapel Hill, I went to work for a company in the oil industry and I advanced into the General Manager position. During the 20 years which I spent managing this large, diversified business with wholesale and retail operations, I took the initiative in building the first 10-minute oil change unit in VA. After acting as sales manager and developing the commercial fleet business, I sold the business to the Jiffy Lube franchise for a profit.

I can assure you that I am a tireless hard worker who thoroughly enjoys selling and developing a new marketing program as well as a great product/service. Although much of my experience has been in petroleum operations/sales and in automotive parts/sales with specialized knowledge of lubricants sales, I have proven my ability to sell products in other industries. As a Sales Representative of insurance products, I exceeded all quotas and was named a National Quick Start winner.

A naturally outgoing individual with a proven ability to lead and motivate others, I have been active in numerous leadership capacities in my community. I am a former past president of the Rotary Club and former director of the Chamber of Commerce. If you can use my considerable sales and management abilities, I hope you will write or call me to suggest a time when we could meet in person.

Sincerely,

Wallace Jackson

WALLACE JACKSON

1110½ Hay Street, Fayetteville, NC 28305 • preppub@aol.com • (910) 483-6611

OBJECTIVE   To benefit an organization which can use a dynamic communicator and creative sales professional with outstanding negotiating and management skills along with a proven ability to transform ideas into operating realties while maximizing profit and market share.

EXPERIENCE   **PRESIDENT & SALES MANAGER.** Tidewater Sales & Rentals, Richmond, VA (1995-present). Utilized my entrepreneurial ability, aggressive sales orientation, strategic planning capabilities, and management skills to start a pre-owned car business "from scratch."
- Although I have been successful in starting up and managing a profitable business, I have decided to sell the company and seek a full-time sales situation.

SALES REPRESENTATIVE. State Farm Insurance, Richmond, VA (1993-1995). As a Property and Casualty Insurance Sales Professional for State Farm, handled "Family Insurance Checkups" and personal lines.
- Excelled in my first sales experience outside the automotive and petroleum industry; was selected as a National Quick Start winner in 1993; received a company-paid excursion to Los Angeles, CA, for advanced training.
- Exceeded quotas and boosted insurance sales by introducing a unique insurance concept: a membership benefits package for independent business owners which provided clients with maximum insurance coverage through membership in the National Association for the Self-Employed (NASE) or other association programs.

GENERAL MANAGER. Jackson Oil Company Inc., Tidewater, VA (1973-1993). In my first job out of college, began with Mayfield Oil Company and advanced into the General Manager position; provided leadership in turning around a marginally profitable company and then helped it to achieve higher levels of sales and profitability each year; negotiated the buyout of key assets of Mayfield Oil Company by Jackson Oil Company in 1989 and continued as the corporation's chief executive officer.
- At the head of a diversified multiplex consisting of an oil company and a chain of convenience stores, worked at the wholesale buying level of the petroleum industry while gaining experience in managing a chain of retail convenience stores.
- Oversaw staffing, sales, purchasing, bookkeeping, financial management including accounts receivable/payable, vendor relations, and inventory control.
- Transformed a business with only 5 employees into a leading competitor in the region with a 40+ work force and profits which multiplied sevenfold.
- Took the initiative in building the first 10-minute oil change unit in VA and developed the operation from start-up to 35 cars a day; developed the commercial fleet accounts and then sold the business to the Fast Lube franchise for a profit in 1985!
- Established and managed a profitable automatic car wash business.

EDUCATION   Completed two years of college coursework, University of North Carolina at Chapel Hill, 1971-73.
Sales Training: Completed extensive sales and management seminars since 1973 including Dale Carnegie and A.L. Williams Management Seminars.
Technical Training: Completed numerous petroleum industry seminars and training programs sponsored by automotive and oil industry giants

AFFILIATIONS   Former President, Rotary Club of the Tidewater Region. Membership Chairman, Social Chairman, and Chairman of the Board.
Other: Chairman of Miss Tidewater Pageant; Chairman of Tidewater Christmas Parade for five years; Chairman, Tidewater Centennial Parade; Co-Chairman of the Tidewater Heart Fund Drive; Member Tidewater ABC Advisory Board for five years.

PERSONAL   Enjoy hunting, salt-water fishing, golf, and UNC athletic events. Outstanding references.

Date

Exact Name of Person
Title or Position
Name of Company
Address (no., street)
Address (city, state, zip)

**Entrepreneur and
Business Manager**

This businessman offers experience
in establishing a successful
company and then selling it to a
chain. He may attract the attention
of a small or medium-size company
that would like to be turned into a
viable acquisition candidate. On the
other hand, a large company may
be attracted to his creativity and
proven ability to "make it happen."

Dear Exact Name of Person: (or Dear Sir or Madam if answering a blind ad.)

I would appreciate an opportunity to talk with you soon about how I could contribute to your organization through my business management, sales, and communication skills.

As you will see from my resume, I have founded successful businesses, tripled the sales volume of an existing company, and directed projects which required someone who could take a concept and turn it into an operating reality. While excelling as a retailer and importer of products that included oriental rugs and English antiques, I have become accustomed to working with a discriminating customer base of people regionally who trust my taste and character. In addition to a proven "track record" of producing a profit, I have earned a reputation for honesty and reliability. I believe there is no substitute in business for a good reputation.

I am ready for a new challenge, and that is why I have, in the last several months, closed two of my business locations and turned over the management of the third operation to a family member. I want to apply my seasoned business judgement, along with my problem-solving and opportunity-finding skills, to new areas.

If you can use the expertise of a savvy and creative professional who is skilled at handling every aspect of business management, from sales and marketing to personnel and finance, I would enjoy talking with you informally about your needs and goals. A flexible and adaptable person who feels comfortable stepping into new situations, I am able to "size up" problems and opportunities quickly through the "lens" of experience. I pride myself on my ability to deal tactfully and effectively with everyone.

I hope you will welcome my call soon to arrange a brief meeting at your convenience to discuss your current and future needs and how I might serve them. Thank you in advance for your time.

Sincerely yours,

Desmond Vaughn

DESMOND VAUGHN

1110½ Hay Street, Fayetteville, NC 28305 • preppub@aol.com • (910) 483-6611

OBJECTIVE

To add value to an organization that can use a resourceful entrepreneur and manager who offers a proven ability to start up successful new ventures and transform ailing operations into profitable ones through applying my sales, communication, and administrative skills.

EDUCATION

Earned a **B.A. degree in Sociology**, University of Pennsylvania, Philadelphia, PA.
Completed numerous executive development courses in business management and sales.

AFFILIATIONS & COMMUNITY LEADERSHIP

Have served by invitation on the Board of Directors of the following organizations:

Philadelphia Business Guild   Heart Association
Olde Philadelphia Association   Philadelphia Family Life Center
Philadelphia Hospital Pastoral Foundation   New South River Association
City of Philadelphia Downtown Revitalization Commission

Have earned a reputation as a creative strategist with the ability to transform ideas into operating realities and with the communication and leadership skills necessary to instill enthusiasm in others.

EXPERIENCE

FOUNDER & MANAGER. The Captain's Den, Philadelphia, PA (1979-present). Established "from scratch" this business which grew to three locations with sales in seven figures; developed a product line which I bought from sources worldwide, and developed a customer base which included discriminating purchasers from all over the east coast.

- Refined my expertise in all aspects of business management, including financial planning and reporting, hiring and training personnel, designing advertising and marketing plans, selling products valued at up to thousands of dollars, and overseeing accounts payable and receivable.
- From 1981-85, simultaneously acted as an **Importer** and **Management Consultant** for an English antiques business; traveled to England three times a year as an importer.
- From 1979-81, after being recruited as **Development Director** by the Methodist State Convention, took on the paid job of coordinating the pledging and collection of $1.5 million to construct a dormitory and cafeteria for the Methodist State Convention; set up all systems and procedures and managed funds until construction was finished.
- Recently closed down the center city locations of The Captain's Den, and have turned over the midtown location to a family member.

ENTREPRENEUR. Desmond Vaughn, Inc., Philadelphia, PA (1990-95). While simultaneously managing the Captain's Den, was successful in this separate entrepreneurial venture; after extensive market research to determine the viability of establishing a business in the gifts and accessories niche, set up a store in the affluent midtown district which rapidly became successful through innovative promotions, vigorous marketing, and word of mouth.

- In less than two years, the business was producing sales in the low six figures.
- Sold the business to a large chain in the gifts and accessories industry.

SALES MANAGER. Solomon's Carpet Co., Inc., Philadelphia, PA (1971-79). Took over the management of an existing business and tripled the sales volume while increasing the staff from four to 11 employees.

- Used radio and newspaper in innovative ways which boosted traffic and sales.
- Supervised a five-person sales staff and trained them in techniques related to prospecting, closing the sale, overcoming objections, and solving customer concerns.

Other experience: **CAPTAIN & COMPANY COMMANDER**. U.S. Army. Was awarded the Bronze Star and Army Commendation Medal for service in Vietnam.

PERSONAL

Offer a proven ability to manage several functional areas and projects at the same time.

Date

Mr. Jerry Vestry
American Express Financial Services
Suite 2220
Tampa, FL 33062

**Financial Consultant
and Commodities Broker**

This resume and cover letter
could also have been shown in
the Junior Manager Section.
Notice that this career letter has
a philosophical style.

Dear Mr. Vestry:

With the enclosed resume, I am responding to your ad in the *Wall Street Journal* for a Financial Services Coordinator.

As you will see from my resume, I have most recently excelled as a Financial Consultant with one of the leading financial services companies in the nation.

Your ad mentioned that your ideal candidate "will have some understanding of commodities markets and will possess a proven ability to use technical knowledge in a creative way." Prior to becoming a Financial Consultant, I worked as a Commodities Broker, and I possess an expert understanding of commodities markets.

After years of studying different markets and many charts, I have noticed that all markets exhibit the same natural recurring tendencies. My ideas and systems revolve around these principles. My investment objectives are simple: to make as much money as the markets will yield during a given time frame. Constantly evolving and changing, markets go through lively phases and dead, illiquid phases. While some markets are best daytraded, others are good for position trades only. Other markets are good for being short option premium and nothing else. No one trading system works all the time. Conditions must be appraised before any objective, strategy, or individual trading tactic can be employed. I have devised systems and principles to be used during different market environments, and I have used them successfully in reaping huge financial rewards.

If you are seeking someone who offers extensive experience in nearly every type of financial market, I would enjoy the opportunity to meet with you in person to discuss further details of the position you advertised. I can provide excellent personal and professional references, including from my current employer, but I would prefer that you not contact my current employer until after we meet in person to discuss your needs. Thank you in advance for your time and your consideration.

Sincerely yours,

Hugh Dudley

HUGH DUDLEY

1110½ Hay Street, Fayetteville, NC 28305 • preppub@aol.com • (910) 483-6611

OBJECTIVE	To benefit an organization that can use an experienced manager with strong consulting skills along with expert knowledge of financial products including investments, savings, and protection and credit products.
LICENSES	Have the following NASD licenses: Series 7 — General Securities Agent Series 65 — Uniform Investment Adviser Series 63 — Uniform Securities Agent Became a registered Commodities Broker as of February, 1993. Became a member, Chicago Board of Trade and the Chicago Board Options Exchange, 1988; acquired seats on and received my license to trade on both exchanges.
EDUCATION	Graduated *cum laude* with a B.A. degree in Business Administration and Accounting, Tufts University, Medford, MA, 1986; member, Alpha Chi National Honorary. • Entered college as a biology major; upon taking my first investment course, discovered my love of the investment business, and made 37 A's out of 38 courses through my senior year.
ELECTED & ACADEMIC HONORS	• Received 1986 *Wall Street Journal* award given to top Business Administration student. • Elected President, Business and Economics Club. • Was the honored recipient of the award given to the top business student. • Won scholarships from two major corporations/institutions.
EXPERIENCE	**FINANCIAL CONSULTANT.** Smith Barney, Panama City, FL (1997-present). Developed a base of clients for whom I devised financial strategies to help them achieve the long-term financial goals which I had helped them identify. • Established portfolios for clients and selected appropriate investments based on client age, desire for asset growth, need for diversification, risk profile, and other factors. • Helped several clients realize very large increases in their total asset base. • Refined my ability to assess financial needs, provide prudent advice, and close a sale. • Excelled in building relationships and cementing trust while gaining valuable sales and customer relations experience in a financial services environment. **COMMODITIES BROKER.** LaFayette Commodities, Chicago, IL (1990-97). Placed customer orders directly to trading pits and worked with customers on investment strategies; became familiar with many "do's and don'ts" of trading by observing customer trading tendencies and through my own experiences. • As a Broker, learned what type of order to use during different market environments. • Have been trading my own account from a home office since July, 1994; have full equipment setup, instant quotes, and direct access to the trading pits by phone. **OEX MARKET MAKER.** CBC Options, Chicago Board Options Exchange, Chicago, IL (1988). Trained to become a floor trader and learned how to execute trades and manage investment/portfolio risks; applied different strategies while managing an equity trading account and refined my ability to make sound investment decisions in a fast-paced environment; became regarded as an "expert" on the options market and its strategies.

Date

Exact Name of Person
Title or Position
Name of Company
Address (number and street)
Address (city, state, and zip)

General Manager, Garden and Lawn Business

This successful entrepreneur started a lawn and garden business which grossed $250,000 in its fourth year. She could stay comfortably where she is, but she finds herself in a small town missing the "action" of a larger company and a larger town. She has decided to sell her business and job-hunt in a large metropolitan area.

Dear Exact Name of Person: (or Sir or Madam if answering a blind ad.)

With the enclosed resume, I would like to acquaint you with my background and begin the process of exploring opportunities within your organization which could utilize my versatile strengths in management, marketing, and financial control.

As you will see from my resume, after graduating from Alabama University I obtained my Real Estate Broker's License and was consistently in the Top Ten in my county with sales and listings of over $5 million annually. After a sustained track record of outstanding performance, I became involved in large-scale industrial development; I initiated and directed the design of a high-tech digital global telecommunications system which required me to organize extensive collaboration and cooperation among engineers from various competing telecommunications giants. With a partner, I pioneered the concept of and then developed Alabama's first "business incubator" for start-up businesses; after we transformed the concept into a successful operating reality, I became a consultant to 25 foreign countries and a guest lecturer on entrepreneurism at Alabama University's School of Business.

Subsequently, I was recruited by a consulting firm to market and sell industrial buildings and sites for clients such as Burlington Industries, Cone Mills, Jefferson Pilot, and NationsBank. In addition to utilizing my strong negotiating and communication skills, I was involved in planning Alabama's largest commercial development, and I provided leadership in creating a state-of-the-art retirement community based on extensive input from both the public and private sectors.

Most recently I have utilized my proven visionary thinking skills and creative conceptual abilities in simultaneous jobs as a Business Manager/Property Manager and General Manager for two separate businesses. Although I am excelling in handling these responsibilities, I am eager to take on new challenges. I am single and will cheerfully relocate and travel as your needs require. With an outstanding personal and professional reputation, I offer a proven ability to take an idea and transform it into a viable operating entity.

I could make valuable contributions to your organization, and I hope you will contact me. I have a strong bottom-line orientation and outstanding references.

Sincerely,

Martha Woolcott

MARTHA WOOLCOTT

1110½ Hay Street, Fayetteville, NC 28305 • preppub@aol.com • (910) 483-6611

OBJECTIVE

To benefit an organization that can use a creative problem-solver and resourceful manager with excellent negotiating skills along with a proven ability to transform ideas into operating realities while maximizing profitability and satisfying customers.

EDUCATION

B.S. in Political Science, *magna cum laude*, Alabama University, Macon, AL, 1980. Numerous executive development courses in communication/supervision, 1980-1997.

AFFILIATIONS

Have been prominent as a leader in state, local, and business organizations:
- Appointed to a Macon County Strategic Planning Commission; was active in site selection for a major shopping center; recruited new business to the county; and am developing feasibility plans for a small industrial and business park.
- Developed Alabama's first business incubator for start-up businesses; became a leading spokesperson in the state for entrepreneurial development and also became a consultant on the federal and state level to 25 foreign countries.
- Sold 2,000 acres of land for construction of an innovative and comprehensive new retirement community after working extensively with legislators, retirement groups, and numerous public officials to sell them on the concept.

EXPERIENCE

Am excelling in management roles in two separate organizations:
1993-present: **GENERAL MANAGER.** Quality Lawn & Garden, Macon, AL. Combined my strategic planning skills with my management ability in identifying a need and a niche for this successful business; started "from scratch" a business which grossed $250,000 in its fourth year.
- Manage a diversified company which provides landscaping services to 50 new homes annually while managing a retail garden center which sells top-quality trees, flowers, and gardening supplies; also operate a related side business which rakes, bales, and markets 50,000 bales of pine straw a year.
- Hired, trained, and managed a work force of between 6-10 employees.

1991-present: **BUSINESS MANAGER/PROPERTY MANAGER.** Bryson's, Inc., Macon, AL. Represent a diversified multiplex consisting of a furniture store, grocery store, and rental properties; negotiated the multimillion-dollar sale of 200 acres of prime commercial property; developed infrastructure plans and obtained permits/inspections in spite of complicated county procedures.
- Sold prime commercial sites for a service station and an auto parts business.

VICE PRESIDENT & BROKER. XYZ Industrial Relations, Lincoln, AL (1986-91). Marketed and sold industrial buildings and sites for such clients as Burlington Industries, Cone Mills, Jefferson Pilot, and NationsBank while providing the key leadership in two major projects:
- *Project 1:* Assembled a 28,000-acre parcel of land, devised plan for infrastructure and funding and then wrote and presented a proposal to the Governor for Alabama's largest planned commercial development.
- *Project 2:* Pioneered the development of new concepts now routinely used in many retirement communities; obtained several patents on designs for handicapped bathrooms and kitchens while also inventing new concepts in financing retirement living which banks and insurance companies now accept; sold 2,000 acres of land for a new "model" retirement village after engaging public and private sector leaders in "think-tank" activities which ultimately led to their support of the project.

REAL ESTATE BROKER. Trainor Realtors, Duluth, AL (1981-86). Was consistently in the Top Ten in the county in sales and listings with over $5 million annually.

PERSONAL

Can provide outstanding personal and professional references. Single and will relocate.

Date

Exact Name of Person
Title or Position
Name of Company
Address (number and street)
Address (city, state, and zip)

**General Manager,
Firearms Business**

This entrepreneur found himself
in a job hunt because his wife
graduated from college and her
job took them to a new city. He
decided to try to represent one
of the product lines which he
used to purchase when he
owned his own business.

Dear Sir or Madam:

With the enclosed resume, I would like to introduce the proven sales skills and extensive firearms industry knowledge which I could put at the disposal of your company.

As you will see, I recently sold a gun store which I transformed from an unprofitable company saddled with debt into a very profitable business with an excellent reputation.

As a former dealer, I am very familiar with your company's products, and I have dealt personally with salesmen and sales representatives from all manufacturers and distributors. I strongly believe that my sales skills and congenial personality were the keys to my success as a dealer, and I am certain I could be a highly effective representative of your products.

I have grown up around guns since I was a child. Before my father became a Baptist minister, he owned the largest firearms business in eastern KY, and I helped him with everything in the store. I have used the products of every manufacturer.

I attend gun shows frequently and have developed an extensive network of contacts and friends within the industry who know me and my fine personal reputation. I feel certain that I could make significant contributions to your bottom line through my expert product knowledge, outstanding personal reputation, and exceptional sales abilities. I am writing to you because I am familiar with your company's fine reputation, and I feel it would be a pleasure to become associated with your product line.

If you can use a dynamic and hard-working individual to complement your sales team, please contact me to suggest a time when we might meet to discuss your needs and how I could help you. I am married with no children, and I can travel as extensively as your needs require. Thank you for your consideration, and I look forward to hearing from you.

Sincerely,

Robbie J. Goins

ROBBIE J. GOINS

1110½ Hay Street, Fayetteville, NC 28305 • preppub@aol.com • (910) 483-6611

OBJECTIVE

To contribute to an organization that can use an experienced sales professional with expert knowledge of firearms products along with a network of outstanding relationships which I have developed with firearms dealers, manufacturers, and distributors who know of my fine reputation and trust me personally.

EXPERIENCE

Since 1989-present, have been associated with Select Firearms Sports, Inc.:
GENERAL MANAGER & SALESMAN. Carolina Firearms Sports, Inc., Matthews, SD (1989-present). In 1991, bought this company after working for the company as a Salesman for two years; continued as General Manager after selling the business in 1999.

- When I purchased the company, it was unprofitable and in debt; I relocated the company to a better market and utilized effective sales and management techniques to transform an ailing organization into a highly profitable and respected company which I sold in 1999.
- Combined my expert knowledge of manufacturers and distributors with my marketing sense in determining the correct inventory for the store; carried more than 1,000 individual guns and accessories needed by shooters.
- As a dealer, have become very familiar with the products, product lines, and sales policies of all manufacturers including Smith and Wesson, Ruger, Weatherby, Colt, Browning, and Winchester.
- Worked with distributors including Outdoor Sports Headquarters, Inc., Nationwide, Bill Hicks, Go Sportsman, Bangers, and Acusport.
- On a daily basis, used my common sense in solving uncommon problems.
- Strongly believe that my sales skills and congenial personality were the keys to my success in this business.

Other experience:
- **MANAGER.** Traders Antiques, Vass, SD (1984-89). Managed all aspects of a small furniture refinishing business; personally handled sales and customer service.
- **SALESMAN.** Furniture Traders, Rowland, SD (1982-84). Upon graduation from high school, became employed by a furniture refinishing business and rapidly discovered that I have exceptional sales and customer relations skills.
- **GUN STORE ASSISTANT.** Quaker Neck Gun Exchange, Greenville, KY. As a young boy, grew up around guns since my father, who later became a Baptist minister, owned the largest firearms business in eastern KY.
- **LAW ENFORCEMENT OFFICER—Reserve.** (1988-97). As an unpaid volunteer, served as a reserve Law Enforcement Officer helping to enforce the law and keep the peace.

MEMBERSHIPS

Member, National Rifle Association; Member, Capel Baptist Church.

HOBBIES

Hunting, shooting, reloading, and collecting.

EDUCATION

Completed numerous courses in Law Enforcement, Matthews Technical Community College, Matthews, SD.

PERSONAL

Can provide outstanding references inside and outside the firearms industry. Am married with no children; will travel extensively if needed. Excel in establishing strong relationships.

Date

Exact Name of Person
Title or Position
Name of Company
Address (number and street)
Address (city, state, and ZIP)

**General Manager,
Industrial Supply Business**

After more than 18 years in his
own business, this entrepreneur
has diversified management and
sales abilities which could enhance
numerous organizations.

Dear Exact Name of Person: (or Dear Sir or Madam if answering a blind ad.)

With the enclosed resume, I would like to indicate my interest in your organization and my desire to explore employment opportunities.

As you will see from my enclosed resume, I recently sold a company which I built from a one-man operation into a thriving multimillion-dollar company serving a large base of commercial and industrial customers. I made the decision to sell the company to a large chain because it is my strong desire to utilize my background in sales and marketing for the benefit of a company such as yours.

I hope you will welcome my call soon to arrange a brief meeting at your convenience to discuss your current and future needs and how I might serve them. Thank you in advance for your time.

Sincerely yours,

Arthur Iles

Alternate last paragraph:
I hope you will call or write me soon to suggest a time convenient for us to meet and discuss your current and future needs and how I might serve them. Thank you in advance for your time.

ARTHUR ILES

1110½ Hay Street, Fayetteville, NC 28305 • preppub@aol.com • (910) 483-6611

OBJECTIVE	To benefit an organization that can use an experienced manager with proven entrepreneurial abilities along with a reputation as a dynamic individual with an ability to develop and maintain outstanding working relationships.
EDUCATION	B.S. degree in Business, University of Pennsylvania, Philadelphia, PA, 1973.
EXPERIENCE	**GENERAL MANAGER.** Iles Industrial, Inc., Malvern, PA (1979-present). Bought a company which was a one-man operation less than a year old and, after renaming it, transformed it into a highly successful industrial supply business with sales exceeding $2,500,000 and a customer base of 200 major companies; recently sold the company and am embarking on a career in sales.

- **Personnel Administration**: Hired, trained, and motivated a staff of 14 employees, and was successful in maintaining a very low personnel turnover rate.
- **Financial Management**: Developed all internal accounting and financial management systems for accounts receivable, accountable payable, and other areas.
- **Purchasing and Inventory Control**: Handled all purchasing of equipment and supplies.
- **Vendor Relations**: Established and maintained an excellent credit reputation in the process of developing and maintaining effective working relationships with suppliers of equipment and materials; worked with suppliers from across the U.S.
- **Sales and Marketing**: In addition to hiring, training, and managing many inside and outside sales professionals, personally prospected for and obtained many clients through my personal contacts, referrals, and word-of-mouth from satisfied customers; became skilled in prospecting for high-volume corporate accounts and aggressively utilized all types of marketing tools including telemarketing and direct mail.
- **Shipping and Receiving**: Established and managed superior shipping and receiving operations which we continuously improved in order to assure customer satisfaction.
- **Total Quality Management**: Became known for my dedication to customer service and customer satisfaction through my hands-on management style, and continuously monitored the company's quality performance in all areas.

SENIOR BUYER. Pennsylvania Utility Co., Malvern, PA (1974-79). Excelled in a job which required me to handle responsibilities for purchasing various products for fossil and nuclear power plants.

- Became skilled in the bidding process including all aspects of examining extensive bids and evaluating vendors.
- Handled all aspects of purchase order placement, and oversaw the progress of bids including all follow-up; became skilled in solving problems from the initial bid phase to completion.
- Developed "instincts" for anticipating and avoiding problems before they occurred.
- From 1973-74 in my first job out of college, began as a **Marketing/Customer Service Representative** and was rapidly promoted to Senior Buyer; learned how to market electric heat, became knowledgeable of new construction power hookups, and excelled in every aspect of customer service and problem solving.

PERSONAL	Can provide outstanding references. Exceptionally skilled communicator, motivator, sales professional. Would cheerfully relocate and travel extensively if needed.

Exact Name of Person
Title or Position
Name of Company
Address (no., street)
Address (city, state, zip)

**General Manager,
Service Business**

Her husband's transfer to another
city is what prompted this
entrepreneur to seek employment
with a company other than the
one she started and managed.

Dear Sir or Madam:

With the enclosed resume, I would like to initiate the process of being considered for employment within your organization. A Rhode Island native, I have recently married and relocated with my husband to Cambridge, Massachusetts, which is now our permanent new home.

In my most recent job I actually founded and managed a successful small business which provided quality services to business and residential customers. I hired, trained, and managed four people and molded them into a hard-working team which helped the business earn a name for reliability, honesty, and quality work. I believe my outgoing personality and hard-working nature as well as my ability to deal graciously and tactfully with customers were the keys to my success in that business.

My previous jobs gave me the foundation which I needed to manage and grow a successful small business. Previously I excelled in jobs as a Hospital Supply Manager and as an Office Manager. In one job with a radio station as an Account Executive, I prospected for and landed the largest account in the station's history—a $100,000 account with Alaska Railroad. I have a knack for establishing and maintaining strong business relationships.

Now that my husband and I are making our permanent home in Cambridge, I am eager to find a company that I contribute to and grow with on a long-term basis. If you meet me in person, you will see that I have excellent public relations and customer service skills along with a proven ability to use tact and diplomacy in solving difficult customer problems. I can provide outstanding personal and professional references.

If you can use a hard worker with a strong bottom-line orientation, I hope you will contact me to suggest a time when I can make myself available for a personal interview at your convenience. Thank you in advance for your time.

Sincerely,

Elaine Cercone

ELAINE CERCONE

1110½ Hay Street, Fayetteville, NC 28305 • preppub@aol.com • (910) 483-6611

OBJECTIVE	To become a valuable member of an organization that can use an outgoing and highly motivated individual who offers a proven ability to produce a profit, control costs, satisfy customers, as well as coordinate billing and accounting.
EDUCATION	Studied **Computer Technology,** 1994-95; and studied **Medical Terminology**, Jamestown Vocational Technology, 1993-94; Jamestown, RI. Completed numerous courses sponsored by Nissan related to product features, automobile financing, prospecting and selling techniques, and customer service. Refined my public speaking skills in the Dale Carnegie Course, 1998.
EXPERIENCE	**GENERAL MANAGER.** Cleaning Solutions, Jamestown, RI (1993-99). Established "from scratch" and then managed the daily operations of a business which provided janitorial services; initially developed a base of residential customers and gradually phased out all residential accounts as I developed a customer base of business and industrial accounts with which I negotiated long-term contracts.

- Hired, trained, motivated, and managed four individuals who became a hard-working team of people which helped the business earn a reputation for reliability, honesty, and quality service.
- Designed and implemented all systems for billing, accounting, and payroll administration.
- Prospected for new accounts through telemarketing and through personal sales calls; after the first year, enjoyed a strong word-of-mouth business as well as loyal, repeat customers.
- Gained valuable experience in managing the operations of a busy office and in scheduling employees for maximum productivity.
- Believe that—in addition to hard work—my outgoing personality and my ability to deal with people and solve their problems in a tactful and gracious manner were the main keys to success in this entrepreneurial venture.

Excelled in simultaneously handling the following two positions at Jamestown Hospital, Jamestown, RI:

MEDICAL ASSISTANT/COMPUTER OPERATOR. (1991-93). Assisted doctors with minor medical procedures and diagnostic examinations.

- Was commended for my ability to put patients at ease and to explain their medical procedures in a way that lessened their anxiety.

HOSPITAL SUPPLY MANAGER. (1990-93). Was the first woman ever hired for this position and excelled in managing the ordering of hospital supplies.

- Negotiated with vendors; assured vendor compliance with contract terms.
- Became respected by hospital department heads for my outstanding customer service.
- Oversaw the shipping and receiving function; coordinated with accounting.

Highlights of other experience:

- **SALES ASSOCIATE/ACCOUNT EXECUTIVE.** Was Top Sales Associate several months at a car dealership.
- **OFFICE MANAGER.** For a business equipment company, excelled as a sales representative while also managing the office and eight employees.

PERSONAL	Am skilled at dealing with people and earning their confidence. Am a member, National Association of Female Executives. Excellent references.

Date

Exact Name of Person
Exact Title
Name of Company
Address (no., street)
Address (city, state, zip)

Dear Sir or Madam:

Entrepreneurs often have established an excellent reputation within their communities, and his active community leadership is one of the distinguishing features of this individual. A prospective employer likes an employee who comes with a substantial "network" of associates, because that could be a ready-made customer referral base.

With the enclosed resume, I would like to initiate the process of being considered for employment within your organization.

When you look at my resume, you will see that I have demonstrated a proven ability to transform ideas into operating realities and to improve the profitability and productivity of existing ventures. In my current position, I have developed "from scratch" a highly profitable business which now enjoys an excellent reputation while serving customers throughout Ohio.

With an outstanding personal and professional reputation, I am known as an excellent communicator and dedicated community leader. In Dayton County, I was elected to the Board of Education and then elected by my peers to act as Vice Chairman of the Board.

I am certain I could become a valuable asset to your organization, and if you can use my considerable talents please contact me to suggest a time when we might meet to discuss your needs and goals and how I might serve them.

Thank you in advance for your time.

Yours sincerely,

Jonathan Da Silva

JONATHAN DA SILVA

1110½ Hay Street, Fayetteville, NC 28305 • preppub@aol.com • (910) 483-6611

OBJECTIVE

To benefit an organization that can use an experienced manager with a proven ability to improve profitability while providing outstanding customer service, training and motivating employees, and transforming new ideas into operating realities.

HONORS

Am an active community leader, and have served Dayton County in these ways: Vice Chairman, Board of Education, 1996-present: Was elected by my fellow board members to serve in this leadership capacity.
- Member, Board of Education, 1994-present: Elected by the people of Dayton County because of my leadership ability and commitment to quality education.
- Am a trusted public official known for outstanding communication and leadership skills.

EDUCATION & LICENSES

Received a Bachelor of Science degree as an **Honor Graduate,** Turf Grass Management Program, Ohio State University, Columbus, OH, 1979.
- Completed professional development courses related to business management, personnel supervision, financial administration, and other areas.
- Obtained Ohio Department of Agriculture Pesticide **License** after extensive technical training by the N.C.D.A. related to the identification and control of insects, diseases, and weeds in ornamentals and turf.
- Received Ohio Registered Landscape Contractor License #348, February 1989.

EXPERIENCE

GENERAL MANAGER. Finescaping, Inc., Dayton, OH (1988-present). Have utilized my extensive technical expertise as well as my general management skills in building "from scratch" a business which employs up to five people while providing quality landscaping services to residential and commercial customers.
- *Financial Management*: Developed all internal accounting and financial management systems for accounts receivable, accountable payable, and financial control.
- *Purchasing and Inventory Control:* Handled all purchasing of equipment and supplies.
- *Vendor Relations*: Established and maintained an excellent credit reputation in the process of developing and maintaining effective working relationships with suppliers of equipment and materials; worked with suppliers from across the U.S.
- *Sales and Marketing*: Obtained many clients initially through my outstanding personal and professional reputation and then through referrals and word-of-mouth from satisfied customers; aggressively prospected for new customers through telemarketing, direct mail, and personal sales.
- *Safety Management:* Emphasized superior safety practices, and continuously trained equipment operators in safety procedures.
- *Personnel Administration*: Hired, trained, and motivated all employees including foremen and supervisors.
- *Total Quality Management:* Have a hands-on management style, and continuously monitor progress to assure the company's quality performance in all areas.
- *"Do it right the first time:"* Have learned that doing a job right the first time is often the key to customer satisfaction and repeat business, and try to instill this attitude in all employees.

SUPERINTENDENT. Garden & Lawn, Dayton, OH (1982-88). Supervised employees in all phases of installing landscape and irrigation systems, and managed projects ranging from $5,000 projects to $100,000 projects.

PERSONAL

Outstanding references can be provided. Adaptable individual with versatile skills.

LEE EVANOVICH

1110½ Hay Street, Fayetteville, NC 28305 • preppub@aol.com • (910) 483-6611

OBJECTIVE

To offer my experience as a chef and management professional as well as my educational background in culinary arts to an organization that can use an individual who enjoys the challenge of creating a productive and positive environment where continual learning and personal growth are encouraged.

EDUCATION

Earned an A.A.S. degree in *Culinary Arts* from the Culinary Institute of America (CIA), Hyde Park, NY, 1993.
Completed Associate of Management degree from Mercer College, Trenton, NJ, 1990.

EXPERIENCE

HEAD CHEF and **MANAGING PARTNER.** Graceland Café Restaurant, Los Angeles, CA (1996-present). For this popular dining facility which has become one of "the" places to dine in this city with an international population, have built a prospering business from the ground up and have seen it grow to take in more than $1 million dollars annually; recently sold the business and am continuing for a brief period of transition as General Manager.
- Provided the creative spark which allowed this restaurant to develop and grow.
- Developed new menu items and oversaw all aspects of restaurant operations.
- Hired, trained, and managed the staff which now numbers about 30 employees.
- Developed the restaurant layout and actual physical design.
- Designed menus including layout and making price determinations; oversaw all stages of food preparation and daily á la carte service.
- Handled full responsibility for all bottom-line profits, expenses, and payroll processing.
- Managed the inventory control process including ordering perishable and non-perishable food items and equipment.
- Monitored all aspects of restaurant operations to ensure the highest quality of customer service and food preparation.

Accomplishments:
- During its third year, led the Graceland Café Restaurant to win these 1999 honors:
   People's Choice Award for Best Restaurant
   "Best Entrée Award" in the March of Dimes Chef's Auction

SOUS CHEF. Don Luis Italian Restaurant, New Orleans, LA (1993-96). Learned to produce quality products in a high-volume kitchen while applying my skills in food preparation at all work stations within the kitchen.
- Contributed ideas and suggestions in menu development and design.
- Assisted in inventory control by coordinating ordering for products each day in order to prepare adequately.
- Scheduled, hired, trained, counseled, and terminated employees.
- Applied my creativity and knowledge while developing recipes and testing them to ensure consistency and quality.
- Prepared soups, stocks, sauces, and specials.

STUDENT CHEF. Lani's Restaurant, Atlanta, GA (1992). As a Culinary Institute of America student, received an excellent introduction and training in the proper basic fundamentals of cooking.
- Gained exposure to the quality control environment in a professional kitchen under the classical brigade system.
- Handled preparation and production in line stations.
- Learned basic baking and pastry skills needed to build a base for the future.
- Assisted in supporting private parties and special functions which were a separate activity from á la carte service.

PERSONAL

Excellent personal and professional references on request. Will relocate worldwide.

Date

Exact Name of Person
Title or Position
Name of Company
Address (number and street)
Address (city, state, and zip)

President and General Manager

This successful automobile industry entrepreneur is seeking a new challenge after a career which has included starting up dealerships, troubleshooting problems in existing dealerships as a consultant, and managing large-scale operations.

To whom it may concern:

With the enclosed resume, I would like to make you aware of my interest in contributing to your organization through my considerable management experience as well as my proven motivational, sales, and organizational skills.

Although most of my business savvy has come from "real-world" experience, I do hold an M.S. degree in Business Administration, a Master's degree in Guidance and Counseling, and a B.S. degree. After earning my college degree, I worked for several years as a High School Teacher until economics forced me to seek a simultaneous part-time job as a Salesman for used and new cars with a prominent dealership. That part-time job opened my eyes to my talent for selling cars and motivating others, and thus began an impressive career in the automotive industry.

After attending Ford Motor Company's two-year Dealer Trainee Program, I became General Manager of a Ford dealership. I was successful in turning around that dealership which had experienced multimillion-dollar losses in three previous years, and I led it to show a profit of $500,000—its first profit in four years. Subsequently, I served as a Consultant to start-up dealerships and to mature dealerships in need of a strong manager to resolve sales and profitability problems.

As General Sales Manager of another dealership, I played a key role in increasing market penetration by 60%. I was then recruited to serve as President and General Manager of a dealership. I led the company to achieve gross sales of $32 million a year along with a $1 million profit-before-tax income for three consecutive years. We received the Outstanding Dealer's Award for three consecutive years, and were recognized as a five-star dealer—the ultimate achievement in customer service—for two years.

Most recently, I have managed a successful start-up of a used car dealership which became a major force in the market in less than two years.

I can provide excellent personal and professional references at the appropriate time, and I can assure you that I am a dynamic individual with an outstanding reputation within the industry along with an aggressive bottom-line orientation.

Sincerely,

Carson Oleksiw

CARSON OLEKSIW

1110½ Hay Street, Fayetteville, NC 28305 • preppub@aol.com • (910) 483-6611

OBJECTIVE	To benefit an organization that can use a dynamic leader who has excelled in recruiting and training personnel, developing and implementing human resources policies, as well as troubleshooting problems with creative solutions.
EDUCATION	M.S. in Business Administration, University of Tampa, Tampa, FL, 1975. Masters of Science in Guidance and Counseling, Tampa State College, Tampa, FL. B.S. Degree, Macklin University, Macklinburg, GA, 1966. Completed two-year Dealer Trainee Program, Ford Motor Company, Detroit.
EXPERIENCE	**PRESIDENT & GENERAL MANAGER.** Carson's Used Cars, Tampa, FL (1997-99). Supervised 15 individuals including six sales professionals, two finance specialists, one manager, one assistant sales manager, office personnel, and the Recon Department. • Founded a company which rapidly became a major competitor. **PRESIDENT & GENERAL MANAGER.** Beverly Hills BMW, Beverly Hills, FL (1992-97). Supervised 60 individuals who included 18 sales professionals, two finance specialists, the Used Car Manager, the New Car Manager, the Service and Parts Manager, the Service Department, the Recon Department, and the office personnel. • Led the company to achieve gross sales of $32 million a year, and achieved a $1 million profit-before-tax income for three consecutive years. • Became recognized as a Five Star Dealer. • Exceeded all goals and projections for growth, market share, and profitability; for example, doubled assigned market penetration each year for three consecutive years. • Received "Just the Best" award and the Outstanding Dealer's Award for three consecutive years. **GENERAL SALES MANAGER.** Bradenton Subaru, Brandenton, FL (1991-92). Supervised 10 sales professionals including the Used Car Manager, the New Car Manager, and the finance specialist. • For this dealership with a $6 million inventory and gross sales of $25 million per year, increased market penetration by 60%. • Was rated one of the top dealerships in FL. **INTERIM OPERATOR & CONSULTANT.** Ford Motor Company (1983-91). Was recruited to serve as Interim Operator and Consultant by Ford Motor Company and placed in charge of a large dealership until a major buy/sell was negotiated and implemented; also acted as roving consultant and problem solver for new dealerships and for dealerships in trouble. • As a consultant for one dealership in Wisconsin: In 90 days, turned around a franchise which had been losing $100,000 a month and restored it to profitability. • As a consultant for an Indiana dealership: Led a new dealership to achieve phenomenal results in profitability and sales through effective advertising, merchandising, and expense control. • Experience prior to 1983: Excelled in sales management roles with automobile dealerships in FL and WI.
PERSONAL	Excellent personal and professional references. Dynamic and results-oriented.

Date

Exact Name of Person
Title or Position
Name of Company
Address (number and street)
Address (city, state, and zip)

**Real Estate Broker
and General Manager**

This entrepreneur does not say
why he wants to leave the
company he founded which bears
his name, and prospective
employers will certainly ask him
when they meet him. If he is
managing a thriving agency in a
highly competitive market, why is
he looking for a job? Put yourself in
the employer's "shoes" when you
write your resume and cover letter
and you will realize some of the
things you need to talk about in
your cover letter.

Dear Exact Name of Person: (or Sir or Madam if answering a blind ad.)

Can you use an enthusiastic, results-oriented sales manager who offers outstanding communication skills, a talent for reading people, and a reputation for determination and persistence in reaching goals?

With a proven background of success in sales, I have displayed my versatility while selling and marketing a wide variety of products and services including residential real estate and land, new and used automobiles, and financial products/ investment services. In one job I trained and supervised a successful team of mutual fund and insurance sales agents. Most recently as a Real Estate Broker and General Manager of a real estate firm, I achieved the $3 million mark in sales for 1995 while training and developing junior associates who have become top producers. While excelling in all aspects of the business, I have used my experience to create marketing strategies which reached large audiences and generated much business.

Earlier experience gave me an opportunity to refine my sales and communication abilities as well as gain familiarity with business management including finance and collections, inventory control, personnel administration, and customer service. Prior to owning and managing a business which bought, reconditioned, and marketed automobiles, I was one of Houston Buick's most successful sales professionals, earning the distinction of "Salesman of the Month" for 13 consecutive months and "Salesman of the Year."

If you can use a seasoned professional with the ability to solve tough business problems, maximize profitability, and increase market share under highly competitive conditions, I would enjoy an opportunity to meet with you to discuss your needs and how I might serve them. I can provide outstanding references.

I hope you will welcome my call soon to arrange a brief meeting at your convenience. Thank you in advance for your time.

Sincerely,

Keith Toomey

KEITH TOOMEY

1110½ Hay Street, Fayetteville, NC 28305 • preppub@aol.com • (910) 483-6611

OBJECTIVE

To offer a track record of success in sales and managerial roles where outstanding communication skills and the ability to close the sale were key factors in building a reputation as a highly motivated professional oriented toward maximum bottom-line results.

EXPERIENCE

REAL ESTATE BROKER & GENERAL MANAGER. Toomey Real Estate, Inc., Myrtle Beach, SC (1994-present). After founding a real estate firm which bears my name, quickly reached the $3 million personal sales level; hired, trained, and now manage three junior real estate brokers who are playing a key role in boosting overall sales and profitability of a thriving agency in this highly competitive market.
- Have become known for my strong interpersonal and communication skills while coordinating with potential buyers, lending institutions, construction professionals, sellers, and others.
- Negotiate all aspects of financial transactions; deal with mortgage company representatives to arrange financing and with attorneys to handle real estate closings.
- Utilize my expert marketing abilities while creating sales strategies and preparing direct mail materials which capture the interest of prospective clients and generate new business.
- Routinely make presentations to other agents and buyers.
- Have become skilled in all aspects of property evaluation and am skilled in comparing newly available homes with those having comparable features.

SALES AND MARKETING REPRESENTATIVE. Self-employed, Myrtle Beach, SC (1988-94). Trained and then supervised the efforts of as many as 12 agents while also personally marketing and selling mutual funds and insurance; refined my abilities in a competitive field and excelled in developing sales and marketing techniques which resulted in increased sales.

Highlights of earlier experience: Gained versatile experience in sales, inventory control, and customer service in jobs including the following:
FINANCE AND OPERATIONS MANAGER: Became highly effective in handling finances, marketing, and sales as the owner of a business with six sales professionals, a title clerk, a bookkeeper, and 12 employees in the body shop (Gene's Auto Shop, Houston, TX).
- Learned small business management while handling sales, finances, and collections.
- Created marketing and advertising plans and products which were highly effective.

SALES REPRESENTATIVE: For a major automobile dealer, consistently placed in the top three of 22 sales professionals (Houston Buick, Houston, TX).
- Was "Salesman of the Month" for 13 consecutive months and "Salesman of the Year."

FIELD SALES MANAGER: Became the youngest person in the company's history to hold this position after only a year with this national company (Fuller Brush Company, Plattsburgh, NY, and Phoenix, AZ).
- Became skilled in earning the confidence of potential customers and achieved a highly successful rate of positive responses from four out of each five people I approached: increased the amount of sales per customer.

STORE MANAGER & SUPPORT SERVICE SPECIALIST: Gained business management experience and learned to handle inventory control and funds (U.S. Navy).

TRAINING

Completed corporate training programs in areas such as real estate law, brokerage, finance, and securities as well as life, accident, and health insurance.
Am licensed as a real estate salesman, broker, and life/accident/health insurance agent.

PERSONAL

Am known for my ability to see "the big picture" while managing the details.

Date

Exact Name of Person
Title or Position
Name of Company
Address (number and street)
Address (city, state, and zip)

**Retailing Entrepreneur
and General Manager**

This successful entrepreneur
sold his business and is now
seeking a management or sales
position, hopefully in retailing.

Dear Sir or Madam:

With the enclosed resume, I would like to make you aware of my background as a seasoned retail manager with exceptional communication and organizational skills. I offer proven abilities in human resources recruiting and training as well as in purchasing, loss prevention, inventory control, and customer service.

As the founder and General Manager of Heggan's of Santa Rosa, I supervised a staff of 16 associates while overseeing the operation of this busy retail outlet. Through innovative marketing and merchandising strategies as well as through emphasizing the highest levels of customer service, I was able to grow the store's annual sales to more than $2.2 million in a highly competitive market. I aggressively implemented state-of-the-art scanning and bar coding technology which resulted in numerous efficiencies and cost savings, and I automated management reporting. Because of our outstanding reputation in the market and our highly efficient operating systems, Heggan's was acquired by an Arizona-based company.

In an earlier position. I advanced from an entry-level position as a Sales Clerk to General Manager, responsible for the operation of four retail locations and a warehouse distribution center. I managed a combined staff of 20 employees at several different locations, conducting all interviews as well as hiring and training personnel.

If you can use a sales and retail professional with exceptional leadership ability and problem-solving skills, then I hope you will give me a call to suggest a time when we might meet in person. I can assure you in advance that I have much knowledge which could be beneficial to your organization, and I am seeking an opportunity to put my experience and knowledge to use in ways that will maximize profitability and efficiency.

Sincerely,

Parker Heggan

PARKER HEGGAN

1110½ Hay Street, Fayetteville, NC 28305 • preppub@aol.com • (910) 483-6611

OBJECTIVE

To benefit an organization that can use an experienced retail professional with exceptional organizational skills who offers a track record of success in operations management, staff development, and inventory control.

EXPERIENCE

GENERAL MANAGER. Heggan's Inc. of Santa Rosa, CA (1986-present). Started this company "from scratch" and grew its sales to more than $2.2 million annually; the company was then acquired by Brian Enterprises, an Arizona-headquartered company.

- Oversaw and directed all areas of this busy retail store to include managing human and fiscal resources, loss prevention, purchasing, training, inventory control, merchandising, and customer service.
- Provided leadership in implementing state-of-the-art scanning and bar code technology at the earliest opportunity; this technology greatly improved efficiency and reduced inventory loss.
- Led by example, supervising up to 16 associates; as a matter of personal and company philosophy, we aimed for the highest standards of customer service.
- Created innovative and effective marketing and merchandising strategies which resulted in doubling sales from $500,000 to more than $1 million annually.
- Interviewed and hired potential employees; evaluated all personnel.
- Trained all associates; authored detailed training manuals designed to provide step-by-step instruction in all functional areas of performance.
- Computerized all reporting procedures at the management level, including payroll, accounts payable, accounts receivable, purchasing and order tracking, etc.
- Conducted store meetings in order to motivate staff members and foster a team atmosphere while improving and maintaining customer service standards.
- Performed regular inspections of the store to ensure compliance with company policies, appearance standards, and merchandising plans.

Began with Major Supply Outlet as a Sales Clerk and advanced to positions of increasing responsibility:

1981-86: **GENERAL MANAGER.** Santa Rosa, CA. Promoted to General Manager after ably serving the company; within two years of assuming a leadership role, transformed an organization that had not shown a profit in five years into a profitable operation.

- Entrusted with total responsibility for the operation of four retail stores and a warehouse distribution center; managed as many as 20 associates at several different locations.
- Interviewed, hired, and trained all personnel; conducted employee performance appraisals and counseled employees to improve performance.
- Oversaw all aspects of purchasing and inventory control, contacted and conducted negotiations with various vendors.

PERSONAL

Excellent personal and professional references are available upon request.

Date

Exact Name of Person
Title or Position
Name of Company
Address (number and street)
Address (city, state, and zip)

Dear Exact Name of Person: (or Dear Sir or Madam if answering a blind ad.)

With the enclosed resume, I would like to indicate my interest in your organization and my desire to explore employment opportunities.

As you will see from my enclosed resume, I have most recently founded a restaurant which grew into a thriving business grossing more than $1 million annually. In addition to providing the creative spark which allowed the restaurant to thrive, I hired and trained all staff while acting as Head Chef. I have recently sold the business and am interested in joining a large organization which can make use of my considerable management ability and sales skills.

I hope you will welcome my call soon to arrange a brief meeting at your convenience to discuss your current and future needs and how I might serve them. Thank you in advance for your time.

Sincerely yours,

Lee Evanovich

Alternate last paragraph:
I hope you will call or write me soon to suggest a time convenient for us to meet and discuss your current and future needs and how I might serve them. Thank you in advance for your time.

Exact Name of Person
Title or Position
Name of Company
Address (number and street)
Address (city, state, and zip)

President and Sales Manager, Landscaping Business

Although he doesn't reveal this fact in his cover letter or resume, this entrepreneur lost his zest for his business when two of his employees got killed on the job. He is seeking a sales or management position in a large company.

Dear Exact Name of Person: (or Dear Sir or Madam if answering a blind ad.)

With the enclosed resume, I would like to introduce you to the proven leadership ability, management skills, and sales/marketing experience which I could put to work for your organization.

Through my strong sales and management skills, I built a business "from scratch" which rapidly grew into a profitable venture grossing more than $2 million last year. I am a very hard-working individual and am highly confident in my ability to sell any type of service or product to any type of individual or organization.

You will see from my resume that I offer a proven ability to prospect not only for new customers and new accounts but also for new business opportunities and new niches, markets, and segments in which to position a product and grow market share. Although I established a residential landscaping business, I rapidly perceived of new sales opportunities and became a major force in the wholesale and retail sod brokerage business. Through my ability to deal with people and establish strong personal relationships, I became a respected individual who was often called in on complex commercial projects after a low bidder or initial contractor had botched the job. I am experienced in negotiating large commercial projects.

Although I am a very successful businessman who is effective in hiring and retaining quality employees, I have decided that I wish to become involved full-time in sales and marketing, since I feel that is where my strongest abilities lie.

If you can use a dedicated person with an outstanding personal and professional reputation to enhance your growth and profitability, I hope you will give me a call to suggest a time when we might meet to discuss your needs and how I might help you. Thank you in advance for your time.

Sincerely,

William Goldman

WILLIAM GOLDMAN

1110½ Hay Street, Fayetteville, NC 28305 • preppub@aol.com • (910) 483-6611

OBJECTIVE	To contribute to an organization which can use a motivated professional with exceptionally strong sales, leadership, stress management, and customer relations skills along with proven abilities related to managing operations, boosting profitability, and solving problems.
EXPERIENCE	**PRESIDENT & SALES MANAGER.** Quality Turf, Inc., Virginia Beach, VA (1990-1999). With only a pickup truck and an aggressive sales orientation, started "from scratch" a business which grew from $54,000 in gross revenue in its first year to over $2 million last year; started out by providing residential landscaping services and then expanded and diversified into other areas as I gained knowledge, experience, and a reputation for reliability and quality.

- Once established in residential landscaping, identified an opportunity for statewide sod sales; became a broker and eventually serviced customers from Atlanta to Washington, DC while providing quality sod and grading services to prominent golf courses.
- As a large sod wholesaler and retailer, achieved an 80% market share in the Virginia Beach market; serviced most landscapers and gardeners.
- Negotiated numerous multimillion-dollar contracts for services provided to organizations such as AT&T, the City of Virginia Beach, privately owned golf courses, Target Stores, Home Depot Stores, and large construction companies.
- Expanded the company into the tree surgery business, and personally completed extensive formal training which resulted in my becoming a Certified Arborist (tree surgeon); became a member of the International Society of Arboculture.
- Acquired a million-dollar inventory of pickup trucks, dump trucks, tractors, fork lifts, front-end loaders, tree chippers, and other equipment.
- Employed up to 40 people including three crew foremen while always acting as General Sales Manager and negotiating all commercial contracts.
- Gained extensive experience in bidding on government and commercial contracts; on numerous occasions was called in on a job after a low bidder had mishandled and often abandoned the project.

COMMUNICATIONS TECHNICIAN. U.S. Army, Ft. Bragg, NC (1987-90). Received an Honorable Discharge and several medals for exceptional performance while serving my country as a Radio Technician.

FOREMAN. Bekins Moving and Storage, Phoenix, AZ (1985-87). In my first job after high school, began working for one of the world's largest moving and storage companies, and became the company's youngest-ever full-time employee and youngest-ever foreman.

- Supervised 30 individuals involved in moving office and industrial goods.

EDUCATION	Completed extensive management and technical training sponsored by the U.S. Army. Excelled in numerous executive development programs related to sales and marketing, effective communications, and operations management.
PERSONAL	Am a highly motivated hard worker who excels in communicating with others. In sales situations, have always sold my strengths rather than my competitor's weaknesses. Believe that establishing a personal relationship based on trust is the key to sales success. Have a visionary approach to business; am able to troubleshoot problems before they arise.

Date

Exact Name of Person
Exact Title
Exact Name of Company
Address
City, State, Zip

Dear Exact Name of Person (or Dear Sir or Madam if answering a blind ad):

I would appreciate an opportunity to talk with you soon about how I could contribute to your organization through my experience as a golf course superintendent with a reputation as a creative and innovative manager of resources.

As you will see from my enclosed resume, I offer a strong history as a golf course superintendent with more than 15 years of experience at several successful and heavily played courses in the Maryland and New York areas. I was highly effective in taking on the challenge of renovating and refurbishing courses which were in need of improvements. For two 150-acre courses located in residential developments and one private club, I brought about significant changes which transformed struggling facilities. While rebuilding these facilities, I applied abilities in areas which included hiring and training personnel, coordinating the renovation of capital equipment, planning for long-range success, and completing design projects for sprinkler layout, drainage, and reconstruction of greens, tees, and fairways. I also oversaw the design and installation of water reservoirs for irrigation, including a 110-acre reservoir.

My organizational and time management skills have been displayed more recently while attending college full-time, excelling academically while simultaneously creating a successful residential landscape design business. Building on my earlier A.A. degree in Agronomy and Turf Production and golf course experience, I recently earned a B.S. in Agribusiness and Environmental Resources.

Since graduation, I have relocated permanently to the Atlanta area to be near family members. If you can use an experienced golf course superintendent with a broad base of experience and well-developed abilities, I hope you will contact me to suggest a time when we might meet to discuss your needs. I can assure you in advance that I could rapidly become an asset to your organization.

Sincerely,

James Besecker

JAMES BESECKER

1110½ Hay Street, Fayetteville, NC 28305 • preppub@aol.com • (910) 483-6611

OBJECTIVE

To contribute through a versatile history of accomplishments in positions where initiative and innovative thinking along with knowledge of budgeting, capital improvements, planning, and management can combine to produce exceptional quality results and a healthy bottom line.

EDUCATION

B.S., Agribusiness and Environmental Resources with a minor in Geography, Colorado State University, Denver, CO, 1999.
- Received a prestigious award from the School of Agribusiness and Environmental Resources in recognition of my leadership and scholastic excellence.
- Was awarded a university Legislative Internship for my scholastic achievements.
- Excelled in specialized course work which included world agriculture development, crop management and production, sales and merchandising, marketing, and finance.

A.A., Agronomy and Turf Production, University of Maryland, College Park, MD, 1973.

EXPERIENCE

FOUNDER and **PRESIDENT.** Crayton Concepts, Denver, CO (1992-99). While excelling academically as a full-time college student, coordinated the complete start-up and operation of a successful landscape design business including hiring and training a staff.

FOUNDER and **PRESIDENT.** Marshall Outdoor Services, College Park, MD (1986-91). Planned and coordinated the complete start-up and operation of a service business and built a satisfied customer base which included Holiday Inn and Carnation.
- Built annual company sales to more than $250,000.
- Developed, designed, and presented project estimates to potential clients followed by negotiating, acquiring, and securing contracts.
- Hired, trained, and supervised a 10-person staff; procured $75,000 in capital equipment.

CLASS "A" GOLF SUPERINTENDENT. Diamond Golf & Country Club, College Park, MD (1984-86). Transformed and refurbished this 150-acre golf course and residential property into one of the state's top golf facilities.
- Coordinated project management in turf, shrub, and tree production.
- Managed turf development through fertilizer, herbicide, pesticide, and fungicide applications including completing chemical calculations.

HEAD GOLF COURSE SUPERINTENDENT. Ivy League Golf Course, Forest Hills, NY (1978-84). Was credited with successfully refurbishing a 150-acre golf course and 1,300-acre residential development and turning it into a well-managed and highly played facility.
- Coordinated project design techniques in sprinkler layout, drainage, and reconstruction of greens, tees, and fairways; developed a 110-acre water reservoir for irrigation.
- Hired and trained staff members; coordinated and renovated all capital equipment.

HEAD GOLF COURSE SUPERINTENDENT. Prestige Golf & Country Club, Forest Hills, NY (1974-78). Brought about the successful renovation of a 150-acre private club through landscape design and the installation of trees and shrubbery.

PERSONAL

Offer knowledge in turf, and chemical, and biological management for all seasons/climates. Can provide excellent personal and professional references.

Senior managers and executives share unique advantages and disadvantages in a job hunt. Yet they face many of the common issues all managers face when they go out into the job market.

Problems faced by the senior manager and executive in a job hunt

Ask senior managers and executives what they believe to be their biggest problem in their job hunt and they will tell you this: They are afraid companies will discriminate against them because of their age, and they believe companies will hire the less expensive junior manager over the senior manager in many situations. Their fears are often based on reality.

Not emphasizing age on the senior manager's resume

Although it is never appropriate to misrepresent anything on a resume, it is often to the advantage of the senior manager to decrease the emphasis on his or her age. Generally it is recommended that a resume show the last 10 or 15 years of experience, and experience prior to that, if shown, can be highlighted in an "Other Experience" section without dates. When you look at the resumes in this section, you will see low-key techniques used to de-emphasize the age of many of these senior managers and executives. Since experience is often more important than education in terms of what the senior manager is offering, the Education section is usually near the bottom of the senior manager's resume, and sometimes the year dates showing when degrees were earned are omitted. The senior manager is not trying to disguise his age; he or she is simply trying to de-emphasize it and avoid being screened out because of seniority.

Seniority and experience can be a positive thing!

Experience, as they say, is the best teacher, and experience can be a valuable asset to any organization. Companies are not ignorant of that fact, and they know that experience usually comes with age, so the important facts to show on a resume are one's results, accomplishments, and achievements. Indeed, many companies actually seek the mature and seasoned employee. For example, a number of financial services firms say they look for individuals with "a little grey in their hair," because age and maturity seem to connote wisdom in that industry.

Senior managers can be in career change, too!

Several of the senior managers in this section are in the career-change mode. As we mentioned previously in this book, most of us working people are expected to have at least three different careers in our lifetimes. You will be seeing people in this section who are embarking on their third career!

Date

Exact Name of Person
Exact Title of Person
Exact Name of Organization
Address
City, State zip

Airport Manager

Although this professional enjoyed the fast pace of airport management, he is now looking for excitement in the sales and marketing area. Even though he is an experienced manager, he is in this particular job hunt selling his "potential" to do something he's never done before.

Dear Exact Name (or Dear Sir or Madam if answering a blind ad):

With the enclosed resume, I would like to make you aware of my interest in utilizing my outstanding sales, marketing, communication, and management skills for the benefit of your organization.

Although I most recently have been working in the aviation industry and am excelling in my current position, I have decided to embark on a radical career change. I have a strong desire to work in a professional position in which I can combine my extroverted personality and "natural" sales ability with my customer relations and problem-solving ability.

My recent experience in airport management, air traffic control, and in piloting advanced attack aircraft may not appear relevant to your needs, but my stable work history also includes several jobs which, I believe, illustrate my versatility. In one job I excelled as a Juvenile Counselor and thoroughly enjoyed the experience of providing a strong role model for troubled youth who had essentially been kicked out of their homes and labeled as "uncontrollable." In another job in California, I was part of the movie-making industry as I worked as a double for Mel Gibson. I also worked previously as a professional model. A wine expert and gourmet cook, I grew up in an Italian family which was in the restaurant business so I learned customer service at a young age!

In my current job involved in managing people and key areas related to airport management at one of the military's busiest airlift centers, I am continually using my problem-solving and decision-making skills. I am confident that my management ability, resourcefulness, and ability to relate effectively to others are qualities which could transfer to any field. In one of my jobs in the aviation industry, I managed a $3.5 million budget with outstanding results, and I offer a strong bottom-line orientation.

If you can use a highly motivated self-starter known for unlimited personal initiative and a creative problem-solving style, I hope you will contact me to suggest a time when we might meet to discuss your needs. I am single and would relocate and travel extensively as your needs require, and I can provide outstanding references at the appropriate time. Thank you in advance for your consideration.

Yours sincerely,

James Brown

JAMES BROWN

1110½ Hay Street, Fayetteville, NC 28305 • preppub@aol.com • (910) 483-6611

OBJECTIVE

To benefit an organization that can use an outgoing professional with excellent sales and marketing skills who has excelled in executive positions through applying my strong problem-solving, decision-making, communication, and management skills.

EDUCATION

Earned **A.A.S. degree in Logistics Management**, Community College of the Air Force, 1989; and an **A.A.S. degree in Liberal Arts**, Texas Central University, 1988.
Completed Pilot training; graduated **with honors,** top 10% of my class, 1991.
Excelled in executive development programs for military officers.

EXPERIENCE

AIRPORT MANAGER. Department of Defense, Neilson AFB, CA (1992-present). At one of the Air Force's busiest airlift hubs, am making significant contributions to efficiency and safety through my managerial abilities and interpersonal skills.
- Reduced personnel costs by 35% while resolving critical staffing issues.
- Supervise airport management personnel; through my background as a pilot, have strengthened the knowledge of airfield management staff and increased their understanding of aircrew concerns; through my staff development expertise, morale is at an all-time high.
- Coordinate responses to flight emergencies, ground accidents, and contingency operations; am known for my ability to remain calm in a crisis.
- Simultaneously from 1991-present, have served in the Reserves as an **Attack Flight Pilot** and **Utility Pilot**, flying some of the world's most advanced aircraft.

RESOURCE MANAGER. Department of Defense, Los Alamitos, CA (1990-92). Managed a $3.5 million budget while coordinating the utilization of human and aviation assets for specific flights on flight schedules.
- Learned to make decisions among competing priorities as I managed a multimillion-dollar budget divided into six sections and then subdivided into 34 sub areas in each section.
- Performed liaison with numerous state and federal agencies including the California Drug Team Task Force.
- Became skilled in managing multiple priorities in changing circumstances.

JUVENILE COUNSELOR. Concord Training School, Concord, SC (1989-90). At a school for troubled youth whose families could not control or provide for them, worked with teenagers and helped them develop realistic long-range and short-term goals for their lives.
- Thoroughly enjoyed providing a positive role model for children, and according to statistics, was more successful than most counselors in this job: my success rate for repeat offenders was 50%, which was better than my fellow counselors.

QUALITY CONTROL INSPECTOR. U.S. Air Force, Pope AFB, NC (1983-89). Performed in-flight, pre-flight, and post-flight checks in a role similar to that of an Inspector; acted as the technical expert during ground and in-flight emergencies.
- Supervised loading of passengers and cargo; accountable for the safety of all.

Other experience and skills:
- **Movie acting**: For one year, worked as a double for Mel Gibson.
- **Modeling:** Was a professional model.
- **Gourmet cooking:** Learned to cook growing up in an Italian family in the restaurant business; have expert knowledge related to fine wines and gourmet cooking.

PERSONAL

Am known for my ability to relate easily to others and to establish trust. Single. Would relocate and/or travel extensively according to my employer's needs.

Date

Exact Name of Person
Exact Title of Person
Exact Name of Organization
Address
City, State zip

Dear Exact Name (or Dear Sir or Madam if answering a blind ad):

I would appreciate an opportunity to talk with you soon about how I could contribute to your organization through my extensive management experience in most functional areas of accounting, human resources, operations, and banking.

As you will see from my resume, I have enjoyed a track record of promotion with National Consumer Bank, one of the leading financial institutions in the South. I have often worn multiple "hats" and am known for my ability to oversee complex responsibilities in numerous areas simultaneously. For example, in my current position as a vice president, I oversee the Operations and Compliance areas for the bank, and I actually developed the bank's Deposit Compliance Program.

If you feel your management team could benefit from my in-depth experience, creative problem-solving style, and reputation as a strategist and visionary, I would be delighted to make myself available at your convenience to discuss your needs and goals and how I might help you achieve them. I do wish to point out that I will be relocating to the Houston area in order to be closer to my family who all live in or near Houston.

I hope you will welcome my call soon to arrange a brief meeting to discuss your current and future needs and how I might serve them. Thank you in advance for your time.

Sincerely,

Anne Wade

ANNE WADE

Present: 1110 Hay Street, Fayetteville, NC 28305
Permanent: 1605 California Street, Houston, TX 78345

(910) 483-6611
(823) 522-3400

OBJECTIVE

To contribute to an organization that can use an innovative manager who believes that "the sky is the limit" when persistence, creativity, and attention to detail are combined with superior planning, time management, communication, and problem-solving skills.

EXPERIENCE

For more than 14 years, have built a "track record" of accomplishment in positions of increasing responsibility at National Consumer Bank, Virginia Beach, VA;
VICE PRESIDENT, OPERATIONS & COMPLIANCE (1995-present). Was promoted to handle additional responsibilities related to consumer compliance while continuing to handle responsibilities described in the Assistant Vice President job below.

- Developed Deposit Compliance Program for consumer law and regulation.
- Personally conduct compliance testing (audits) and the training program; have trained approximately 40 employees in this specific area.
- Have become very experienced in internal auditing for compliance.

ASSISTANT VICE PRESIDENT OF OPERATIONS & HUMAN RESOURCES. (1991-95). In this highly visible, fast-paced position reporting to the bank president, wore "three hats," balancing multiple responsibilities in human resources, operations, and investments.

- *Management:* Directly supervised five people, ensuring that assigned responsibilities were executed in a systematic and effective manner.
- *Operations:* In coordination with top management, developed/implemented plans and policies that affected accounting, bookkeeping, and data processing of main office and two branches.
- *Human Resources:* Applied my expert knowledge to develop, maintain, and administer all personnel policies as they applied to 40 bank employees; oversaw EEO compliance, recruitment, safety & health.
- *Benefits Administration*: Oversaw all salary and benefit functions, including 401(k) pension plan and Blue Cross/Blue Shield health plan.
- *Finances*: Managed an investment portfolio utilizing excess funds per day while efficiently planning and administering the department's budget.
- *Training:* Coordinated in-house programs on personnel policies; organized training on compliance with demand deposit, direct deposit, bank privacy, and other regulations.

OPERATIONS OFFICER. (1986-1991). Excelled in directing all aspects of the Operations Department because of my versatile management skills; supervised five employees.

- Reviewed surveys of community banks and made recommendations on competitively pricing various banking products.
- As a member, Strategic Planning Committee, offered input on personnel and operations.
- Managed all day-to-day bookkeeping functions and monitored the bank's cash position, making investments or borrowing funds as appropriate.

HEAD BOOKKEEPER. (1985-1986). Ensured the highest standards of customer service while supervising and reviewing the work of five assistants; balanced general ledger accounts; processed overdrafts, returns items, and ACH debits and credits.

EDUCATION

B.S., Accounting, Virginia State University, Virginia Beach, VA, 1999.
Excelled in courses in Accounting, Introduction to Computers, Banking & Finance, Business Communication, Supervision, and Principles of Management.
Attended seminars on sexual harassment, interviewing & hiring, state and federal wages, personnel policies (developing/implementing), public speaking, and check processing.

PERSONAL

Self-motivated, dedicated professional with a reputation as a team leader.

Date

Exact Name of Person
Title or Position
Name of Company
Address (number and street)
Address (city, state, and zip)

Dear Exact Name of Person: (or Sir or Madam if answering a blind ad.)

With the enclosed resume, I would like to formally make you aware of my interest in exploring employment opportunities within your organization.

As you will see from my resume, I have excelled in a variety of assignments which required outstanding accounting, customer service, and management skills. In my current position as Controller, I prepare monthly financial statements and year-end financials while also supervising ten people in the accounting department including an assistant controller as well as the MIS and accounts payable/receivable personnel. I wrote this 30-year-old company's first policies and procedures manual. While in control of $5 million in inventory, I developed procedures which led the company to process inventory by barcode at its nine locations.

In my prior job, I rose to Chief Financial Officer for a diversified corporation with holdings in the construction industry and restaurant business. For one of the company's divisions, I was personally responsible for leading the limited partnership's reorganization out of Chapter 11 bankruptcy and, after leading the company out of bankruptcy, the company posted a 7% net profit within the first year.

I am knowledgeable of software including Depreciation Solution, Computer Systems Dynamics (CSD) programs, and Microsoft Office 97. I have demonstrated my capabilities in operational areas including contract development and negotiation, debt structure reorganization, and information systems/data processing administration.

If you can use a hard-working professional with knowledge in numerous operational areas, I hope you will contact me to suggest a time when we might meet to discuss your needs and how I might serve them. I can provide outstanding personal and professional references. Thank you in advance for your time, and I would appreciate your holding my interest in your company in the strictest confidence at this point.

Yours sincerely,

Michelle Bazaldua

MICHELLE BAZALDUA

1110½ Hay Street, Fayetteville, NC 28305 • preppub@aol.com • (910) 483-6611

OBJECTIVE	To contribute to an organization that can use a skilled accounting professional with experience related to financial analysis and financial statement preparation, auditing, cash management, AR/AP, general ledger, payroll, collections, and automated systems.
EXPERIENCE	**CONTROLLER.** Quality Building Supply, Springfield, VA (1993-present). Prepare monthly financial statements and year-end financials while supervising ten people in the accounting department including an assistant controller, AP and AR personnel, and the MIS Director.

- For this 30-year-old company, wrote its first policies and procedures manual.
- Implemented new computer systems for automated payroll with swipe cards.
- Am in control of over $5 million in inventory; developed procedures in processing inventory by barcode for the company's nine locations.
- Implemented new software called CSD, a program for the building supply industry.

For The Jason G. Roth Company, was promoted from Controller to Chief Financial Officer, and worked in two main divisions of the company (1985-93):

1991-93: CHIEF FINANCIAL OFFICER & GENERAL MANAGER. Stone Mountain, GA.

- For a chain of three premier restaurants, was personally responsible for leading the limited partnership's reorganization out of Chapter 11 bankruptcy; personally renegotiated the company debt structure and reduced food, labor, and liquor costs by as much as 12% within six months.
- After leading the company out of bankruptcy, achieved a 7% net profit within the first year.
- Supervised all business operations at three establishments which employed more than 150 employees while producing annual sales of $4.6 million.
- Was the hands-on manager in charge of daily operations, marketing and promotions, purchasing, inventory control, and alcohol management.
- Was in charge of transition planning as the businesses were readied for sale to a new management team; directed the liquidation of assets not included in the sale.

1985-1991: CONTROLLER and PROPERTY & PROJECT MANAGER. Lester Springs, GA. For the Real Estate Development Division, oversaw on-site and off-site construction of new buildings and tenant improvements in addition to performing all financial and property management functions for 32 industrial properties valued at $128 million.

- Collaborated with the owner and architects during the preliminary planning stages of each project; took bids, awarded contracts, and provided oversight of the construction phase through completion.
- Marketed properties, negotiated leases, and handled all property management duties.
- Was in charge of all accounting for this entire real estate portfolio; in addition to managing investment instruments, negotiated secured/unsecured loans up to $41 million.
- Oversaw cash management, mortgage management, and auditing.
- Served as liaison to company attorneys and accountants.
- Supervised projects valued at $61 million, saving $1.2 million as general contractor.
- Generated more than $7 million in net profits through the careful management of company-owned stocks, bonds, and mutual funds.

ACCOUNT CLERK II. County of Siddell, In-Home Supportive Services, Siddell, GA (1982-85). Prepared regular financial reports for the State of Georgia while also reviewing, auditing, and approving grants valued at $10.8 million on a bimonthly basis.

- Initiated and implemented the county's first computerized Medi-Cal care issuance system.

EDUCATION	Associate of Arts Degree in Accounting, Hazelton Junior College, GA.
PERSONAL	Knowledgeable of software including Depreciation Solution, CSD, and Microsoft Office 97.

Date

Exact Name of Person
Exact Title
Exact Name of Company
Address
City, State, Zip

**Controller,
Trucking Industry**

His employer of more than 26
years has restructured and, to keep
his job with the company, he must
move to Richmond. He has decided
to resign from the company and
seek employment elsewhere.

Dear Exact Name of Person (or Dear Sir or Madam if answering a blind ad):

With the enclosed resume, I would like to make you aware of my considerable experience in the area of accounting, finance, budgeting, and controlling.

As you will see from my resume, I have a rather unusual work history, since I have worked for only one company. I began with Quality Truck Rental, Inc. in 1974 and was promoted through the ranks until in 1980 I became a District Controller for one of Quality's 70 districts. For a district with a fleet of 800 vehicles, I received extensive recognition for exemplary performance in accounts receivable management as well as prudent accounting management in all areas.

Since 1998, Quality has been engaged in a process of eliminating administrative services performed at the district level and moving them to Richmond. I have played a key role in helping customers and staff adapt to the new concept. Although I have been strongly encouraged to be part of the restructured organization, I do not wish to move to Richmond. I can provide outstanding references at the appropriate time.

If you can use a professional with extensive experience in managing people while managing the bottom line for maximum profitability, I hope you will contact me to suggest a time when we might meet to discuss your needs. I am confident that I could become a valuable addition to your management team.

Yours sincerely,

Owens Kober

OWENS KOBER

1110½ Hay Street, Fayetteville, NC 28305 • preppub@aol.com • (910) 483-6611

OBJECTIVE	To benefit an organization that can use an experienced manager who offers a background in accounting, finance, budgeting, and forecasting along with a proven ability to adapt to change while implementing new systems to enhance growth and profitability.
COMPUTERS	Highly proficient in utilizing computer software for financial analysis and word processing; extensive experience with software programs including Microsoft Excel, Microsoft Word, and Lotus 1-2-3.
EDUCATION	**Associate in Applied Science in Business Administration,** Sidona Technical Institute, Sidona, AZ 1974; named as class **Honor Student.**. • Excelled in professional training programs sponsored by Quality Truck Rental, Inc. related to cost accounting, financial analysis, forecasting, and budget preparation.
EXPERIENCE	**Excelled in handling a variety of special projects and multiple responsibilities while working for Quality Truck Rental, (Quality Transportation Services), locations in AZ, 1974-2000:** • Quality has restructured nationally, moving central support activities from its 70 districts to Richmond; I have played a key role in helping the company restructure and, although I have spent 26 enjoyable years with the company, I have decided not to relocate to Richmond. • Can provide outstanding references from individuals at all company levels. **REGIONAL CONTROLLER.** Tempe, AZ (1998-present). Assisted the General Manager with matters pertaining to financial analysis of the business while answering customer questions, resolving billing problems, and supporting the sales staff in obtaining answers and resolving problems related to the "migration" of administrative functions from the Tempe District to the Richmond Shared Services Center. • Demonstrated my loyalty to Quality by helping both customers and sales staff accept and develop enthusiasm for the new concept of the Shared Services Center in Richmond; was instrumental in training and developing a new General Manager. **DISTRICT CONTROLLER.** Tempe, AZ (1980-98). Excelled as District Controller of one of Quality's 70 districts, and managed up to seven Accounting Clerks in activities including accounts receivable and payable, repair expense accounting, vehicle cost records, vehicle licensing and permitting, and computer system administration. • Ensured proper control of company assets in this $25 million district; oversaw $20 million in annual revenues while supporting the District Manager and General Managers with forecasting, budgeting, financial analyses of operations, general ledger maintenance, as well as monthly profit and loss statements. • Prepared the district's annual financial plan, and am proud of our track record in nearly always exceeding profitability and revenue goals. • Led the district to achieve outstanding results in internal audits conducted every 12-24 months by Quality officials. • Received recognition for exemplary performance in accounts receivable management; was recognized for my initiative in implementing accounting controls. • Provided the leadership in implementing PCs in the district, and served unofficially in the role of System Administrator. • For a fleet of 800 vehicles, provided oversight of licensing for interstate operations. • Analyzed financial statements including balance sheets and income statements. *Other Quality experience:* **OFFICE MANAGER.** Milestown, AZ (1977-80).
PERSONAL	Excellent reputation and can provide outstanding personal and professional references.

Date

Exact Name of Person
Title or Position
Name of Company
Address (number and street)
Address (city, state, and zip)

**Credit Card Company
Executive**

Senior managers and
executives often face the
problem of deciding which of
their many accomplishments to
show on a one-page resume.
Nice problem to have!

Dear Exact Name of Person: (or Dear Sir or Madam if answering a blind ad.)

With the enclosed resume, I would like to indicate my interest in your organization and my desire to explore employment opportunities.

As you will see from my enclosed resume, in my current job as Vice President of Customer Service and Sales, I have supervised an 800-person workforce and improved customer satisfaction from 79% to 95%. Although I am held in high regard by my current employer, my wife and I have decided to relocate to the east coast to be closer to our aging parents.

If you can use an experienced credit card manager with extensive quality assurance knowledge, I hope you will welcome my call soon to arrange a brief meeting at your convenience to discuss your current and future needs and how I might serve them. Thank you in advance for your time.

Sincerely yours.

Denford Hanby

Alternate last paragraph:
I hope you will call or write me soon to suggest a time convenient for us to meet and discuss your current and future needs and how I might serve them. Thank you in advance for your time.

DENFORD HANBY

1110½ Hay Street, Fayetteville, NC 28305 • preppub@aol.com • (910) 483-6611

OBJECTIVE   To add value to an organization that can use an energetic and innovative executive who offers a dynamic communication style, superior motivational skills, as well as problem-solving and decision-making abilities refined as a corporate executive.

EDUCATION   Completed **Graduate Management Training Program**, MasterCard, 1991.
M.B.A., San Diego State University, CA, 1990; Led a team of MBAs to earn honors in a state competition solving profitability problems of real companies.
B.S. in Business Administration, Georgia State University, SC, 1983.
- Received a full athletic scholarship; was captain of the track team.

EXPERIENCE   **VICE PRESIDENT, CUSTOMER SERVICE & SALES**. MasterCard, San Diego, CA (1997-present). Lead and develop strategies for one of three major customer service and sales centers located in the United States; responsible for serving over 20 million cardmembers with exclusive relationship management responsibilities for customers that hold co-branded MasterCard cards like the Travelers Group product while controlling a $36 million annual operating budget.
- Supervise 800-person workforce; improved customer satisfaction from 79% to 95%.
- Achieved best annual employee satisfaction scores in the company's history to date.
- Improved revenue attainment by 6% in customer service "concept test."

REGIONAL SALES DIRECTOR. Sprint, Huntington Beach, CA (1994-97). After excelling as Regional Sales Director in Huntington Beach from 1994-96, was handpicked to manage the consolidation of two offices with a total of more than 300 employees which involved managing sensitive customer relations for Sprint residential customers while controlling a $35 million annual budget.
- Supervised 1,100 employees operating out of two remote customer contact centers.
- Improved revenue attainment 15% and customer satisfaction 10% while meeting a $190 million revenue objective.
- Provided the leadership which allowed the region to achieve first-place honors in tough competition with the seven other regions throughout the country.
- At Huntington Beach, improved revenue attainment 20%, customer satisfaction 5%, and productivity 30% while managing customer service and sales relationships with more than 200,000 small business customers; supervised 200 employees located in a remote business sales center operating on a $9 million budget while working as a key member of a team to achieve a $40 million corporate revenue objective; cut expenses by $300,000.

Previous MasterCard experience: Was promoted in this track record:
1990-94: **RE-ENGINEERING DIRECTOR**. Managed re-engineering project portfolio worth $3 million in savings; redesigned work flows and eliminated activities that did not add value to the process of delivering excellent customer service.
- Aggressively managed re-engineering projects, reaping over $2 million in savings; consulted with retailers on streamlining credit card operations to improve customer service.
- Developed innovative concept for resolving customer inquiries that saved $500,000.

1984-90: **CUSTOMER SERVICE DIRECTOR**. Began as a Customer Service Manager managing 85 employees, settling cardholder-retailer disputes, and controlling a $2 million budget; then was promoted to manage customer relationships with over 400,000 retail merchants nationwide to develop strategies for improving service levels and re-engineering workflows.
- Re-engineered workflows; reduced by 50% the correspondence time for selected retailers.

Date

Exact Name of Person
Title or Position
Name of Company
Address (number and street)
Address (city, state, and zip)

Day Care Center Manager

A prominent corporation advertised for a Director of Child Care Services, and this experienced day care professional is curious about what the company has in mind. In order to satisfy her curiosity, she must "get in the door" for an interview, and that requires a great resume and cover letter.

Dear Sir or Madam:

I am writing to express my interest in the job you recently advertised for a Director of Child Care Services.

As you will see from my resume, I am a proven performer in the child care services field. Since 1985, I have enjoyed a track record of increasing advancement with Quality Day Care Centers, which operates more than 2,000 facilities nationwide. In my current position as a center director which I have held since 1986, I have reduced staff turnover, increased profits, and led our 200-child center to win numerous awards for excellence. In the evenings during 1994 and 1995, I was a college instructor and taught classes for up to 25 day care providers. As company needs have required, I have filled in as an Interim District Manager and I frequently travel in my current job to train new center directors throughout the South. The center which I manage is considered a model of what a quality day care center should be.

In addition to the college teaching I have described, my educational background includes the Child Development Associate (CDA) Certificate, which is the equivalent of an associate's degree. I have also completed more than two years of other college-level coursework including one year of coursework in Elementary Education University as well as numerous professional workshops and seminars.

I feel certain you would find me in person to be a congenial individual who relates well to staff, employees, parents, regulators, and children. I have a genuine love for the day care field and am proud of the contributions I have made to the early childhood years of thousands of children.

I hope you will write or call me soon to suggest a time when we might meet to discuss your current and future needs and how I might serve them. Thank you in advance for your time.

Yours sincerely,

Clarice Stoeckley

CLARICE STOECKLEY

1110½ Hay Street, Fayetteville, NC 28305 • preppub@aol.com • (910) 483-6611

OBJECTIVE

To offer my creativity, enthusiasm, and love for the field of child care and development combined with my experience in managing day care facilities and training day care providers.

CERTIFICATE

Received Child Development Associate (CDA) Certificate; this is the equivalent of an Associate's degree in Child Care Services.

EXPERIENCE

Have excelled in positions of increasing responsibility with Quality Day Care Centers, various locations.

DIRECTOR. Charlotte, NC (1986-present). For this nationwide chain with 2,000 centers all over the U.S., have increased profits and enrollment since taking over center; in addition to managing total operations of the center and providing quality day care for up to 200 children, travel frequently in order to train new center directors throughout the state.

- Received the annual **"Manager's Excellence Award"** every year since 1986.
- Have further enhanced my problem-solving, motivational and management abilities which is evidenced by a low turnover in staff.
- Manage total center operation, providing care/education for up to 200 children.
- Hire, train, manage, and evaluate up to 20 staff members and ensure their continued training and development.
- Ensure that facility and daily activities meet or exceed state and local regulations.
- Plan and prepare for annual re-licensing evaluation.
- Collect and process $10,000 weekly while handling accounts payable and receivable, payroll and other supplies; oversee maintenance activities.
- As a **COLLEGE INSTRUCTOR** with Charlotte Technical Community College in the evenings from 1994-95, taught courses including "Day Care Discipline" and "Directing a Day Care Center" to classes of up to 25 day care professionals.

INTERIM DISTRICT MANAGER. NC and SC (1986-present). On an as-needed basis, frequently handle short-term assignments related to setting up new centers and troubleshooting problems in existing ones; interview, select, and monitor new center directors; have assisted District Manager in training new staff and center directors in Charleston, Greenville, Fayetteville, Charlotte, Wilmington, Raleigh, and Greensboro.

- Set up marketing fairs throughout NC and SC; monitored Child Care Assistants and acted as a Management Consultant for centers throughout those two states.

DIRECTOR. Lumberton, NC (1985). Center showed an increase in enrollment in only six months; responsibilities similar to current duties.

Other experience:
- **TEACHER'S AIDE**. The Sinclair Elementary School, Charlotte, NC (1982-84). Assisted a Third Grade Teacher in all areas of classroom instruction. Successfully organized a Teacher's Assistant Association for the City School System.
- **PRE-SCHOOL AIDE**. American Creative School, Charlotte, NC (1980-82). Taught a class of four-year-olds.

EDUCATION

Completed Elementary Education coursework, Charlotte University, Charlotte, NC (1978-80).

AFFILIATIONS & CERTIFICATION

Member, North Carolina Day Care Association, Charlotte Jaycees
Certified in CPR and First Aid.

Date

Exact Name of Person
Exact Title
Exact Name of Company
Address
City, State, Zip

**Director of Operations,
Restaurant Industry**

If a previous employer recruited
you, go ahead and say so.
Employers are trying to find the
employees that other
companies want to hire, too.

Dear Exact Name of Person (or Dear Sir or Madam if answering a blind ad):

With the enclosed resume, I would like to make you aware of an experienced food service professional with exceptional motivational, communication, and organizational skills as well as a background as a restaurant General Manager and Director of Operations who has demonstrated the ability to produce extraordinary "bottom-line" results.

With Bennigan's, I was aggressively recruited and hired to design, coordinate the construction of and manage the kitchen for the opening of this location. My management skills were quickly recognized, and I was promoted to Director of Operations, with accountability for all aspects of the operation of a busy restaurant with annual sales of $1.5 million. I train and supervise the Kitchen Manager, Bar Manager, and Front End manager as well as the kitchen, wait and bar staff, totaling 65 employees. I prepare and manage the monthly operations budget, evaluating all expenses to maximize profits and ensure budget compliance.

In a previous position, I coordinated the construction and development of a family restaurant, and a few years later was actively sought out by the owners to "turn around" the operation, taking over at a time when it was on the verge of bankruptcy. Using the same innovative, cost-cutting inventory control procedures I had implemented when I first worked for the company, I quickly transformed the restaurant into a popular and profitable organization with a $200,000 increase in sales.

If you can use an experienced General Manager and Director of Operations whose supervisory and leadership skills have been tested in a variety of restaurant environments, I would enjoy hearing from you. I can assure you in advance that I have an excellent reputation and would quickly become a valuable asset to your company.

Sincerely,

David North Omori

DAVID NORTH OMORI

1110½ Hay Street, Fayetteville, NC 28305 • preppub@aol.com • (910) 483-6611

OBJECTIVE   To benefit an organization that can use an experienced food service professional who can produce extraordinary "bottom-line" results through applying sales and management skills gained in a variety of restaurant General Manager and Operations Manager positions.

EXPERIENCE   **DIRECTOR OF OPERATIONS.** Bennigan's, Sierra Vista, AZ (1992-present). Aggressively recruited to design and manage the kitchen for this newly-opened restaurant; quickly advanced to Director of Operations, responsible for all aspects of the operation of this busy local eatery with annual sales of $1.5 million.
- Train and direct the activities of three managers, including the Bar Manager, Kitchen Manager, and Front End Manager.
- Supervise the bar, kitchen, and wait staff, totaling more than 60 employees.
- Prepare and manage monthly operations budget, evaluating all expenses to ensure budget compliance and maximize profits.
- Oversee the creation and development of innovative marketing plans and promotions to increase catering and banquet sales.
- As Kitchen Manager, directed the construction, maintenance, and purchasing of all equipment for the initial set-up of the cooking stations and preparation areas.

OWNER-OPERATOR. Omori's Restaurant & Tavern, Sierra Vista, AZ (1991-1992). Opened, managed, and oversaw the operation of a busy local restaurant and tavern.

GENERAL MANAGER. Faison's Surf & Turf, Sierra Vista, AZ (1989-1991). Actively recruited by my former employer, I took over at a time when this restaurant was on the brink of bankruptcy. Quickly transformed it into a popular and profitable organization with a $200,000 increase in sales; supervised a staff of 25 employees.
- Applied my exceptional motivational skills and my expert purchasing and cost-control know-how to produce dramatic results, quickly "turning around" this ailing operation.
- Trained and motivated employees who became known for exceptional customer service.

MANAGER. Huggmugger's, locations in AZ and CO (1988-1989). Excelled in a variety of management roles in this large restaurant chain.
- *Kitchen Manager:* Prepared and managed a budget of $200,000; by increasing efficiency and controlling waste, made this restaurant one of the most profitable in 11 states.
- *Service Manager:* Trained and motivated 70 bar and wait staff personnel; carefully budgeted labor hours; controlled liquor costs.
- *Manager Trainee:* Played a key role in this location being named #1 of 41 restaurants for two consecutive months.

GENERAL MANAGER. Faison's Surf & Turf, Sierra Vista, AZ (1986-1988). After coordinating the construction and development of this family restaurant and creating its menu, excelled in making it one of the area's most popular.
- Decreased food and labor costs with no loss of quality in food or service.
- Implemented innovative, cost-cutting inventory control procedures.

EDUCATION   Attended the University of Arizona at Sierra Vista.
Completed the National Restaurant Association Seminar on Catering.

Date

Mr. James Brown
Regional Sales Manager
Excalibur Company
190 Decatur Road
Houston, TX 90235

District Sales Manager,
Consumer Products

This consumer products
professional is exploring
opportunities with leading
companies. Notice that he is
"name dropping" in the first
paragraph, trying to inspire
confidence and establish
rapport in the first sentence.

Dear Mr. Brown:

Upon the strong recommendation of Ann Williams with The Bessemer Company, I am faxing you my resume.

As you will see, I have an outstanding track record in producing sales and profit for Frito-Lay Company, where I have worked since 1988. You will see from my resume that I have won numerous awards including Manager of the Year several times. I believe my fine personal reputation as well as my extensive knowledge of convenience store operations in TX could be of value to the Excalibur Company, and I would enjoy an opportunity to speak with you in confidence about employment opportunities.

At the appropriate time, I can provide exceptionally strong personal and professional references, including from Frito-Lay Company, but I would appreciate your not contacting Frito-Lay until after we have a chance to talk.

I pride myself on high standards of loyalty and integrity, and I am well known within my industry for delivering on whatever promises I make.

Please let me know if you would be interested in discussing the possibility of putting my talents, knowledge, sales skills, contacts, and background to use. In advance I send warm holiday greetings and best wishes for the New Year.

Sincerely,

Joe Vieira

JOE VIEIRA

1110½ Hay Street, Fayetteville, NC 28305 • preppub@aol.com • (910) 483-6611

OBJECTIVE

To benefit an organization that can use a loyal and dedicated sales professional who offers versatile skills in sales management, extensive knowledge of convenience store operations in Texas, as well as a "track record" of achievement in maximizing sales and profit.

TRAINING

Excelled in extensive executive development course work sponsored by Frito-Lay Company and previous employers; areas studied included merchandising, advertising, budgeting, buying, marketing, sales, inventory control, quality control, shrinkage control, and human resources administration.
- Was born and raised in Austin, TX, and graduated from Austin High School.

EXPERIENCE

DISTRICT SALES MANAGER. Frito-Lay Company, Austin, TX (1988-present).
Began with this company as a warehouseman and was rapidly promoted to Route Sales Representative; then advanced quickly into management: was named supervisor of five sales representatives and in 1992 was promoted to District Sales Manager.
- From 1992-99, built the existing territory from five to 22 routes; the parent company then divided up the huge territory I had created and I was named **Regional Sales Manager of the Year in 1999.**
- Currently supervise 10 sales representatives and two spare reps.
- Plan and administer a budget of $2 million annually.
- In 1998, doubled projected profit for my territory; exceeded the sales budget by 20%.
- In 1998, was named **National District Manager of the Year** as well as **Regional District Manager of the Year.**
- Accomplished an historical sales record within Frito-Lay of $124,000 net sales for one week, and was the first and only district manager to ever exceed quarterly sales of $1 million.
- Am completely familiar with convenience store operations in TX, having made headquarters calls and presentations to buyers and owners.
- Offer extensive knowledge of the chain convenience stores such as Quik Stop, Scotchman, and Short Stops.

Other experience:
- As a manager for a shoe division, opened three stores and trained the managers, assistant managers, and other personnel.
- As an insurance salesman, was named **Top Salesman** for the year for the eastern Texas region.

REFERENCES

Outstanding personal and professional references available upon request.

PERSONAL

Believe in the pursuit of excellence in all areas of life, and have become skilled in motivating employees to give their best effort. Have excellent contacts throughout Texas.

Date

Operations Management
Attn: Box 2668
Minneapolis, MN 98023

District Training Manager

There is always a reason to make an exception to a rule. As a rule, one does not send out letters of reference or recommendation with one's resume. However, this professional has done just that and mentions that fact in his cover letter. It may be the kind of attention-getting technique or gimmick which can blow some doors open for him. (Beware of doing this, however; it could make it appear that your job hunt is widespread knowledge, and you could make prospective employers feel that your job hunt is being encouraged by your current employer.)

Dear Sir or Madam:

I would appreciate an opportunity to talk with you soon about how I could contribute to your organization through my well-developed managerial skills and emphasis on training, team building, and customer service which together produce high-quality retail operations.

As you will see from my enclosed resume, I am known for my team building, time management, and organizational abilities. Most recently with BestBuy Family Clothing and earlier with Family Dollar Stores, Inc., I was singled out to manage complex projects including overseeing store openings from hiring and staffing locations, to opening them, to operational oversight. I have also been involved in managing a project to remodel 12 stores and in another situation was involved in corporate strategic planning.

I am also enclosing a copy of a letter of commendation I recently received from a Regional Manager with whom I worked closely. I feel that this letter touches on several of the strengths I would want a prospective employer to be aware of. One thing she emphasized is my "remarkable sense of urgency" in seeing that all jobs were done quickly so that deadlines were met and goals achieved. My drive for putting forth the effort which allowed the operation to advance to the next level, being handpicked as the district's training specialist for incoming management personnel, and my abilities as a troubleshooter and analytical problem solver were also addressed.

My extensive experience in retail store management has also afforded me opportunities to oversee and participate in all operational environments in retail settings: human resources and personnel management, purchasing and inventory control, customer service, public relations, merchandising, office operations, and loss prevention. Having been in management for approximately 17 years, I have refined my expertise in numerous areas and am confident that I offer the abilities and experience which make me a professional capable of contributing successfully to your organization's "bottom line."

I hope you will call or write me soon to suggest a time convenient for us to meet and discuss your current and future needs and how I might serve them. Thank you in advance for your time.

Sincerely,

Dixon Williamson

DIXON WILLIAMSON

1110½ Hay Street, Fayetteville, NC 28305 • preppub@aol.com • (910) 483-6611

OBJECTIVE To benefit an organization that can use an articulate manager who excels in supervising, training, and communicating with others while building strong teams, exceeding sales goals, prioritizing tasks, and meeting schedules.

EXPERIENCE **STORE MANAGER** and **DISTRICT TRAINING MANAGER.** BestBuy Family Clothing, Eden Prairie, MN (1994-99). Completed two months of corporate familiarization training before taking over a new location and building it to be recognized as one of the most profitable and successful locations in the 100-store region.
- Conducted interviews and selected the store's 130 associates including training and developing the management team which led to successful store operations.
- Handpicked as **District Training Manager**, personally carried out the training of all new store managers in a nine-store area.
- Achieved one of the ten lowest shrinkage percentages in a 100-store region as well as earning a 94% score during a recent corporate audit.
- Was cited by the Regional Manager as **"by far one of the greatest managers I had the opportunity to work with in my eleven years with the company"** for my role in not only managing a $3 million store but also assisting in all phases of several other store openings from the hiring process, to the grand opening, to operational support.

Advanced in managerial roles with the Family Dollar Stores, Inc.
STORE MANAGER. Ed Prairie, MN (1982-94). Carried out daily planning while staffing and supervising employees and directing all phases of operations so that each store consistently reached high levels of profitability while averaging under 2% shrinkage throughout an 11-year period.
- Trained and supervised an average of 100 associates in each store.
- Singled out as the coordinator of special projects for the district, managed remodeling activities at 12 stores and was involved in corporate-level strategic planning.
- Earned awards including **"Best Store Appearance in District"** and **"Best Sales Increase"** in the zone, both in 1991.
- Consistently met sales goals of $7 million annually and controlled million-dollar annual operating budgets.

Highlights of earlier experience with Family Dollar Stores:
- **SENIOR ASSISTANT MANAGER.** Assisted in employee supervision while overseeing merchandising, loss prevention, personnel staffing, and training for a store with 100 associates; special areas of emphasis were inventory shrinkage prevention and sales.
- **ASSISTANT STORE MANAGER.** Provided leadership in merchandising and operational areas of the store while contributing to growth and profitability of an 80-employee store.
- **MANAGEMENT TRAINEE.** Completed assignments in merchandising and operations after being selected for management training based on my accomplishments during two years as a sales associate, stockroom manager, and department manager.

EDUCATION Associate's degree in Business Administration, Eden Prairie Community College, MN. Received awards as an inspirational and motivational speaker from the Dale Carnegie program.

PERSONAL Possess skills which result in top sales results and quality customer service.

Date

Exact Name of Person
Title or Position
Name of Company
Address (no., street)
Address (city, state, zip)

**Engineering Manager and
Industrial Manager**

This successful manager cites
numerous accomplishments in cost
reduction, and he is seeking his
next challenging assignment as an
Industrial Engineer.

Dear Exact Name of Person: (or Dear Sir or Madam if answering a blind ad.)

I would appreciate an opportunity to talk with you soon about how I could contribute to your organization through my industrial engineering background including my experience in managing cost reduction programs, planning capital expenditures, and supporting new product design.

In my current job as an Industrial Engineer and Cost Reduction Manager, I have implemented the new manufacturing concept known as continuous process flow cells and have functioned as the "in-house expert" in training my associates in this area. While managing a $700,000 cost reduction program, I investigate and implement cost reductions through alternative materials and manufacturing processes as well as design modifications. I am involved on a daily basis in on-the-floor problem solving, costing of component processing, tooling and gaging, and capital equipment acquisitions. I have had extensive experience in project management.

Prior to graduating with my B.S. degree in Industrial Engineering, I worked my way through college in jobs in which I was involved in producing computer-aided drawings and participating in new product design. Although I worked my way through college, financing 80% of my education, I excelled academically and received the Outstanding Senior Award.

I am knowledgeable of numerous popular software and drafting packages. I offer a proven ability to rapidly master new software and adapt it for specific purposes and environments.

Single and willing to relocate, I can provide outstanding personal and professional references. I am highly regarded by my current employer and have been credited with making numerous contributions to the company through solving problems, cutting costs, determining needed capital equipment, and implementing new processes. I am making this inquiry to your company in confidence because I feel there might be a fit between your needs and my versatile areas of expertise.

I hope you will call or write me soon to suggest a time convenient for us to meet and discuss your current and future needs and how I might serve them. Thank you in advance for you time.

Sincerely yours,

Douglas Atkinson

DOUGLAS ATKINSON

1110½ Hay Street, Fayetteville, NC 28305 • preppub@aol.com • (910) 483-6611

OBJECTIVE

To add value to an organization that can use an accomplished young industrial engineer who offers specialized know-how in coordinating cost reductions, experience in both manufacturing and process engineering, proven skills in project management, and extensive interaction with product design, quality control, vendor relations, and capital expenditures.

EDUCATION

Bachelor of Science (B.S.) degree, Industrial Engineering Major; concentration in manufacturing, Western Carolina University, Asheville, NC, 1990.
- Achieved a 3.5 GPA (3.8 in my major); inducted into National Honor Fraternity.
- Received Outstanding Senior Award in manufacturing concentration.
- Worked throughout college and financed 80% of my education.

Associate of Applied Science (A.A.S.) degree, Mechanical Engineering and Design Technology Major, Richmond Community College, Richmond, VA, 1986; 3.7 GPA.

From 1990-present, completed business minor at St. Andrews Presbyterian College. Participated in continuing education sponsored by Ingersoll-Rand, Ford Motor Company, and the George Group in these and other areas:

ISO 9000 Internal Auditing	Root Cause Analysis
Total Quality Management	Value Engineering/Value Analysis
Continuous Flow Manufacturing	Synchronous Manufacturing

TECHNICAL KNOWLEDGE

Software: Quattro Pro, Freelance, Harvard Graphics, WordPerfect, Fox Pro
Drafting: VERSACAD, CADCAM, Cascade, Intergraph, Unigraphics Machining
Knowledge of machining processes and tooling and gaging equipment; experience in programming CNC equipment.
Certification: Certified Manufacturing Technologist; Certified ISO 9000 Internal Auditor

EXPERIENCE

INDUSTRIAL ENGINEER & COST REDUCTION MANAGER. Delbert Smith Co., Virginia Beach, VA (1992-present). Manage the processing of machined components from raw material to finished product while also coordinating a $700,000 annual cost reduction program; investigate and implement cost reductions by exploring the possibility of alternative materials, other manufacturing processes, and design modifications.
- Involved on a daily basis in on-the-floor problem solving, costing of component processing, tooling and gaging, and capital equipment acquisitions.
- Implemented and coordinated continuous process flow cells, a new concept in the manufacturing area; completed extensive training and trained my associates.
- Performed cost justifications and complete equipment installs for capital equipment acquisitions totaling half million dollars.
- Continuously interact with new product teams, problem-solving groups, purchasing specialists, vendors, as well as manufacturing and quality control personnel.
- Evaluated ergonomic equipment in assembly environment to reduce operator fatigue.

Other experience:
- **DESIGNER.** For the Precision Controls Division of Dana Corporation, produced computer-aided drawings and actively participated in new product design while interacting with engineering and manufacturing. Was part of the team that introduced the first microprocessor controlled cruise control.
- **DEPARTMENT ASSISTANT.** On a part-time work scholarship, produced drawings on VERSACAD computer-aided drafting system for Richmond Community College.

PERSONAL

Society of Manufacturing Engineers, Roanoke Division; National Association of Industrial Technology; Epsilon Pi Tau International Honorary Fraternity for Education in Technology

Date

Exact Name of Person
Title or Position
Name of Company
Address (number and street)
Address (city, state, and zip)

Dear Exact Name of Person: (or Sir or Madam if answering a blind ad.)

With the enclosed resume, I would like to introduce myself and my desire to explore suitable positions within your organization which can utilize my experience in providing leadership to non-profit organizations. I am relocating back to the Seattle area where I own a townhouse, and I believe my extensive background in non-profit management may be of interest to you.

As you will see from my resume, I have most recently served as Executive Director of an organization in San Diego, where I have managed recruitment and training of a 65-person volunteer staff while also supervising three professional staff personnel. I have developed effective collaborative efforts among numerous community organizations while simultaneously identifying gaps in community services and developing programs to fill those needs.

In my previous position in Mission Viejo, I was promoted from Community Services Coordinator to Assistant Director and then to Director of a community shelter with a staff of 30 human services professionals and paraprofessionals. In addition to developing and maintaining the $800,000 budget, I was active in grant writing and in numerous community activities which raised the shelter's profile.

I am the recipient of numerous awards and honors for my contributions and service, and I have enjoyed the respect of my colleagues in being elected to leadership positions in professional organizations and high-profile committees. I am widely respected for my ability to develop and maintain effective working relationships, organizational partnerships, and collaborative efforts.

If you can use my considerable leadership abilities and team building skills, I hope you will contact me to suggest a time when we might meet to discuss your needs and goals and how I might meet them. Thank you in advance for your time.

Sincerely,

Miyoko Hutchings

MIYOKO HUTCHINGS

1110½ Hay Street, Fayetteville, NC 28305 • preppub@aol.com • (910) 483-6611

OBJECTIVE   To offer my proven track record in fund-raising, community relations, and program development to an organization that can use an experienced director of non-profit programs, crisis intervention services, and volunteer activities.

EXPERIENCE   **EXECUTIVE DIRECTOR**. Rape Crisis Center of San Diego, San Diego, (1997-present). When I relocated back to San Diego, was immediately re-hired by Rape Crisis Volunteers of San Diego as Direct Services Coordinator; was promoted to Executive Director in 1998.
- Gained widespread respect for my leadership and ability to build collaborative coalitions and viable partnerships.
- Monitor and direct all aspects of a major crisis intervention agency: implementing policies, determining budgetary requirements, guiding various programs and functions, and managing an organizational budget of $500,000 for a program providing counseling, support groups, advocacy, and referral for victims of sexual assault 24 hours a day, 7 days a week.
- Identified gaps in services and created new programs to fill those gaps.
- Oversaw recruitment and training of a staff of 65 volunteers.

Mission Viejo Shelter, Mission Viejo, CA (1985-1997). *Was promoted in the following "track record" of advancement by a community shelter with an annual budget of $800,000.*
DIRECTOR. While managing the shelter, directed a staff of 30 human services professionals and paraprofessionals. Acted as liaison between the shelter and the community, establishing relationships with the voluntary Advisory Council, local organizations, and the business community. Developed and maintained an $800,000 budget. Effective fund-raising through grant writing, solicitations, and special events generated ten percent of the annual budget.

ASSISTANT DIRECTOR. Effectively managed existing services and developed new services for the homeless, maintaining compliance with the shelter program and funding requirements. Supervised a staff of 7 social workers, developed new programs, conducted volunteer recruitment program, determined funding requirements, and served as a liaison to the advisory council and local government agencies.

COMMUNITY SERVICES COORDINATOR. Directed and supervised a program with more than 150 volunteers, providing preventive, restorative, and aftercare services to the homeless.

DIRECT SERVICES COORDINATOR. Rape Crisis Volunteers of San Diego, CA (1981-1985). Supervised, recruited, and trained volunteers in an agency program meeting the needs of sexual assault survivors. Responsible for planning, organizing, and implementing direct services to meet the needs of primary and secondary victims of sexual assault.

EDUCATION   Enrolled in **University of California's Non-Profit Management Program:** a program of executive education for leading professionals in the non-profit organizational management field.
Earned **Bachelor of Arts, Sociology** – University of North Carolina at Chapel Hill.
Program included internships in geriatric and alcohol rehabilitation centers.

PERSONAL   Can provide outstanding personal and professional references upon request. Am known for my ability to develop strong organizational alliances.

Date

Exact Name of Person
Exact Title
Exact Name of Company
Address
City, State, Zip

Executive Director,
Arts Organization

If you want to see another
resume of a non-profit executive,
look at the resume and cover
letter of Ms. Hutchings on the
previous page. This accomplished
senior manager has specialized
experience in the arts.

Dear Exact Name of Person (or Dear Sir or Madam if answering a blind ad):

With the enclosed resume, I would like to make you aware of my background as an arts management professional with exceptional communication, organizational, and motivational skills. I offer the proven ability to recruit, train, and manage volunteers; direct grant writing and fundraising activities; and increase public awareness and involvement in the arts.

In my most recent position, I served as Executive for the seventh largest arts council in Oregon, which has an annual operating budget of nearly $800,000. With the West Linn Arts Council, I developed and implemented a number of new programs, including a comprehensive dance program that generated more than $10,000 annually in class fees, and a drama troupe for teenagers which was funded by an annual grant that I secured. In addition to events planning and coordination, I also excelled in marketing and public relations, designing brochures, press releases, and program books while raising community awareness of the Arts Council's programs and services.

In a previous job as Executive Director for another Arts Council, I created and implemented the first-ever Very Special Arts Festival for mentally handicapped children and adults in that county.

As you will see, I have earned my Bachelor of Science in Theatre Arts, and I have supplemented my degree program with additional courses in Arts Management. I am currently completing the Certificate in Non-Profit Management program at Oregon State University.

If you can use a motivated and experienced arts management professional whose skills in volunteer management, fundraising, and program development have been proven in challenging positions, then I look forward to hearing from you soon. I have an outstanding reputation and could become a valuable asset to your organization.

Sincerely,

Allyson Shook

ALLYSON SHOOK

1110½ Hay Street, Fayetteville, NC 28305 • preppub@aol.com • (910) 483-6611

OBJECTIVE	To benefit an organization that can use a dynamic, experienced non-profit director with exceptional communication and organizational skills who offers the proven ability to recruit, train, and manage volunteers as well as direct grant-writing and fund-raising activities
EDUCATION	Bachelor of Science in Theatre Arts, Oregon State University, Ponca City, OR, 1993. Graduated with a 3.6 GPA; minored in Dance and Music. Additional courses in Arts Management, Weymouth, OR, 1997. Completing Oregon State University Certificate in Non-Profit Management program.
AFFILIATIONS	Member, North Carolina Theatre Conference, 1993-present. Silver Arts committee, North Carolina Senior Games, 1995-present. Member of the Board of Directors, West Linn Special Olympics, 1995-1997.

EXPERIENCE

EXECUTIVE DIRECTOR. West Linn Arts Council, West Linn, OR (1997-1999). Excelled as Executive Director for the seventh largest arts council in Oregon with an annual budget of nearly $800,000; became known as an innovator in the areas of program development; recruiting, training, and supervision of volunteers; and fund-raising.

- Oversaw the planning, development, and implementation of new and existing arts programs; created resourceful marketing plans and publicity materials.
- Recruited and supervised 20 volunteers, training them to assist in the administrative operations of the organization as well as teaching them details of stage production so they could provide technical assistance at events.
- Developed a comprehensive dance program which was attended by more than 100 students in its first year, generating more than $10,000 in annual revenue.
- Established a drama troupe for teenagers, securing a $10,000 yearly grant for the company and collaborating with youth in the community on program development; the troupe received more than 30 invitations to perform for local organizations.
- Coordinated the Oregon Children's Theatre Circuit Showcase, scheduling over 50 groups to perform before 100 representatives of arts councils and related agencies; designed and produced press releases, brochures, and programs for the event.

EXECUTIVE DIRECTOR. Mount Prospect Community Arts Council, Mount Prospect, IL (1995-1997). Oversaw all operational aspects of this county-wide organization; provided supervisory and administrative support in addition to acting as liaison between the Arts Council and local schools, arts organizations, and local government.

- Collaborated with the members of the Board of Directors to formulate policies; prepared and administered the yearly arts agenda.
- Developed and managed an annual operational budget of $100,000.
- Prepared applications and gave recommendations for a local sub-granting program.
- Planned, organized, coordinated, and promoted two major festivals; served as coordinator for the Senior Games Program.
- Developed new training procedures for arts council board members, including designing and producing all printed training materials, information packets, etc.
- Created and implemented the first Very Special Arts Festival for mentally handicapped children and adults.

DRAMA TEACHER. Menasha County Schools, Menasha, WI (1993-1995). Taught six classes daily in drama and dance, as well as directing and producing plays for public performance; served as chairperson for electives teachers.

- Organized and collaborated with the chorus class to produce a musical as a fund-raiser.

PERSONAL   Excellent personal and professional references are available upon request.

Exact Name of Person
Exact Title
Exact Name of Company
Address
City, State, Zip

Executive Sous Chef

A recent relocation to Atlanta is what has sparked the job hunt of this accomplished culinary professional. His affiliations are numerous and require a separate section on his resume.

Dear Sir or Madam:

   With the enclosed resume describing my experience and skills, I would like to formally initiate the process of being considered for a culinary position within your organization.

   As you will see from my resume, I have excelled as an Executive Chef and Executive Sous Chef and have been a Certified Executive Chef since 1981. I am a member of numerous professional organizations including the American Culinary Federation of Chefs, the Academy of Chefs, the American Culinary Federation, the Canadian Chef Federation, as well as other clubs for the world's top culinary experts.

   I have recently relocated to Atlanta and am seeking a permanent position with an organization that can make use of my versatile management and culinary skills. Since moving to Atlanta I have worked with a culinary temporary service and have excelled in short-term assignments filling in for chefs who are on vacation.

   You will see that my previous job was Executive Sous Chef with a prestigious hotel, where I managed an 18-person staff and was extensively involved in the production of banquets and special events ranging from weddings to corporate functions. In previous positions I have excelled as Chef for an athletic club, as Executive Chef for a yacht club, and as Executive Chef for both hotels and businesses.

   You would find me in person to be a congenial individual who prides myself on doing every job to the best of my ability. I have managed budgets, people, and special projects with flair as well as with an aggressive bottom-line orientation.

   If you can use a culinary professional with my expert technical skills and extensive management experience, I hope you will call or write me to suggest a time when we could meet in person to discuss your needs and how I might serve them. I can provide excellent references at the appropriate time.

Yours sincerely,

Dimitri Charbonneau

DIMITRI CHARBONNEAU, CEC

1110½ Hay Street, Fayetteville, NC 28305 • preppub@aol.com • (910) 483-6611

OBJECTIVE
To benefit an organization that can use an imaginative chef with experience in budgeting and financial control, personnel training and management, marketing and promotion, as well as club and hotel administration.

EDUCATION
CHEF. Premier Catering Service, Atlanta, GA (1999-present). For a temporary service which provides culinary personnel to various organizations, have worked on major assignments filling in for chefs who are on vacation.

EXECUTIVE SOUS CHEF. Hyatt Regency, Richmond, VA (1996-1999). Added an international touch to the cuisine of this fine hotel through my extensive culinary background; trained and re-trained key staff people with the result that the kitchen is now operating more harmoniously and efficiently.
- Managed an 18-person staff; was extensively involved in the production of banquets and special events ranging from weddings to corporate functions.

CHEF. San Diego Athletic Club, San Diego, CA (1994-95). Planned and directed all food services related to both restaurant operations as well as special banquets for a club with a membership of 1200 along with a full athletic staff.
- Served luncheons daily to include banquets for up to 500 people.
- Served wedding parties every weekend through 1994 and 1995.
- Created an aggressive performance appraisal system which increased guest and member satisfaction.
- Dramatically cut food costs as a percentage of total budget while actually increasing food quality and customer satisfaction; maintained 28% food cost and 17% labor cost.

EXECUTIVE CHEF. Mantle Enterprises, Inc., Cupertino, CA (1992-94). Served 2,500 employee meals each day for this corporation.
- Produced outstanding meals considered excellent quality for the money.
- Based on average purchase of $4.75, maintained a 38% food cost and 45% labor cost.

EXECUTIVE CHEF. New York Club, New York, NY (1979-92). At a private yacht club with 2,600 members around the world, managed food preparation and food service provided six days a week at two restaurants, each with its own menu and in a different geographical location.
- Oversaw food sales totaling $2.3 annually at the yacht club.
- Developed regionally acclaimed menus and an elegant style of food service which has helped the restaurants garner top-notch reputations.

AFFILIATIONS
Certified Executive Chef since 1981
American Culinary Federation of Chefs since 1985
Member of the Academy of Chefs since 1982
Member of American Culinary Federation since 1970
Member of Canadian Chef Federation since 1967
Member of Pacific Coast Chefs in San Francisco since 1984
Member of Gastrome Club in New York since 1984
Les Topues Blanches International Club in Carmel and Monterey, CA since 1990

EDUCATION
Completed Trade School for Cooking and Pastry Apprenticeship

PERSONAL
Offer a culinary background with kitchen proficiency in German, English, and Spanish. Excellent references. Extensive P & L responsibility.

Exact Name of Person
Title or Position
Name of Company
Address (number and street)
Address (city, state, and zip)

Farm Manager

This farm manager is seeking a position in a new industry, and he believes his management and problem-solving skills are transferable to numerous fields.

Dear Exact Name of Person: (or Sir or Madam if answering a blind ad.)

With the enclosed resume, I would like to formally make you aware of my interest in exploring employment opportunities within your organization.

As you will see from my resume, I have excelled in management positions within the agricultural industry and have earned a reputation as an innovative professional who knows how to deal resourcefully with matters ranging from personnel issues to budgeting and cash flow. Although I am highly regarded in my current position and am being groomed for further rapid promotion, I am interested in transferring my management skills to a different industry.

I am skilled at training, motivating, and managing personnel from all backgrounds and socio-economic levels, and I have become adept at working with the Hispanic population. On several occasions, I have managed a staff which was entirely Spanish speaking.

Since I have worked in the agricultural industry where the best of plans are often assaulted by unexpected weather conditions, I have learned how to think quickly in order to save livestock, reduce operational costs, and assure a top-quality product. In our highly regulated industry, I have become skilled at dealing with regulators and inspectors.

I feel certain that my excellent problem-solving and troubleshooting skills could be transferable to any other industry and to your company in particular. If you can use a take-charge manager who is accustomed to facing unexpected challenges each day and developing common sense plans for resolving those problems, I hope you will contact me. I can provide outstanding personal and professional references at the appropriate time.

Thank you in advance for your time.

Yours sincerely,

Andrew R. Harris

ANDREW R. HARRIS

1110½ Hay Street, Fayetteville, NC 28305 • preppub@aol.com • (910) 483-6611

OBJECTIVE	To apply my ability to maximize human and fiscal resources to an organization that can use an assertive, articulate, and dedicated manager with excellent motivational abilities, experience in training and motivating employees, as well as skills in budgeting and cash flow.

EXPERIENCE

FARM MANAGER. Hartmans of Greenville, Greenville, KY (1997-present). Was originally hired as a Department Head on a 1,500-head sow farm and, within four months, was promoted to supervise between five to eight people; then promoted in February 1998 to Assistant Manager supervising nine people on a 1,000-head sow farm, and in 1999 to Farm Manager in charge of 22 individuals.
- Am in charge of all aspects of production as well as personnel problems/employee issues.
- Have excelled in managing a staff which is totally Hispanic.

GENERAL MANAGER. Harris Farms, DuVall County, KY (1988-1997). Handled all aspects of running a family farm including financial planning and budgeting, payroll accounting, short-term and long-range planning, and the supervision of four full-time and 30 six-month seasonal employees.
- Decreased fertilizer expenses 10% and at the same time increased the quality, quantity, and sale price of crops through close attention and constant awareness of market conditions.
- Took care of financial matters including payroll, loan procurement, accounts payable, and accounts receivable.
- Supervised the care of 3,600 swine in containment buildings.
- Assisted with the care of 150 beef cattle.
- Became fluent in Spanish and excelled in motivating/relating to Spanish-speaking workers.

OPERATIONS SUPERVISOR. Barrington Farms, Louisville, KY (1986-88). Supervised 15 full-time workers and as many as 300 seasonal employees on a 2,000-acre produce farm.
- Refined supervisor and managerial skills on a large farming operation where areas of responsibilities included monitoring soil fertility and seeing that sweet corn and cucumbers were properly planted and harvested.
- Scheduled irrigation and crop rotations so that all crops were given the optimum growing conditions.
- Provided the farm owner with the freedom to spend more of his time in planning and financial management while taking care of day-to-day activities.

GENERAL MANAGER. Harris Farms, Duvall County, KY (1979-86). Learned to apply what had been learned in college in a family farm environment while supervising two full-time and 15 seasonal workers taking care of 150 beef cattle, 200 sows on the ground, and a variety of crops.

EDUCATION

Associate in Applied Science degree in General Agriculture, Kentucky State University, Lexington, KY 1979.
- Course work emphasized field crops as well as hogs, poultry, and cattle.
- Was honored with a Phillip Morris scholarship.

LANGUAGES

Speak and understand Spanish which allows me to better relate to Spanish-speaking workers and motivate them.

PERSONAL

Am a persuasive, articulate speaker who excels in motivating others to work to maximum productivity. Excellent analytical and problem-solving skills.

Date

Mr. Frank McKinney
District Manager
Fashion First, Inc.

By fax to: 910-483-2439

Dear Mr. McKinney:

I would appreciate an opportunity to talk with you soon about how I could contribute to the Fashion First management team through my well-rounded background, experience, and track record of success in roles calling for financial expertise, training and personnel management skills, and a strong bottom-line orientation.

As you will see from my enclosed resume, I am presently excelling as General Manager/Training Manager for two restaurants in the large chain known as Hanford's of St. Louis. With full responsibility for profit and loss, in my four years with this organization I have reduced food costs 5% and cut employee turnover in half. Heavily involved in training, I interview and make hiring decisions. Then I provide new employee orientation and training for these locations which have a total of approximately 50 employees.

With proven organizational abilities, an eye for the bottom line, and a strong customer service orientation I am confident that I have a great deal to offer any organization needing an experienced manager. I pride myself on my ability to creatively solve problems, make prudent and timely decisions, and ensure that employees are working to their highest personal levels.

I hope after reviewing my resume you will be interested in setting up a brief meeting to discuss my qualifications for a managerial role with your organization. I look forward to talking with you soon to discuss your current and future needs and how I might serve them. Thank you in advance for your time.

Sincerely,

Annette Bolleg

Date

Exact Name of Person
Exact Title
Exact Name of Company
Address
City, State, Zip

Head Football Coach

Dear

This cover letter is set up a little differently than many others in this book. The subheads identify key qualities or experience which this high school coach hopes will persuade the colleges he is approaching that he is "college coach" material.

With the enclosed resume, I would like to make you aware of my strong desire to become a college coach at your institution. I offer 23 years of experience in coaching, teaching, and directing athletic programs which I could put to work for your program. I can provide outstanding references at the appropriate time.

Coaching success

Since 1996, I have excelled as Head Football Coach and Instructor at Bristol High School, and I have led the school to its first state playoffs since 1991 while being voted **Coach of the Year, 1999** by my peers. While I am held in high regard in this community, I am very selectively exploring opportunities to coach at the college level. You will see from my resume that I have excelled in earlier positions as Head Football Coach, Offensive Coordinator, and Athletic Director.

Teaching experience and educational credentials

In addition to being a winning coach, I am also an excellent teacher, administrator, and communicator. I hold SC, VA, and KY Teaching Certificates G-19 as well as my M.A.Ed. degree and B.S. degree. I am proud of the fact that I have earned a reputation as a powerful communicator and motivator in the classroom as well as on the ball field.

Reputation as a powerful motivator

A versatile professional who was "MVP" of my high school football team and who won a Merit Scholarship to the University of South Carolina, I have coached track, basketball, wrestling, and golf. I am confident that I could play a key role in strengthening any sports program while guiding young people to prosper academically and grow in character through athletics. I am extremely effective in molding groups of young people into productive, winning teams. For example, when I became the youngest 4A Head Coach at Moravia High School, I quickly produced a team with the most conference wins in the school's history. It is now my strong desire to do this at the college level.

I hope you will call or write me soon to suggest a time convenient for us to meet and discuss your current and future needs and how I might serve them. Thank you in advance for your time.

Sincerely yours,

Ben Kourofsky

ANNETTE BOLLEG

1110½ Hay Street, Fayetteville, NC 28305 • preppub@aol.com • (910) 483-6611

OBJECTIVE	To benefit an organization that can use dynamic professional who offers financial expertise, strong interpersonal skills, as well as experience in developing and implementing training and personnel development programs.
EXPERIENCE	**GENERAL MANAGER & TRAINING MANAGER.** Hanford's of St. Louis, St. Louis, MO (1992-present). Direct all phases of activities which impact on the restaurant's profitability for two locations with a total of 50 employees; have been highly effective in increasing average daily customer transactions and amounts spent per customer through the development of more focused local marketing campaigns.

- Refined my ability to read people and make decisions on their suitability for employment while interviewing and hiring new employees.
- Dealt with corporate executives on a regular basis while keeping them informed of store operations; interacted with vendor representatives.
- Developed orientation programs for new hires and trained them on corporate policies and activities which impacted on them.
- Reduced food costs 5% through the development of improvements to the purchasing and inventory control procedures.
- Cut employee turnover in half in an industry where rapid turnover is pretty much the norm: made employees aware of the level of performance I expected from them and was known for treating people in a fair but firm manner.
- Oversaw administrative activities including the development of monthly budgets, ordering of food and other supplies, and facility maintenance.
- Prepared weekly profit and loss reports.

BRANCH OPERATIONS SUPERVISOR. U.S. Army Library, Germany (1988-91). Was cited with several certificates of appreciation for my versatile skills demonstrated while overseeing areas including public relations, circulation, patron services, training and program management, and collection development for two geographically separate branch libraries serving American military personnel and their families.

- Established standards of accuracy and consistency in cataloging and shelving materiels.
- Maintained 80,000 books, tapes, and videos; prepared regular reports on library utilization figures.
- Explained and interpreted regulations and procedures to members of the public as well as being called on to assist other staff members.
- Applied my organizational and research skills while locating and retrieving information in response to requests for specific facts or items.
- Wrote publicity releases concerning activities being held in the library facilities and new material available.

SUBSTANCE ABUSE PROGRAM COUNSELOR/NURSE. St. Louis, MO (1987). Coordinated, monitored, and assessed activities in a 25-bed adolescent substance abuse unit while making certain that everything was being done to ensure the safety and security of the patients physically, medically, and psychologically.

EDUCATION	B.S., Nursing, University of Rhode Island, Providence, RI, 1987. Completed U.S. Army-sponsored training programs which emphasized the prevention of sex discrimination and elimination of sexual harassment.
PERSONAL	Apply innovative, creative ideas while solving problems and making decisions.

Date

Exact Name of Person
Title or Position
Name of Company
Address (number and street)
Address (city, state, and zip)

Dear Exact Name of Person: (or Sir or Madam if answering a blind ad.)

Senior managers often want to "test the waters," even when they enjoy their current position and responsibilities. That's what has motivated this senior manager to approach a select number of employers in industries which interest him. Notice that he has only one job on his resume, and his numerous functional responsibilities are highlighted within his chronological resume.

With the enclosed resume, I would like to make you aware of my interest in discussing the possibility of employment with your organization.

As you will see from my enclosed resume, I have been excelling in a track record of accomplishment with a 50-year-old company that produces gross revenue of more than $100 million annually. While earning a reputation as a dedicated businessman known for honesty and intelligence, I provided the leadership in helping this company strengthen its market share and improve its ability to serve its customers in a timely fashion. On my own initiative I took on the task of building a trucking division within the organization so that the company could be more responsive to customer needs and be able to rapidly take advantage of business opportunities. The company now has a 12-truck fleet and gross sales have increased by nearly 40% during the past six years.

I have earned a reputation as an outstanding communicator, and I have found that my communication skills have enabled me to tactfully resolve difficult customer problem, find remedies to employee issues, as well as aggressively develop new business and new accounts.

You would find me in person to be a congenial, straightforward individual who is skilled in every aspect of public relations and customer service. I can provide outstanding personal and professional references within the auto auction industry, banking community, and from numerous other sources.

If you can use a go-getter with exceptionally strong sales and marketing abilities along with a strong make-it-happen attitude and aggressive bottom-line orientation, I hope you will contact me to suggest a time when we might meet to discuss your goals and how I might help you achieve them.

Yours sincerely,

Neil Harriss

WILLIAM McGOWAN

1110½ Hay Street, Fayetteville, NC 28305 • preppub@aol.com • (910) 483-6611

OBJECTIVE	To benefit an organization that can use a strong manager with expert knowledge of inventory, wage, and shrinkage control as well as a well-developed sense of the value of customer service and satisfaction.
TRAINING	Continually add to my knowledge by reading and taking tests which have earned me approximately 1,000 continuing education units awarded by the Food World corporation.
EXPERIENCE	*Have built a track record of advancement with a large retail supermarket chain, Food World, which is headquartered in Macon, GA:*

STORE MANAGER. Duluth, GA (1997-present). Increased sales and profitability in a store with $14 million in annual sales while managing six department heads and overseeing the day-to-day performance of 70 employees.
- Am providing the leadership which has allowed this location to see a year-to-date shrinkage rate of +0.14% and a 21% sales increase.
- Increased this store's bottom-line profitability by 4%.
- Oversee all phases of store operations ranging from wage control and processing, to inventory control and supply, to utilities, to maintenance, to security and safety, to cleaning and sanitation, to merchandising.
- Hire, train, and schedule employees.

STORE MANAGER. Smithfield, GA (1994-97). Increased sales 8% a year in a store which had an average annual sales volume of $10 million while supervising five department heads and 50 employees.
- Demonstrated my dedication to the success of store operations by working an average of 60 to 70 hours a week.
- Maintained outstanding results in all measurable areas of wages, shrinkage reduction, and bottom-line profitability.
- Oversaw all operational areas to include wage control and payroll actions, inventory control and supply, utilities management, building maintenance, security and safety, cleaning and sanitation, and merchandising as well as hiring, training, and scheduling.

STORE MANAGER. Crayfish, GA (1992-94). Supervised five department heads and 50 employees in a store which posted sales of $9 million annually.
- Increased sales; learned to share responsibilities with my department heads while still working an average of 60-70 hours a week; and maintained high levels in all measured areas of operation (wages, shrinkage, and profitability).

ASSISTANT MANAGER. Malvern, GA (1991-92). Supervised one department head and seven employees in the grocery department while working as acting manager in his absence for a store with a $10 million annual sales volume.
- Was recognized for my excellent inventory control abilities as well as for my skills in scheduling, ordering, and building displays.

SKILLS	Through my years of retail experience, have become familiar with equipment and procedures which include using computerized cash registers and automated systems for recordkeeping and inventory control.
PERSONAL	Earned numerous "Outstanding Performance Awards" based on sales increases, inventory control, and customer satisfaction surveys. Have not missed one day of work due to illness in ten years with Food World.

BEN KOUROFSKY

1110½ Hay Street, Fayetteville, NC 28305 • preppub@aol.com • (910) 483-6611

OBJECTIVE

To offer my positive leadership style, along with my experience in building and coaching winning teams, to an ambitious high school or college that can use an enthusiastic, intelligent professional with a reputation for the highest ethics.

EXPERIENCE

Offer a track record of more than 100 wins as a football head coach and assistant coach in a 23-year career as an athletic director and coach; have guided teams to the state playoffs eight years:

HEAD FOOTBALL COACH and **INSTRUCTOR.** Bristol High School, Richmond, VA (1996-present). Have successfully rebuilt a football program and transformed a group of average players into champions with strong competitive spirits and the will to win in the tough Central 4A conference; teach physical conditioning and P.E.
- Doubled the level of participation by both parents and players in three years.
- Coached back-to-back winning seasons at Bristol High for the first time in 20 years: 6-5 in 1997 and 7-5 in 1998.
- Was voted **"Coach of the Year, 1999"** by my peers; led Bristol High to its first state playoff since 1991.
- Increased football gate receipts from $18,000 in 1995, to $24,000 in 1996, and to $38,000 in 1997 and 1998.

OFFENSIVE COORDINATOR and **PHYSICAL EDUCATION TEACHER.** Mason Senior High School, Mason, VA (1994-96). Was hired as offensive coordinator for a football team which built an impressive record of wins in a conference recognized as the toughest and most competitive in the state.
- Averaged 10 wins a year over two seasons while building teams that worked well together under pressure.
- Contributed intelligence, leadership, and knowledge of the game of football as a member of a coaching staff which was effective in winning "the big games."
- In two years, guided the team to an impressive streak of scoring in double figures for 21 consecutive games, a fact publicized by the *High School Football PREP News.*

HEAD FOOTBALL COACH and **ATHLETIC DIRECTOR.** Cameron Senior High School, Cameron, KY (1991-93). Provided the management and guidance for a project in which three high schools combined; then coached the football program and directed all other sports for the consolidated school.

HEAD FOOTBALL COACH and **ATHLETIC DIRECTOR.** Davidson High School, KY (1987-91). Led the state's smallest 4A school to four consecutive playoffs in the state's toughest league; was administrator of the school's total athletic program.

HEAD FOOTBALL COACH and **INSTRUCTOR.** Moravia High School, Moravia, SC (1979-87). Joined this organization as the youngest 4A high school head coach in the state; led the team to break several school records; supervised and trained an eight-person staff.

EDUCATION

M.A.Ed. degree, East Carolina University, Greenville, NC, 1984.
B.S., Physical Education, University of South Carolina, Mason, SC, 1979.
Hold SC, KY, and VA Teaching Certificates G-19.

FOOTBALL COACHING EXPERTISE

In my coaching career, have gained experience in these areas:

offensive and defensive coordination

special team coordination

formulation of game plans

fundamentals in all positions

PERSONAL

Was "MVP" of my high school football team. Work well under pressure.

Date

Director of Human Resources Position
c/o Management Consultants Inc.
89 Forsythe Building, Suite 45
Gainesville, FL 90213

Human Resources Director

Here you see the human resources director of a mental health organization seeking the recently-advertised position of human resources director for the city of Gainesville. Her resume is full of accomplishments and achievements.

Dear Sir or Madam:

With the enclosed resume, I would like to make you aware of my interest in the position of Human Resources Director for the City of Gainesville. In my current position as Human Resources Director of the Gainesville County Mental Health Center overseeing 395 people in 20 locations, I have earned widespread respect for my skill at all aspects of human resources management. I have earned a reputation as a skilled problem solver in personnel matters as well as an insightful administrator and strategic planner.

A lifelong resident of Gainesville, I offer a broad base of contacts in and knowledge of the people and the resources available in this city. I have been very effective in managing all functional areas of the human resources activities of the County Mental Health Center through my excellent communication and leadership skills. This organization has allowed me opportunities to establish goals and policies, solve problems, and develop time- and money-saving improvements in a variety of areas. Examples of my accomplishments include the creation of an annual training program for new supervisors, automation of all position and personnel files, development of guidelines adopted by the area mental health authority, and creation of a new department for staff development.

I am confident that I possess the human relations management expertise, education, and communication skills you expect in a candidate for such an important role. I hope you will contact me to suggest a time when I might meet with you in person to discuss my strong qualifications for this position. I take great pride in the many milestones and achievements which have been accomplished at the Mental Health Center under my leadership, and it would be a great pleasure to serve the City of Gainesville.

Sincerely,

Ivana Hufstader

IVANA HUFSTADER

1110½ Hay Street, Fayetteville, NC 28305 • preppub@aol.com • (910) 483-6611

OBJECTIVE To offer my experience in human resources management and knowledge of local government personnel administration and employment law to an organization that would benefit from an insightful problem solver and planner.

EDUCATION & TRAINING

B.S. and A.A. in Business Administration, Florida State University, 1988.
- Graduated *magna cum laude.*

Received certificates in a variety of subject areas including computers, insurance, short-hand, typing, and taxes, Gainesville Technical Community College, Gainesville, FL.

Attended professional development training programs—sponsored by such organizations as the State of Florida, Office of State Personnel, and the University of Florida Institute of Government.

EXPERIENCE

Advanced to positions of increasing responsibility in the field of human resources and administrative operations with the Mental Health Center, Gainesville, FL (1971-present):

HUMAN RESOURCES DIRECTOR. (since 1982). Oversee 800 people in 40 locations while providing outstanding leadership, organizational, and management skills in the process of directing the recruiting and hiring of personnel as well as ensuring compliance with federal and state employment law and center policy.
- Created and implemented an annual training program for new supervisors.
- Managed a major project during which information in all position and personnel files was automated—accomplished this time-saving improvement on my own with no assistance from outside consultants or vendors.
- Handpicked for a work group, played a key role in applying for certification for Alcohol, Drug, and Crisis Stabilization programs which resulted in accreditation in October, 1999.
- Developed and wrote personnel policy and procedural guidelines which were adopted for use by the area mental health authority.
- Created a new department (Staff Development Department) established to oversee the training for all employees and for center programs.
- Provided oversight for the development of the personnel department's annual budget.
- Directed functional areas which included Workman's Compensation and Unemployment Compensation claims along with the program which provided performance evaluations.
- Was appointed to serve on the Human Rights Committee of the International Personnel Management Association and earned this honor again in 1999 after serving in 1998.
- In evaluations, have been described as "consistently exceeding standards."

Highlights of Mental Health Center employment (1971-76): Originally hired as Secretary to the Director, was promoted to Administrative Secretary and Administrative Assistant before advancing to Administrative Officer and Staff Development Specialist.
- Gained experience in supervising a staff and developing budgets.

AFFILIATIONS Hold membership in the International Personnel Management Association and in the state chapter and in the Society for Human Resource Management.

Exact Name of Person
Title or Position
Name of Company
Address (number and street)
Address (city, state, and zip)

**Multi-Unit Restaurant Manager
and International Consultant**

This top-level professional with
management and international
consulting experience is open to
worldwide relocation.

Dear Exact Name of Person: (or Sir or Madam if answering a blind ad.)

With the enclosed resume, I would like to make you aware of my interest in joining your management team in some capacity which could utilize my proven skills in strategic planning, operations management, new venture start-up, and troubled unit turn-around.

As you will see from my enclosed resume, I am currently working as a Multi-Unit Manager with the KYC Restaurant Group in eastern California, where I have made dramatic improvements in lowering food costs while increasing unit controllable income, boosting unit net income, and strengthening customer service. In addition to re-training employees and developing three new General Managers who are excelling in their jobs, I have led the company in producing the highest gross profit margin.

From 1987-97, I worked in Japan. I speak Japanese proficiently. While working for Crawford Consulting in Tokyo, I earned a reputation as a creative and resourceful management consultant. I enjoyed helping business executives make wise investments in the Asian market and I trained numerous area supervisors in effective management techniques. Projects in which I was involved included establishing a 47-unit restaurant facility in Tokyo; developing the strategic plan for an $11 million restaurant; and transforming a downtown bus station in Seoul into a 32-floor Hilton Hotel with restaurants on nine different floors.

Before I was recruited by Crawford Consulting, I prospered in a job as a Multi-Unit Restaurant Manager when I helped Burger King establish its first 35 restaurants in the Japanese market. In that position I oversaw a 450-person work force which was only 5% American.

With a reputation as a dynamic and creative manager with unlimited personal initiative and superior problem-solving skills, I am confident that I could become a valuable addition to your outstanding management team. If you can use a top performer with the proven ability to positively impact the bottom line, I hope you will contact me to suggest a time when we might meet to discuss your goals and how I might help you achieve them. I can provide outstanding personal and professional references at the appropriate time.

Sincerely,

Dudley Brady

DUDLEY BRADY

1110½ Hay Street, Fayetteville, NC 28305 • preppub@aol.com • (910) 483-6611

OBJECTIVE	To benefit an organization that can use a vivacious and enthusiastic problem solver who has excelled in both management consulting and line management positions internationally while helping companies in the hospitality industry to improve their sales, customer service, quality assurance, profitability, market share, cost control, as well as strategic positioning.
EXPERIENCE	**MULTI-UNIT MANAGER.** KYC Restaurant Group, Eastern CA (1997-present). For this 1,100-unit restaurant concern, have combined my leadership skills and technical expertise in producing the following results in six units in eastern CA.

- Reduced food costs by 6% ($120,000 yearly); lowered food costs from 29% to 23.02%.
- Raised average sales ticket by 15%; increased unit controllable income by 4% ($245,000 yearly) and boosted net unit income by 15% ($150,000) annually.
- Retrained employees and developed three new General Managers who are excelling.
- Produced the highest gross profit in the company (73.15% versus 65% industry standard).

OPERATIONS CONSULTANT. Crawford Consulting, Tokyo, Japan (1996-97). As a management consultant for this international consulting group, played a key role in helping business executives make wise investments in the Asian market while also training area supervisors to utilize effective management styles; was involved in these and other areas:

Concept adaptation from English to Japanese	Service operations training
Multi-Unit management training	Project management
New venture start-ups	Turning around unprofitable units
Market analysis, sales, and pricing decisions	Profitability management

- Played a key role in establishing a new 47-unit restaurant facility in Tokyo.
- For the Okinawa Express, helped develop the strategic plan for an $11 million restaurant which achieved $11 million in sales annually (this restaurant serves only two meals a day with a modest capacity of 290 seats!)
- Worked with a client list that included the Kafu Hotel group, Okinawa Express, Fosters Hollywood, and Ashton City.
- From the concept stage to operational reality, provided leadership in transforming a main downtown bus station in Tokyo into a 32-floor Hilton Hotel with restaurants on nine different floors; oversaw strategic planning regarding food concessions and contracts.

MULTI-UNIT RESTAURANT MANAGER. Department of Defense, Japan (1990-96). In this international environment, managed 15 restaurants as well as six school cafeterias.

- Hired, trained, managed, and continuously developed 450 employees in a work force which was only 5% American.
- Was Central Warehouse Custodian for a multimillion-dollar equipment and food inventory.
- Helped Burger King establish its first 35 restaurants in the Japanese market, and functioned as a consultant in helping Burger King maximize profitability.
- In Japan, opened the largest food court ever located on a U.S. military installation; with 18,000 sq. ft., the facility produced $8 million in annual sales.
- Acted as the liaison between the Burger King corporation and the base commander, who viewed me as his "food guru" and sought my advice on a wide range of matters related to menus, catering services, and special events.

EDUCATION	Extensive executive development training sponsored by organizations including Burger King, Crawford Consulting, Army and Air Force Exchange Service (AAFES), and other organizations.
PERSONAL	Excellent references. My strong interest in restaurant management and cooking began when I was a youth, and I credit my mother and aunts, outstanding cooks, as my inspiration.

Date

ATTN: Box 3151
c/o Oklahoma City Publishing Company
P.O. Box 902
Oklahoma City, OK 89723

Dear Sir or Madam:

With the enclosed resume, I would like to make you aware of my interest in utilizing my considerable experience in health care management within your organization.

As you will see from my enclosed resume, I served Elder Village of Oklahoma City as its Licensed Nursing Home Administrator for the past 19 years. In 1999, I resigned from that position in order to seek new opportunities and new challenges. Currently I am working with an in-home care organization as a consultant on a special project which involves its marketing program as well as the correction of several deficiencies recently noted by the Division of Facility Services.

I excelled in every aspect of my job at Elder Village, from public relations, to budgeting, to Medicare and Medicaid insurance billing, to human resources and personnel administration. I am an expert in dealing with matters pertaining to regulation and compliance, and I am proud of the fact that, in May 1999, the Division of Facility Services inspected Elder Village on all state and federal compliance and gave the facility a 100% deficiency-free inspection survey result—an almost unheard-of accomplishment.

As I look back over my accomplishments at Elder Village, I am especially proud of my achievements related to human resources administration and personnel management. It was my responsibility to manage a staff of up to 170 people, who included 35 licensed nurses as well as employees involved in dietary, housekeeping, social services, physical therapy, and other activities. I created the organization's human resources policies and procedures, oversaw the development of the organization's first employee manuals, and maintained constant vigilance over personnel files to assure employee compliance with all regulations pertaining to licenses, certifications, and other matters.

If you can use a hard-working professional with vast knowledge related to health care management, I hope you will contact me to suggest a time when we could meet. I can assure you in advance that I have a strong bottom-line orientation and am known for my highly creative approach to problem solving and decision making.

Sincerely,

Myrna Joan Reese

MYRNA JOAN REESE

1110½ Hay Street, Fayetteville, NC 28305 • preppub@aol.com • (910) 483-6611

OBJECTIVE	To offer my management, public relations, and customer service skills to an organization that can use a respected manager with proven versatility in business administration.
LICENSE & CERTIFICATIONS	Licensed Nursing Home Administrator by the State of Oklahoma All areas of health care as it relates to long-term skilled care including certified in CPR, Fire Safety, Drug Management, and other areas
EDUCATION	Bachelor of Science degree, Oklahoma State University. Completed extensive ongoing professional education in all areas related to health care trends and management as well as business administration including budgeting and finance, human resources administration, other areas.
EXPERIENCE	*For 19 years, was the administrator of Elder Village of Oklahoma City, a nursing home and medical facility known for the highest quality standards; resigned from this position in order to pursue other opportunities. In May 1999, the Division of Facility Services inspected Elder Village on all state and federal regulations compliance; the facility was given a 100% deficiency free inspection/survey result. With more than 600 regulations to comply with, this is considered an almost impossible task to accomplish, and my management skills were considered the key to this rare accomplishment.* **ADMINISTRATOR.** Elder Village of Oklahoma City, Oklahoma City, OK (1980-99). Took over the management of this facility in 1980 and directed its growth over the next 19 years; Elder Village is a skilled nursing care and heavy rehabilitation facility which employs up to 170 people while providing nursing care and services for 159 patients.

- **State-of-the-art facility:** Provided oversight for numerous renovations and construction projects which resulted in a comfortable home for the 159 residents of this facility that provides services including round-the-clock nursing and physical therapy.
- **Human resources administration**: Developed all human resources policies and procedures; oversaw the development of the organization's first employee manuals. Take pride in the fact that many of the facility's current employees have worked at Elder Village for nearly 20 years.
- **Staff:** Hired and managed the 170-person staff which included 35 licensed nurses as well as employees in all functional areas.
- **Personnel Administration:** Maintained continuous vigilance over personnel files to assure up-to-date compliance of all personnel with regulations pertaining to their licenses, certifications, current CPR, health cards, TB testing, documentation of all time sheet discrepancies, vacation days, paid leave days, leaves of absence, family medical leave, inservice certification, drug testing, and any drug rehabilitation programs.
- **Medicare and Medicaid Insurance billing:** Provided stringent oversight for billing for this facility which was Medicare, Medicaid, and VA Certified.
- **Budgeting and Finance:** Managed budgeting related to $7 million in annual revenues; figured payroll calculations for every payroll period.
- **Quality Assurance:** Developed continuous Quality Improvement Programs for each department and was vigilant in maintaining quality assurance in all departments.
- **Outstanding Reputation in the community and with regulators:** Maintained excellent public relations with physicians, hospitals, health organizations, and patients' families and friends; was monitored by 52 licensing agencies, and handled numerous regulatory visits, announced and unannounced, from the Division of Facility Services, Department of Social Services, Department of Human Resources, Fire Marshal, Health Department, others.

PERSONAL	Hardworking. Creative. Honest. Detail Person. People Person. Superior communicator. Am in excellent health and ready for a new challenge for my management abilities!

Date

Exact Name
Exact Title
Exact Name of Organization
Exact Address
City, State zip

Nursing Home Administrator

If you want to compare the resumes and cover letters of two nursing home administrators, compare this resume with the resume of Ms. Reese on the previous page. Ms. Spears, unlike Ms. Reese, has worked for numerous organizations.

Dear Exact Name of Person: (or Dear Sir or Madam if answering a blind ad):

With the enclosed resume and this cover letter, I would like to make you aware of my interest in being considered for the position of Long-Term Care State Facilitator. In addition to my expert knowledge of nursing center administration and long-term care, I offer a reputation as a highly effective communicator, creative problem-solver, and skilled crisis manager.

As you will see from my resume, I am a Licensed Nursing Home Administrator (L.N.H.A.) and have excelled in administrative positions within the nursing care field. In most of my jobs, I have taken on a wide range of problems and have developed and implemented solutions that improved the census, boosted morale, improved staff skills, and resolved a wide range of problems which had resulted in deficiencies.

In my current position, I have decreased deficiencies from eight to one while increasing the census from 87% to 99%. In my previous position, I increased the census from 90% to 97% while decreasing deficiencies from 14 to five. I am skilled at planning, organizing, and directing administrative functions and monitoring conformance to regulatory guidelines. In one job, I took over the management of an organization which was experiencing a variety of staffing problems and I restored confidence in the staff while improving public relations and profits.

I am well aware of the many significant contributions your organization makes to the long-term care industry. As an administrator, I have utilized the services you provide in inservice training as well as in mediation and problem solving. Based on my understanding of your role within the nursing home and long-term care industry, I feel I could make valuable contributions through my ability to establish and maintain outstanding relationships as well as through my highly professional approach to solving problems within our very unique industry.

I hope you will give me the opportunity to talk with you in person about my interest in this position. I can provide outstanding personal and professional references at the appropriate time, and I can assure you in advance that I am a loyal and hard-working professional who would be a valuable addition to your team. Thank you in advance for your time.

Yours sincerely,

Maureen Spears, L.N.H.A.

MAUREEN SPEARS, L.N.H.A.

1110½ Hay Street, Fayetteville, NC 28305 • preppub@aol.com • (910) 483-6611

OBJECTIVE   To offer my exceptionally strong problem-solving, public relations, marketing, and communication skills to an organization that can use a skilled administrator with expert knowledge of nursing center administration and long-term care.

EXPERIENCE   **ADMINISTRATOR.** NC Nursing Center, Charlotte, NC (1996-present). Through my public relations, leadership, and strong administrative abilities, have accomplished numerous ambitious goals which included boosting patient and staff morale, improving staff training and effectiveness, strengthening community relations, and making facility improvements.
- Cut deficiencies from eight to one; increased census from 87% to 99%.

ADMINISTRATOR. Dunn Nursing Center, Dunn, NC (1995-96). Took over the management of this organization which experienced a suspension of admissions; was given a provisional license and four months later received a permanent license for the first time in its three-year history.
- Increased the census to 97% from 90%.

ADMINISTRATOR. Raleigh Nursing Center, Raleigh, NC (1993-94). Through my management and problem-solving skills, played a key role in "turning around" an 84-bed nursing facility experiencing numerous internal difficulties.
- Just 12 days after I was hired, the facility received its provisional license and, six months later, regained its licensure status; then I recruited, hired, and trained department heads.

ADMINISTRATOR. Primary Care of Raleigh, Raleigh, NC (1992-93). Led this 70-bed long-term care facility to show a profit for the first time in four years while also increasing the census from 90% to 95%; reduced aged receivables to 22% of total receivables.
- Planned, organized, and directed all administrative functions and monitored conformance to guidelines promulgated by regulatory agencies.
- Within one month, hired and trained four new department heads and worked with them to dramatically improve the quality of services provided.

ADMINISTRATOR. The North Carolina Diabetes Institute, Inc., Morganton, NC (1990-92). Took over the management of an organization that was experiencing a variety of staffing problems; stabilized and restored confidence in the staff while improving public relations, increasing the census, and boosting profits.
- Planned and directed administration for this 56-bed long-term facility.

EDUCATION & TRAINING   A.S. degree, Banking and Finance, Whetmore College, Reading, PA, 1989.
Completed 50-week Administrator-in-Training and Medical Terminology Course.
Licensed Nursing Home Administrator (**L.N.H.A.**) and CPR certified.
Completed courses in finance, customer service, word processing, and management.

PERSONAL   Outstanding references. Proven leader with strong human relations and communication skills.

Date

Tallahassee School System
PO Box 53498
Tallahassee, FL 89032

Dear Sir or Madam:

With the enclosed resume, I would like to make you aware of my interest in the position you recently advertised as Executive Director for Child Nutrition for the Tallahassee School System.

As my resume reveals, I offer the extensive knowledge you are seeking in child nutrition along with proven management skills, analytical abilities, and the ability to develop and maintain harmonious working relationships. In my current job as Child Nutrition Supervisor for Tallahassee City Schools which I have held since 1987, I oversee child nutrition programs in 65 school cafeterias while also planning and implementing all staff development for more than 900 employees. I also plan the yearly orientation program and conduct safety training for all child nutrition employers. I offer an outstanding personal and professional reputation and am known for my ability to work well with others at all organizational levels.

In previous jobs I excelled as a Home Economics Teacher and Home Economics Extension Agent, and I also served as a Food Service Director in a 120-person nursing care facility and in a 90-patient retirement home.

My Certifications include Certified Child Nutrition Supervisor and Certified Home Economist. I am a member of numerous associations and federations related to home economics and food service, and I have received many honors in recognition of my leadership, character, and technical knowledge of the nutrition field.

I hope you will give me an opportunity to demonstrate to you in person that I am the hard-working professional you are seeking, and it would be a great honor for me to continue my service to the children of the Tallahassee School System in the role of Executive Director for Child Nutrition. Thank you in advance for your time.

Yours sincerely,

Joan Hocker

JOAN HOCKER

1110½ Hay Street, Fayetteville, NC 28305 • preppub@aol.com • (910) 483-6611

OBJECTIVE   To serve the Tallahassee School System as its Executive Director for Child Nutrition.

EDUCATION   Florida State University, Tallahassee, FL; Post-Graduate Class—1996
Master's of Education in Foods, Nutrition & Food Service Management, University of Florida, Gainesville, FL, 1986.
B.S., Home Economics Education, Florida State University, Tallahassee, FL, 1982.

WORK HISTORY   **CHILD NUTRITION SUPERVISOR.** *Tallahassee City Schools*, Tallahassee, FL (1987-present). Manage 40 Child Nutrition Supervisors providing oversight for 65 school cafeterias.
- Plan and implement all staff development for 900+ employees which includes training in these and other areas:

Human Resources	Management Skills
Baking	Menu Planning
Quality Foods	Procurement
Recordkeeping	Computer Skills

- Responsible for bidding of all snacks for after school day care programs.
- Schedule and design course curriculum as needed by Child Nutrition Services.
- Refined skills in menu planning and purchasing.
- Plan yearly orientation program and conduct safety training for all child nutrition employers.

HOME ECONOMICS EXTENSION AGENT. *FL Agricultural Extension Service*, Gainesville, FL (1985-87).
- Home Economics Extension Agent with responsibility for clothing, foods and nutrition, human development, family resource management, housing and homes furnishings, extension homemakers; was also assigned forestry program responsibility.

FOOD SERVICE DIRECTOR. *Quality Care, Inc.*, Tampa, FL (1983-85).
- Food Service Director for 220-patient nursing care facility.
- Supervised staff of eight.
- Responsible for purchasing supplies, maintaining inventory, menu preparation on a six-week cycle, supervision of food preparation, and participation in patient care conferences.

FOOD SERVICE DIRECTOR. *The Baptist Retirement Home, Inc.*, Durham, NC (1982-83). Food Service Director for 90 patient facility. Supervised five people.

CERTIFICATIONS   Certified Child Nutrition Supervisor, American School Food Service Association, 1988
Certified Home Economist, American Home Economics Association, 1987

HONORS   State Employee Association District Member of the Year—1998
Governor's Award—1996
Outstanding Young Woman of America—1994
Outstanding Young Extension Home Economist of the Year—1986

Date

Ms. Jane Allen
Management Consultants & Executive Recruiters
Beacon Hill
Boston, MA 06713

Dear Ms. Allen:

I would like to make you aware of my interest in a Quality Assurance position within a corporation which can utilize my strong executive skills as well as my proven ability to apply my technical expertise in resourceful ways that improve the bottom line while strengthening customer satisfaction.

As you will see from my resume, I have progressed in a track record of advancement with the Kaysey Corporation, one of the world's leading consumer products manufacturing companies. In my current job, I manage a 29-person QA department in a plant which employs 1,925 people and manufactures personal care products totaling $550 million. While managing a departmental budget of nearly $2.5 million, I have transitioned the plant from a regular production assembly line operation into a team-managed operation in which teams of employees are responsible for individual products. This has shifted QA from a "police" role to a consulting and monitoring role. I have also developed, implemented and managed a Cost-of-Quality Program which achieved 1999 cost savings of $750,000 by identifying and eliminating unnecessary processes.

In my previous job at Quality Assurance Manager at the company's plant in Lawrence, KS, I developed and implemented a Quality Demerit System which the company now uses corporate-wide. The Quality Demerit System transformed four manufacturing plants from a quality level of 67% defect-free product to the consumer in 1992, to 98.2% defect-free in 1999. The targeted goal for 2000 is 99.0% defect-free product.

I offer extensive expertise related to blow molding and injection molding. Both in my current and previous job, I managed Quality Assurance related to blow molding and injection molding. In the plant, we achieved a 10% improvement in lots accepted when using Mil. Std. 105E to determine acceptable quality levels (AQLs).

You would find me in person to be a congenial individual who prides myself on my ability to establish and maintain effective working relationships. I can provide outstanding personal and professional references at the appropriate time. I hope you will contact me to suggest a time when we might meet to discuss your needs as well as my skills, experience, and qualifications.

Sincerely,

Hugh Visco

HUGH VISCO

1110½ Hay Street, Fayetteville, NC 28305 • preppub@aol.com • (910) 483-6611

OBJECTIVE	To benefit an organization that can use a knowledgeable quality assurance executive with a proven ability to lower costs, improve customer satisfaction, reduce defects, and strengthen employee accountability.
EXPERIENCE	*1981-present: Have excelled in the following track record of promotion with Kaysey Corporation, a $1 billion a year Fortune 500 company which recently became a part of Consumer Products USA, a $4 billion corporation.*

QUALITY ASSURANCE MANAGER. (1993-present). Champaign, IL. Manage a 29-person department which includes five QA Supervisors and a Laboratory Manager in a plant which employs 1,925 people and manufactures personal care products totaling $550 million.
- Developed, implemented, and managed a Cost-of-Quality Program which identified and eliminated non-value-added process activities; this process produced a 1999 cost saving of $750,000.
- Implemented analytical and microbiological testing of raw materials and bulk products which instituted QA at the earliest possible point in the process.
- Through aggressive training, have transformed my Quality Assurance Department into the one acknowledged as the best within the corporation.
- Manage a departmental budget which in 1999 was $2.5 million; developed and implemented initiatives which stimulated cost efficiencies and improved worker participation in all facets of QA.
- Transitioned this plant from a regular production assembly line operation into a team-managed operation in which teams are responsible for individual products. This has shifted QA from a "police" role to a consulting role.
- Implemented Employee Information Boards for each team which shows vital information including the top five defects, wastage, and efficiency measures.
- Developed some flexible work schedules which improved customer service.

QUALITY ASSURANCE MANAGER. (1987-93). Lawrence, KS. In a plant that employed 2,500 people, managed and directed plant quality efforts through process evaluations, quality measurements, and cycle time reductions; supervised 42 people and managed a budget of $1.9 million.
- Instituted educational and training programs that improved line efficiencies by 30% and produced cost savings of at least $200,000.
- Developed and implemented a Quality Demerit System which the company now uses corporate-wide; the Quality Demerit System transformed four manufacturing plants from a quality level of 67% defect-free product to the consumer in 1982, to 98.2% defect-free in 1999. Goal for 2000 is 99.0% defect-free product.

INSPECTION SUPERVISOR. (1981-87). Wichita, KS. Developed, managed, and directed the vendor certification program with the result that the customer service level was raised to 99%.
- Led efforts to enhance the Just-In-Time (JIT) process which saved millions of dollars in operating costs and lowered inventory carrying costs.

EDUCATION	Completing MBA in my spare time at New Haven University; degree anticipated 2000. B.A. with Major in Psychology, Southern Illinois University, Carbondale, IL, 1981. Numerous executive development courses including training in QA ISO 9001.
AFFILIATIONS	Member, American Management Society; American Society of Quality Control; and Southern Aerosol Technical Association.
PERSONAL	Can provide outstanding personal and professional references.

Date

Exact Name of Person
Title or Position
Name of Company
Address (number and street)
Address (city, state, and zip)

**Regional Manager,
Concrete Industry**

This professional has been
approached by competitors in his
industry, and he is responding
selectively to their approaches.

Dear Exact Name of Person: (or Sir or Madam if answering a blind ad.)

With the enclosed resume, I would like to make you aware of my interest in the possibility of putting my strong management, production operations, and sales background to work for your company. Please treat my enquiry as highly confidential at this point. Although I can provide outstanding personal and professional references at the appropriate time, I do not wish my current employer to be aware of my interest in your company.

As you will see from my enclosed resume, I have been in the multi-purpose concrete applications business my entire working life. I began in entry-level positions with a small concrete business in northern Iowa and was promoted to Plant Manager and Sales Manager. Then I joined Smith & Son, Inc. where I tripled production and transformed that company into an attractive acquisition candidate which caught the attention of Bullworth Concrete. When Bullworth Concrete Company bought Smith & Son in 1992, I became a Division Manager and in 1994 was promoted to Regional Manager.

In my current position I manage operations at 10 divisions while supervising three Division Managers and overseeing activities of 85 people at 10 locations. I also supervise four sales and customer service professionals while preparing budgets for each of the 10 divisions.

If you can use a versatile professional with a thorough understanding of all facets of the concrete applications business, I hope you will contact me to suggest a time when we might meet. Should you have ambitious goals in either the production management or sales area, I feel certain that my extensive industry knowledge and contacts could be useful.

Sincerely,

Harvey Herron

HARVEY HERRON

1110½ Hay Street, Fayetteville, NC 28305 • preppub@aol.com • (910) 483-6611

OBJECTIVE	To benefit an organization that can use an experienced manager with exceptional organizational skills who offers a background in managing multi-plant operations and expertise in multi-purpose concrete applications.
EDUCATION	Business Administration studies, Faison Technical College, Faison, IA, 1974. Completed numerous seminars including AGC Seminars, Capital Associated Industries Seminars; also completed extensive training related to EPA, DOT Procedures Applications, and other areas.
CERTIFICATIONS	ACI Certified; NRMCA Sales Certified
AFFILIATIONS	Member, Homebuilders Association Former President, Iowa Concrete Association, Faison Chapter
EXPERIENCE	*With Bullworth Concrete Company, have been promoted to positions of increasing responsibility by this multi-purpose concrete company while playing a key role in annual sales increases of more than 10%:*

1996-present: **REGIONAL MANAGER.** Faison, IA. Was promoted to this position from Division Manager for this region with multimillion-dollar annual sales; am continuing to provide valuable leadership in producing outstanding sales and profits after helping the company achieve its record year in 1999.
- Manage operations at 10 divisions while supervising three Division Managers and overseeing activities of 85 people at 10 locations.
- Supervise four Customer Service and Sales Representatives.
- Prepare annual budgets for each of the 10 division locations.
- Am accountable for production of 250,000 yards of concrete annually.

1992-96: **DIVISION MANAGER.** Bladen, IA. While overseeing three divisions, provided supervisory oversight of 30 people while directing production, maintenance, safety, and sales activities related to the production of 55,000 cubic yards of concrete annually for such applications as bridges, waste water treatment plants, as well as commercial and industrial buildings.

Joined Bullworth Concrete Company when Bullworth bought Smith and Son, Inc., a northern Iowa company which I had transformed into an attractive acquisition candidate while excelling in the following history of promotion:
1983-92: Was **GENERAL MANAGER** at Smith and Son, Inc., during these years while tripling production from 12,000 cubic yards to 36,000 cubic yards annually; managed ten truck operations.
- Directed operation of central shop for the entire company.

PLANT MANAGER & SALES MANAGER. Granger Concrete, Walton, IA (1974-83). Started with this company as a truck driver and learned the business from the ground up; was promoted to Plant Manager and then to Sales Manager, and made major contributions to the company in both roles.
- Trained and managed two sales people.
- Sold and managed production of 36,000 cubic yards of concrete annually.
- Managed operations with 12 drivers at two sites.
- Before promotion into the management ranks, worked for the company as a Loader Operator and Mechanic in addition to Truck Driver; these early experiences gave me first-hand knowledge of how the concrete industry works on the ground floor of operations.

PERSONAL	Excellent personal and professional references. Outstanding reputation.

Date

Exact Name of Person
Title or Position
Name of Company
Address (number and street)
Address (city, state, and ZIP)

Retail Mall Manager

This senior retailer took an early retirement when it was offered by his employer, but after a few months of golf and tennis, he decided he was too young to retire. He didn't want to resume the rugged schedule he'd worked previously, but he did want to explore the possibility of part-time work and consulting assignments.

Dear Exact Name of Person: (or Dear Sir or Madam if answering a blind ad.)

With the enclosed resume, I would like to indicate my interest in your organization and my desire to explore employment opportunities.

An experienced retailer and multi-unit manager, I recently took an early retirement while working in Europe, but after six months of golf and tennis, I have determined that I am too young and energetic to retire professionally. Therefore, I have decided to explore opportunities with prominent U.S. retailers. I am open to the possibility of serving your needs on a part-time or consulting basis, and I would welcome the opportunity to travel as extensively as your needs require.

I hope you will welcome my call soon to arrange a brief meeting at your convenience to discuss your current and future needs and how I might serve them. Thank you in advance for your time.

Sincerely yours.

Ellis Turner

Alternate last paragraph:
I hope you will call or write me soon to suggest a time convenient for us to meet and discuss your current and future needs and how I might serve them. Thank you in advance for your time.

ELLIS TURNER

1110½ Hay Street, Fayetteville, NC 28305 • preppub@aol.com • (910) 483-6611

OBJECTIVE	I want to contribute to an organization that can use an experienced professional with expertise related to the management of retailing and service operations as well as the design and implementation of systems designed for loss prevention, accountability, and control.
AWARDS	Received seven **Excellence** awards and five **Special Recognition** and **Superior Accomplishment** awards citing my extraordinary achievements in turning around troubled operations, boosting profitability and consumer satisfaction, and generating enthusiastic merchandising presentations.
EXPERIENCE	**RETAIL MANAGER, MAIN STORE.** Army and Air Force Exchange Service (AAFES), Italy (1995-99). Was specially selected to take over a mall-type operation with total annual sales of $9 million which was losing between 2% and 8% yearly as a percentage of gross product; transformed this complex operation with 13 different facilities into an operation that, by 1996, was making an 8% profit after expenses with a more-than-doubled annual sales volume of $20 million.

* Directly managed 175 employees.
* Within a few weeks after taking the job, initiated changes which streamlined operations and reduced unacceptable accountability losses.
* Managed this diversified mall operation including procurement, merchandising, and operations management while managing inventories of up to $30 million per year.
* Oversaw vendor contact to assure timely stock replenishment of open-end and direct-delivery orders; supervised maintenance of inventory management documents.
* Improved the security of cash, fixed assets, and merchandise inventory.
* Became known for my innovative approach to researching and developing marketing ideas; set up retail outlets from scratch and drew up stock assortments, managed fixturization, and all other start-up details.

RETAIL MANAGER. AAFES, Belgium (1989-95). Took over an operation which was losing money and experiencing out-of-control accountability problems and produced sales increases of more than 300% while restoring profitability and acceptable levels of accountability; supervised 94 personnel.

* Boosted annual sales to nearly $15 million.
* Closed smaller outlets and consolidated categories of merchandise into one complex, thereby decreasing costs and improving consumer satisfaction.
* Maintained a very hands-on style in managing the renovations and refixturizations which resulted in a greatly enhanced image and superior merchandising environments.
* Became known for my fair and straightforward management style, and for my knack for attracting reliable, conscientious individuals who became excellent retailers.

Other AAFES experience:
* As a **Supervising Detective**, managed a force of 20 to 25 detectives working at locations in Europe to solve theft and other accountability problems at retail outlets of all sizes.
* Excelled in positions as an **Assistant Retail Manager**, **Sales and Merchandise Manager**, and **Combined Activities Manager.**

EDUCATION	Completed more than four years of executive development training in all areas of retailing and operations management including:

security management	surveillance	loss prevention
sales and merchandising	fashion merchandising	customer service
softlines merchandising	hardlines merchandising	profit protection

PERSONAL	Can provide outstanding personal and professional references.

Date

Mr. Cliff Dawson
Executive Search Unlimited
112 Braer Avenue, Suite 120
Tampa, FL 32087

**Retail General
Merchandise Manager**

If you want to compare the
resumes of two senior
retailers, compare this resume
of Mr. Gomez with the resume
of Mr. Turner on the previous
page. Mr. Gomez is selectively
exploring opportunities with
prominent retailers.

Dear Cliff:

With the enclosed resume, I would like to confidentially express my interest in the senior management position which is available with Filene's Department Store.

As you will see from my resume, as General Merchandise Manager with Macy's, I am currently supervising a 25-store operation. Previously I enjoyed a track record of success with Jason's Department Store, where I excelled as Market Research Director, Buyer, and then as Divisional Sales Manager.

I am known for my innovative approach to retailing and have earned respect throughout the industry for my entrepreneurial spirit, negotiating and communication skills, as well as my extensive financial knowledge.

Although I am held in high regard by Macy's and take much pride in the superior sales and gross margin results I have produced, I am seeking an opportunity to express my strategic thinking skills and leadership ability in a more senior management position within a company which seeks aggressive growth. From what I have learned about Filene's Department Store and its expansion strategy, there may be an excellent fit between my extensive and diversified experience and the goals of the company. I am known for my ability to take a concept and turn it into an operating reality. I offer a proven ability to "make it happen" in retailing.

In addition to my B.S. in Business, I offer vast knowledge of financial products and services, including pensions, annuities, and mutual funds.

I can provide superior personal and professional references, and I would be delighted to make myself available for an interview.

Sincerely,

Milton Gomez

MILTON GOMEZ

1110½ Hay Street, Fayetteville, NC 28305 • preppub@aol.com • (910) 483-6611

OBJECTIVE To benefit an ambitious company that can use an innovative and experienced retailer who has excelled professionally utilizing my strategic planning ability, strong bottom-line orientation, solid management skills, and proven ability to produce captivating merchandising experiences for the consumer.

EXPERIENCE **GENERAL MERCHANDISE MANAGER.** Macy's Department Store, Washington, DC (1994-present). Am excelling in handling responsibilities equivalent to those of a General Merchandise Manager while supervising a 25-store operation.
- Supervise a staff of Buyers, Assistant Buyers, and a Pool Stock Supervisor.
- Am responsible for generating sales and gross margin, merchandise mix, and advertising.
- Achieved eight percent average annual sales growth each year since 1994 with no sacrifice of margin percent.
- Negotiated special events and promotions, including:
     Miller Rogaska Master Cutter Showcase
     Lenox China Command Performance
     Personal Appearances by Miss Teen USA and Mrs. America
     Liz Claiborne Special Event
     Spode Blue Room special event presentation with *Better Homes* Editor
     Audrey Table Linen Trunk Show

DIVISIONAL SALES MANAGER. Homestore and Mens. Jason's Department Store, Tampa, FL (1988-94). Was rehired immediately by Jason's because of my prior excellent performance and placed in a senior management role; supervised 60 personnel including four Area Managers.
- Increased sales, reduced shrinkage, and managed stock content and inventory levels at optimum levels.
- On my own initiative, developed exciting new sales and motivational presentation which improved performance and morale.
- Selected by General Manager to assume additional duties of Operations Manager.
- Received specialized training in the computerized retail management system, and then played a key role in bringing the system online and training in-store personnel.

FINANCIAL REPRESENTATIVE. Florida Life Company, Ft. Lauderdale, FL (1986-88). In a brief career change from retailing, gained vast knowledge of financial products while achieving outstanding results in selling financial products to professionals and businesses.
- Although I was excelling in a new field, I decided that retailing was what I wanted to do, and Jason's welcomed me back and promoted me from my former position.

BUYER & MARKET RESEARCH DIRECTOR. Jason's Department Store, Tampa, FL (1978-85). Excelled in the following track record of promotion:
- *Buyer, Towel and Bath Shop* (1984-85). Had complete financial and merchandising responsibility for the Towel and Bath Shops throughout Jason's $3.8 million 16-store operation; generated sales and developed gross margin and profit; improved annual sales by 20%.
- *Market Research Director.* (1980-84). Played a significant role in many new initiatives while directing the company's strategic planning and strategic thinking; performed analysis of financial, statistical, and marketing data including sales and stock planning, new store site selection, demographic studies, and profit analysis.

EDUCATION **B.S. degree in Business,** University of Pittsburgh, Pittsburgh, PA, 1978.

PERSONAL Former President, Jason's Employees Credit Union. Active in church activities.

Date

Exact Name of Person
Title or Position
Name of Company
Address (number and street)
Address (city, state, and zip)

School Principal

This senior manager has excelled as a principal and has worked in a school environment throughout her career. Now she's curious about the corporate world, and her resume and cover letter are designed to attract the attention of corporations which can use her ability to direct training programs. While this cover letter is designed to explore opportunities in the corporate world, she could use the same resume with a different cover letter designed strictly to seek other principal or administrative positions if she so desires.

Dear Exact Name of Person: (or Dear Sir or Madam if answering a blind ad.)

With the enclosed resume, I would like to indicate my interest in your organization and my desire to explore employment opportunities.

As you will see from my enclosed resume, as an executive in the academic world, I have excelled in supervising and training others as well as in "selling" ideas and concepts to people including public citizens, children, teaching professionals, and school board members. Although I have excelled in my profession and have greatly enjoyed the challenge of educating young minds, I have decided to change careers and embark upon a "second career" in sales and marketing. I am confident that my naturally outgoing personality as well as my proven ability to "win friends and influence people" will enable me to be highly successful in any sales and marketing area.

I hope you will welcome my call soon to arrange a brief meeting at your convenience to discuss your current and future needs and how I might serve them. Thank you in advance for your time.

Sincerely yours.

Myrna Macias

Alternate last paragraph:
I hope you will call or write me soon to suggest a time convenient for us to meet and discuss your current and future needs and how I might serve them. Thank you in advance for your time.

MYRNA MACIAS

1110½ Hay Street, Fayetteville, NC 28305 • preppub@aol.com • (910) 483-6611

OBJECTIVE

To offer a background of achievements in developing innovative and exciting new programs, providing a fair and confident leadership style, and displaying an enthusiastic and open personality to an organization that can use an articulate and talented administrator.

EXPERIENCE

PRINCIPAL. The Casey School, Lawton, OK (1997-present). For a 400-student pre-kindergarten through fourth grade facility, am implementing change in a school which had the same principal for 30 years.

- Provide strong leadership and keep the school operating smoothly despite the fact that half of the staff changes at the end of each school year due to redistricting issues, the opening of new schools, and the normal turnover in a military community.
- Quickly earned the respect and trust of community members in an environment where support was strong for change and progress.
- Have excelled in dealing with budget procedures including keeping within government guidelines for average daily members and per-pupil cost.

PRINCIPAL. Baker School, Milton, OK (1987-97). Developed a number of creative, fun, and interesting programs which helped the school earn a reputation for being "on the cutting edge" with a very real spirit of team work and growth as teachers and staff learned to work together.

- Used a variety of resources and materials to prepare and write programs for staff development activities while focusing on providing staff members with information and the opportunity to earn CEU (continuing education units) credit and to assist them in advancing toward highly original and progressive styles of teaching.
- Played a significant role in developing sources for additional funding by researching and writing grants which resulted in funds for computers, math and science programs, reading programs, and a writing center.

ASSISTANT PRINCIPAL. Findley School, Macon, OK (1982-87). Learned to be a catalyst for change and progress while supervising the kindergarten teachers and custodial staff in a school with approximately 650 students; took on additional responsibilities as a staff development planner, test coordinator, observer/evaluator, and co-administrator.

EDUCATION

Have completed 36 hours in an Ed.D. degree program in Education Administration, University of Oklahoma, adjunct campus in Lawton, OK.
Master's degree in Education Administration, Southern Nazarene University, OK, 1987.
B.S. in Elementary Education, Southern Nazarene University, Bethany, OK, 1981.

TRAINING

Continuously attend training programs, courses, and seminars such as the following:

Higher-level Thinking Skills Workshops	Creative Leadership Workshops
Junior Great Books Leadership Workshops	Hands-on Science Workshops
Technology in Schools Conferences	Science Conferences
National Elementary Principals' Conferences	Multi-age Teaching Seminars

PROGRAMMING EXPERTISE

Applied my creativity and implementational skills in developing a wide range of programs:
Wellness Program—addressed all aspects of physical wellness from nutrition and food preparation, to skin care, to dancing and aerobics.
Publishing Center—motivated students to write a book and publish it—wrote the grant and used funds from the Burlington Corporation to fund the program.
Reading Is Fundamental (RIF)—received funds which allowed the program to distribute free books three times a year (funds were provided through grants from Hallmark and Nestle's).

PERSONAL

Have often been described as decisive, fair, energetic, and supportive. Have a talent for bringing out the best in others. Am familiar with Windows, Word 6.0, and IBM-compatible graphics/word processing software. Dynamic and caring leader. Excellent references.

TO: Search Committee
FROM: John Mertz
RE: Position of Executive Vice President, National Association of Financial Consultants

**Trade Association Program
Director**

Sometimes a letter must be
addressed to multiple readers, as is
the case with Mr. Mertz's cover
letter. He is sending this letter to
the Search Committee comprised
of 10 members which is trying to
find the right candidate to fill the
top spot in a non-profit
organization.

In response to the urging of someone familiar with your search for an Executive Vice President for the National Association of Financial Consultants, I am sending you a resume which summarizes my background. I offer a unique combination of knowledge, experience, and abilities which I believe would ideally suit the requirements of the National Association of Financial Consultants.

Health industry expertise

You will see from my resume that I offer expertise related to health insurance and underwriting. In my current job I have sought out and negotiated contracts with major insurance companies to provide insurance for the organization. On a $1 million budget, I have developed insurance programs which generated $2 million in net income based on $32 million in premium. These highly regarded programs which I developed have brought 6,000 new members into the organization.

Proven executive ability

I offer proven executive ability. I have earned a reputation as someone who has not only strategic vision and imagination but also the tenacity and persistence to follow through on the "nitty-gritty" details of implementing new projects, programs, and concepts. I know how to delegate, and I know how to "micro manage," and I am skilled at tailoring my management style to particular circumstances while always shouldering full responsibility and accountability for results. My current job has involved the responsibility of recruiting, training, and continuously developing a national sales force of brokers throughout the U.S. which broke with the tradition of passive mail solicitation and led to dramatic growth in sales and profitability. With a strong "bottom-line" orientation, I have streamlined headquarters staff and reduced central office expenses to save at least half a million dollars while continuously supervising the association's five regional offices in the recruitment and training of more than 1,200 insurance agents nationally.

Extensive association experience

You will also see from my resume that I am accustomed to "getting things done" within the unique environment of a trade/membership association. I am well known for my ability to attract and retain a cohesive and productive staff, and I am also respected for my exceptional skills in relating to, inspiring, and supporting key volunteer members. A skilled communicator, I have made countless speeches.

I am aware of the requirements defined by the search committee, and I would enjoy the opportunity to discuss this position further with the Executive Committee. I feel certain I could contribute significantly to the growth and financial health of the National Association of Financial Consultants as its Executive Vice President. Thank you for your time and consideration.

JOHN MERTZ

1110½ Hay Street, Fayetteville, NC 28305 • preppub@aol.com • (910) 483-6611

OBJECTIVE

To contribute to the growth and financial health of an organization that needs a savvy, creative executive with expert knowledge of the health insurance/underwriting industry along with a proven ability to innovate, manage, motivate, coordinate, communicate, and troubleshoot within the unique environment of a membership association.

EXPERIENCE

DIRECTOR, MEMBERS' INSURANCE. National Association of Home Builders, Washington, DC (1984-present). Have excelled in originating insurance programs for the members of NAHB; developed highly regarded insurance programs which brought 6,000 new members into the organization while producing millions of dollars in net income.

- Sought out and negotiated contracts with major insurance companies to provide insurance for the organization.
- On a $1 million operating budget, developed insurance programs which generated $2 million in net income based on $32 million in premium.
- Recruited, trained, and continuously developed a national sales force of NAHB brokers throughout the U.S. which first, arrested declining sales that were the result of passive mail solicitations and second, dramatically boosted sales and profitability.
- Streamlined headquarters staff and reduced central office expenses, resulting in a $500,000 savings; developed annual programs of work and budgets.
- Supervise five regional offices in the recruitment and training of more than 1,200 insurance agents nationally.
- Closely monitor government affairs related to health insurance; maintain excellent relationships with governmental regulatory bodies and state departments of insurance.
- Maintain liaison with association personnel in charge of operations, legislation, education, public relations, and communications as well as with the executive committee.
- Am known for my extraordinary ability to attract, develop, and retain a cohesive and productive staff and for my talent in motivating and inspiring key volunteer leadership.

Other experience:

NATIONAL MEMBERSHIP FIELD DIRECTOR. NAHB, Washington, DC. Was promoted to this position after excelling as **Membership Director for Midwestern and Western U.S. and Canada**; formulated and implemented national membership programs and campaigns that led to the development of new units in the U.S. and Canada.

VICE PRESIDENT OF MARKETING. SETCO, Inc., Los Angeles, CA. Developed marketing programs for manufacturing and marketing companies owned by conglomerate.

LIFE AND HEALTH INSURANCE BROKER. Universal Insurance Agency, Chicago, IL. Was a property and casualty underwriter as well as a life and health insurance broker.

EDUCATION & TRAINING

Hold a Bachelor of Arts (B.A.) degree, Drake University, Des Moines, IA.
Complete yearly 15 hours of continuing education to maintain Life and Health Insurance Broker's license.
Took numerous courses to comply with life and health insurance industry requirements.

PERSONAL

Have given numerous speeches and made hundreds of personal appearances. Am known for my ability to ensure optimum utilization of personnel. Offer a reputation for integrity.

Date

Exact Name of Person
Title or Position
Name of Company
Address (number and street)
Address (city, state, and zip)

**Vice President of
Management Information
Systems (MIS)**

This Vice President of
Management Information Systems
gets calls from recruiters all the
time, but if he makes a change, he
wants it to be for a truly superior
job in a superior location. He is
trying to think strategically about
his career and decide whether he
should move to another
applications environment or to a
software design environment,
where he would be at the leading
edge of technology.

Dear Exact Name of Person: (or Dear Sir or Madam if answering a blind ad.)

With the enclosed resume, I would like to make you aware of my considerable background in the management of information systems and in the development of state-of-the-art software and business applications.

As you will see from my resume, I was recruited in 1994 by a fast-growing corporation experiencing rapid expansion to oversee the design and implementation of its MIS activities at 80 store locations. I was promoted to Vice President of Management Information Systems in the process of making major contributions to efficiency, productivity, and profitability. We have replaced store computers with a Windows-based system that reduced manual record keeping and since then I have been designing the implementation of the second phase of this re-engineering project. We are also developing an intranet for stores, supervisors, and other office personnel, and I have personally designed and conducted training and support for all job levels, from top executives, to store management, to entry-level employees.

In my prior position, I was promoted in a track record of advancement with a company which developed software products for the telecommunications industry. During that time I transformed a failing operation which was losing money into an efficient and profitable business while reengineering a product which became the industry's #1 seller.

My software knowledge is vast, as you will also see from my resume, and I offer recent experience with C++ as well as Intranet and HTML.

I can provide outstanding personal and professional references at the appropriate time, and I can assure you in advance that I have a reputation for building and maintaining effective working relationships with people at all organizational levels. If my considerable skills, experience, and talents interest you, please contact me. Thank you in advance for your professional courtesies.

Sincerely,

Robert Schniepp

ROBERT SCHNIEPP

1110½ Hay Street, Fayetteville, NC 28305 • preppub@aol.com • (910) 483-6611

OBJECTIVE   To offer my creative problem-solving approach and experience in management information systems design and implementation to a company that needs a resourceful expert with highly refined supervisory and communication skills.

EXPERIENCE   **VICE PRESIDENT OF MANAGEMENT INFORMATION SYSTEMS (MIS).** Stop Fast Convenience Stores, Lawrence, KS (1994-present). Was recruited by this fast-growing corporation which employs more than 500 people and operates 80 stores grossing over $150 million annually to analyze its current MIS structure and to design MIS systems which would be compatible with strategic goals and accommodate continued rapid growth.
- Began with the company as MIS Manager and was promoted to VP, MIS.
- In 1994 determined that the company's current computer system consisting of an IBM S/36 and store PCs would not facilitate the company's objectives; implemented Novell Network on a UNIX system for corporate accounting.
- Performed extensive research on systems and networks available; selected potential vendors and negotiated the final contract.
- Functioned as co-developer of the implementation strategy with the software vendor in order to reduce standard implementation time by 32%.
- Replaced store computers with a Windows-based system that reduced manual record keeping by store managers while providing for daily transmittal of sales, purchases, cash, and inventory levels to corporate office.
- Have designed the implementation of the second phase of this reengineering project, integrating the gas console, fuel tanks, credit cards, money orders, time clock, and cash registers: this system has resulted in increased store manager time for managing while reducing the number of errors made at the store-level and transmitted to the corporate host system.
- Am developing an **intranet** for stores, supervisors, and other office personnel to utilize for faster communication and more efficient decision making.

DIRECTOR OF DEVELOPMENT. Carbon Industries, Inc., Tampa, FL (1989-94). Was promoted to oversee product development related to software for telecommunications companies; stepped into a situation where we were losing customers and sales because of poor product design and delivery.
- Transformed a failing operation which was losing money and customers into an efficient and profitable business which enjoyed four years of steady growth; the product I reengineered is now the #1 product in its industry.
- Managed a budget of $1.2 million and a development staff of 25 programmers.

VICE-PRESIDENT OF DEVELOPMENT. Kaypro Systems and Analysis, Inc., Jacksonville, FL (1982-89). For a company providing custom software for home health care companies, was responsible for the analysis, design, programming, testing, and support of all products; managed 15 programmers and testers.

SKILLS   **Software**: Visual Basic, Visual C++, C, Progress, Informix, Access, Pascal, COBOL, Micro-Focus COBOL, AcuCOBOL, Assembler, Basic, Fortran, Intranet, HTML
Hardware: HP, Data General AViiONs, IBM RS6000, NCR Tower, NCR 3000 series, Data General MV series, IBM S/36, IBM-PC compatibles
Operating Systems: Literate in most operating systems, with extensive experience in Windows 95, Windows NT, Novell, Windows, UNIX, AIX, HP/UX, DG/UX, XENIX, AOS/VS, MVS, DOS

EDUCATION   Beacon University, Beacon, SC, BS in Computer Science, 1982.

Top executives share common advantages and disadvantages which are unique to their "station" in the work force.

Problems faced by the top executive

Like the senior manager who feels that he might be "punished" in his job hunt for simply being an older job hunter, the top executive feels that age might be a disadvantage. Furthermore, many people look at the top executive and think "expensive." Another problem faced by the top executive is that he simply has fewer possible organizational options because he is seeking a spot on the top levels. The competition is intense for those top spots, especially when you consider that the executive may be an "outsider" rather than an organizational veteran. Research has shown that most chief executive officers (CEOs) get their jobs through a slow promotion over more than 20 years of loyal service to the organization.

A practical problem of the top executive is often how to "cram" all his information onto one page. Should the resume of the top executive be longer than one page? We don't think so, although it certainly is not "against the rules" to have a two-pager. Remember that a resume is usually accompanied by a cover letter and, even if you are a top executive, prospective employers don't want to read more than two pages about you in order to decide if they want to meet you! Remember, too, that the more you tell people at the resume stage, the more opportunity you provide to get yourself "screened out" by some details.

Advantages of the top executive

Almost by definition, the top executive has had an exciting career, so it should be possible for her to open many doors. Showing a track record of accomplishments and achievements is usually not hard for the top executive! The top executive frequently has accumulated an extensive network of contacts both inside and outside her industry, so she can utilize those contacts in opening some doors. Networking works extremely well for top executives in a job hunt.

The top executive, like all the rest of us in the work force, must figure out what he really wants to do next.

Does the top executive job-hunt differently than other workers?

Not really. The top executive may answer ads in his job hunt, just like other job hunters, although many of those ads may be in "The Wall Street Journal" and other prominent business publications. The top executive may seek help from employment placement specialists, but his form of help may be a "headhunter" or executive recruiter rather than a regular employment agency. Like all other job hunters, the top executive would be smart to choose his next employer by deciding if he wants to look (1) by industry or (2) by geography, or both. For example, a top executive may identify employers to approach by deciding that she would like to live in Seattle, Atlanta, or Houston and that she would prefer working in the telecommunications, banking, or credit card industry. By using the "direct approach," the top executive can then identify employers for whom he would like to work and send a resume and cover letter making attractive potential employers aware of his availability and interest in the company. The top executive, like all the rest of us, must try to figure out what he really wants to do next!

Date

Exact Title
Company Name
Address (street and number)
Address (city, state, and zip)

Chief Executive Officer

With classic credentials including the Harvard Business School, this top executive has worked for only two companies. He is seeking a new challenge that will further test his ability to optimize efficiency and maximize profitability.

Dear Exact Name of Person: (or Dear Sir or Madam if answering a blind ad.)

Can you use an experienced top executive with a proven track record of success in transforming small business entities into large-scale, multi-unit operations while assuring that all core systems are carefully designed and implemented to assure maximum profitability and efficiency?

With an MBA from the Harvard Business School, I have most recently led a small three-unit company operating in one state to become a major competitor in its industry while aggressively expanding into 12 states. Even though I am excelling in my job and am held in high regard by the board of directors, I am selectively exploring the possibility of joining a growth-oriented company which can use my proven ability to maximize profit and efficiency while building dynamic teams of highly motivated individuals. Although I can provide outstanding personal and professional references at the appropriate time, I would appreciate your holding my inquiry in confidence at this time.

Prior to assuming my current position, I refined my business skills in a track record of accomplishment in the retailing business. Throughout my more than 20 years of experience, I was effective in training and leading personnel to achieve historical sales records. Through my knowledge of marketing and merchandising, I increased sales and profits in every store and territory I managed and was successful in managing major expansion projects.

If you can use my considerable business acumen and experience, I hope you will call or write me soon to suggest a time when we might meet to discuss your current and future needs and how I might serve them. Thank you in advance for your time.

Sincerely,

Vincent Trossbach

Alternate last paragraph:
I hope you will welcome my call soon to arrange a time for us to discuss your current and future needs and how I might serve them. Thank you in advance for your time.

VINCENT TROSSBACH

1110½ Hay Street, Fayetteville, NC 28305 • preppub@aol.com • (910) 483-6611

OBJECTIVE

To benefit an organization that can use an experienced executive with a history of success in turning around unprofitable locations, designing and implementing cost control systems, and building teams of dedicated workers.

EDUCATION & TRAINING

M.B.A., Harvard Business School, Boston, MA, 1977
B.A. in English, University of North Carolina at Chapel Hill, NC, 1973

EXPERIENCE

CHIEF EXECUTIVE OFFICER AND PRESIDENT. Specialty Products, Inc., Chicago, IL (1991-present). Through my aggressive leadership of a privately owned retailing business, have transformed it from an operation with three stores in one state to 50 stores in 12 states; we are still expanding and I believe that savvy selection and thorough training of the right people is the key to continued growth and profitability.

- Was recruited by this company to assume the CEO position because of my reputation as an innovative leader and retailing executive with an aggressive bottom-line orientation.
- Worked closely with the director of operations to develop job descriptions and business plans, then hired and trained the management personnel for each location.
- While working closely with our advertising agency, have emphasized the creation of exciting sales promotions and advertising campaigns; hired and trained people whom I consider some of the world's finest merchandisers and retailers.
- Hired and worked closely with computer programmers who have established a point-of-sale and automatic replenishment system that is unique in the industry and which has dramatically lowered inventory carrying costs.

Advanced in the following track record of promotion, Gainey Corporation:
VICE PRESIDENT, SOUTHEAST REGION. Bentonville, AR (1989-91). On my own initiative, implemented numerous changes which boosted efficiency and profitability of the 120-store region which I managed and nurtured to its all-time high in sales and profitability.

TERRITORY MANAGER. Huntsville, AL (1988-89). Applied creative management skills which guided this territory to achieve more than $100 million in annual sales in 1989, a 9% increase over 1988.

STORE MANAGER. Decatur, AL (1984-87). Handpicked to take over an 85-90 employee store scheduled to be closed, implemented aggressive promotions and marketing which "saved" the store and subsequently led to a major expansion to 96,000 square feet; transformed it into a record-setting model store which is still in operation today.

- Guided a sales force which led the nation's 1,500 stores in sales; achieved an increase to $1.1 million from $580,000 in sales for the garden center.

STORE MANAGER. McMinnville, TN (1982-84). Challenged by the competition of having a Super K-Mart built only one-fourth of a mile away, increased profit margins 50% and sales from $2 million to $8.5 million during a two-year time period as manager of this 60,000-square-foot store with 55 employees.

Highlights of earlier experience: Advanced in retail management roles as Merchandise Manager and Assistant Manager where my accomplishments included setting up one store's POS system, developing assistant managers in a training store, and day-to-day management of an $18.5 million store.

- Was aggressively recruited by the Gainey Corporation upon graduation from the Harvard Business School; learned the ropes of retailing.

PERSONAL

Have a reputation as a detail-oriented and self-motivated individual. Am skilled in applying common sense and sound judgment to make decisions and develop solutions.

Date

Exact Name of Person
Title or Position
Name of Company
Address (number and street)
Address (city, state, and zip)

Chief Executive Officer

Although this top executive was offered a position by the corporation which acquired his employer, he has decided not to remain with the company. It's best to communicate that fact in the cover letter so that prospective employers don't feel he is being rejected.

Dear Exact Name of Person: (or Sir or Madam if answering a blind ad.)

With the enclosed resume, I would like to make you aware of my interest in joining your management team in some capacity in which you could utilize my proven skills in increasing profit, cutting costs, restructuring operations for greater efficiency, and improving market share.

I was recruited for my most recent position, which involved directing the operations of a home improvements company with two manufacturing plants and a distribution warehouse. Through my leadership, we boosted revenue from $48 million in 1998 to $64 million in 1999 and the company was acquired by Capel Industries. Although I have played a key role in its divestiture, I have decided not to remain with the company.

In my prior experience, I excelled in management positions with the General Electric Corporation and then with Baylor Industries, a $7 billion company which acquired General Electric's $1.1 billion electrical control and motor business. In one job as a Plant Manager, I transformed an unprofitable plant into a profitable one and then grew sales from $52 to $82 million. In another position as a Plant Manager, I increased sales 25% annually, from $83 million in 1994 to $148 million in 1996, while managing 800 employees, eight assembly sites, and $4.5 million in annual capital investments. In earlier jobs as a Product Line Manager with General Electric, I introduced new product lines and modified the way the company did business through its sales channels, customer base structure, investment strategy, pricing structure, and other areas.

If your company can utilize a strong and insightful leader, I would enjoy the opportunity to talk with you in person about your needs and how I might serve them. I offer a reputation as a visionary thinker, aggressive cost cutter, creative strategist, and resourceful opportunity finder. I believe a company must continuously analyze the ways it does business in order to assure maximum efficiency. For example, as a Plant Manager, I profitably outsourced shipping, logistics, mail, document management, and network maintenance functions previously performed internally, and we made highly profitable quality and productivity improvements. I have a strong customer orientation which was derived from my earliest jobs in technical sales and product line management.

If my executive abilities interest you, please contact me. I can provide outstanding references, and I am willing to relocate anywhere in the U.S.

Sincerely,

Milo Germano

MILO GERMANO

1110½ Hay Street, Fayetteville, NC 28305 • preppub@aol.com • (910) 483-6611

OBJECTIVE

To contribute to the profitability of an organization that can use a creative and resourceful executive who has introduced new product lines, restructured operations for greater productivity, and managed internal change in order to cut costs, improve quality, and increase market share.

EXPERIENCE

CHIEF EXECUTIVE OFFICER. Tyson Home Improvements, Winston, SC (1996-99). Was recruited by this home improvement products company with two manufacturing plants and a distribution warehouse; **boosted revenues from $48 million in 1998 to $64 million in 1999.**
- In large measure due to the results achieved through my leadership, the company became an acquisition target and was acquired by Capel, Inc. in 1999; assisted in the transition of the company to new management and was offered a top management role, but I have decided not to remain with Capel, Inc.
- Cut costs by $1 million in 1997; reduced management head count 30%; shrank inventories while simultaneously improving customer satisfaction; established controls to avoid the chronic inventory shortages which had plagued the company.
- Introduced JIT and Kanban while promoting a union-free, multi-racial environment.

Excelled in this "track record" of promotion within the General Electric Corporation, and then within Baylor Industries, a $7 billion company which acquired General Electric's $1.1 billion electrical control and distribution business:
PLANT MANAGER. Baylor Industries, Sheraton, GA (1994-96). Directed the plant during its period of greatest growth; **sales increased by 25% annually, from $83 million in 1994 to $148 million in 1996.** Managed 800 employees, eight sites assembling electrical motor control products, $4.5 million in annual capital investments, and an expense budget of $85 million.
- Introduced two new major product lines representing $115 million in sales.
- Implemented multiple marketing expert systems which reduced cycle times 50% while improving total quality; also introduced JIT II.
- Planned and implemented the consolidation of businesses from five locations to one without the loss of any major customers.
- Profitably invested $6 million in quality and productivity improvements which included advanced robotics, computer, phone, and other productivity equipment.
- Profitably outsourced shipping, logistics, mail, document management, and network maintenance functions previously performed internally.
- Reduced inventory by $2 million (25%) through Kanban, cycle-time improvements, fewer suppliers, and product rationalization; gained ISO 9002 certification on our first attempt.

PLANT MANAGER. General Electric Corporation, Dawson, GA (1988-94). Transformed an unprofitable business into a profitable one in my first year of managing this troubled plant; then **grew sales from $52 million to $82 million** over six years while growing market share by 19% and increasing price realization to become #2 in the market.

PRODUCT LINE MANAGER. General Electric Corporation, Philadelphia, PA (1981-88). Introduced product lines representing $40 million in investment and developed strategies including product migration and rationalization to increase market share.
- Changed customer base from OEM to dealer, which increased operating profit 20%; also shifted the sales channel from corporate direct to independent manufacturer's representatives, which reduced selling expenses by $500,000.
- In previous jobs with General Electric, excelled in **technical sales** and **customer service.**

EDUCATION

B.S. in Industrial Engineering, Virginia Tech, Blacksburg, VA.
Postgraduate courses in management, marketing, finance, and accounting at George Washington University, University of Dallas, University of Virginia, and Michigan State.

Date

Mr. David Frizelle
Personnel Director
City of Monterey
City Square, Suite 110
Monterey, CA 87098

Chief of Police Applicant

It is finally time to apply for the top job in a law enforcement organization, a job for which Mr. Miller has been grooming himself for years.

Dear Mr. Frizelle:

With the enclosed resume, I would like to formally initiate the process of becoming considered for the job of Chief of Police for the City of Monterey.

As you will see from my resume, I am currently serving the Los Angeles Police Department as a Police Captain in charge of one of the city's Patrol Divisions. As one of the department's Captains, I have transformed the city's newest Patrol Division into a highly respected and productive operating unit known for the high morale and productivity of its 192 personnel.

In previous jobs with the City of Los Angeles, I performed with distinction as Lieutenant in charge of both the Major Crimes Investigative Division and Emergency Operations. I began working for the City of Los Angeles as a Patrol Officer in 1978 after serving my country briefly in the U.S. Army as a Military Policeman. I have enjoyed a track record of promotion because of my hard work and common sense, my outstanding police work in all functional areas, as well as my excellent administrative skills and ability to deal articulately and tactfully with everyone, from employees to citizens' groups.

I can provide outstanding references at the appropriate time, and I can assure you that you would find me to be an individual who is known as a gifted strategic thinker, powerful motivator, and fair supervisor.

Please contact me if you would like me to make myself available for a personal interview at your convenience. Although I am held in high regard within the Los Angeles Police Department, I have a strong interest in exploring ways in which my leadership ability and extensive experience in all aspects of police work could be put to use for the City of Monterey as its Chief of Police.

Sincerely,

Daniel W. Miller

DANIEL W. MILLER

1110½ Hay Street, Fayetteville, NC 28305 • preppub@aol.com • (910) 483-6611

OBJECTIVE

I want to contribute to your city as its Chief of Police through my experience in all aspects of police operations as well as through my outstanding community relations skills, administrative abilities, and highly respected personal and professional style.

EXPERIENCE

Have excelled in this track record of promotion to increasing responsibilities within the Los Angeles Police Department, Los Angeles, CA:

POLICE CAPTAIN, PATROL SUPPORT DIVISION. (July 1997-present). In July 1997, was assigned to command the Patrol Support Division and the Police Sub-Station.
- In addition to motivating, supervising and evaluating a 192-person division comprised of Lieutenants, Sergeants, and Officers, skillfully handle a wide range of administrative responsibilities ranging from strategic planning to statistical analysis.
- Develop the overall budget for the Division and Sub-Station.
- Have made vast improvements in all areas under my management including the Traffic Section, Neighborhood Improvement Team, Housing Officers (Safe Streets Program), School Resource Officers, Mounted Police Unit, and Park Unit.

POLICE CAPTAIN, PATROL. (1996-July 1997). In 1996, was promoted to the rank of Captain and became one of the six Captains in this 420-person police department; was placed in charge of the newly formed 3rd Patrol Division and transformed the division's employees into a highly respected and productive operating unit.
- Motivated, supervised, and evaluated a 62-person division comprised of Lieutenants, Sergeants, and Officers.
- Developed portions of the overall annual budget and controlled budgeted expenses.

LIEUTENANT, MAJOR CRIMES INVESTIGATIVE DIVISION. (1995-96). While still serving in 1995 as Lieutenant in charge of Emergency Operations, was selected to take over as Lieutenant of the Major Crimes Investigative Division with nine Officers and one Sergeant.
- Provided leadership to a division in charge of investigating robberies and homicides; we had 100% clearance in homicides and an 84% clearance in robbery cases.

LIEUTENANT, EMERGENCY OPERATIONS. (1993-95). Commanded operations of the department's S.W.A.T. Team and Narcotic Vice Task Force; earned widespread respect for my work in revitalizing this area of police operations; took over a team which had made 200 felony arrests in 1993; led the team to make 365 felony arrests in only four months in 1994.

Highlights of other experience within the Los Angeles Police Department:
- **Unit Supervisor, Major Crimes Investigative Division.** (1990-91). As Sergeant of Police, supervised nine Investigators assigned to Crimes Against Persons and Property and was credited with producing an unusually high arrest rate.
- **Platoon Sergeant, Patrol Division.** (1985-90). Supervised 15 Officers while assigning patrol cases, evaluating effectiveness of divisional operations, and acting as Patrol Supervisor.
- **Sergeant of Police, Street Crimes Unit.** (1984-85). Planned and coordinated unit operations while supervising five Officers; also worked on active investigations.
- **Investigator, Street Crimes Unit.** (1982-84). Handled a wide range of duties as an Investigator related to vice, narcotics, drug operations, and intelligence gathering.
- **Field Training Officer.** (1980-82). Handled general patrol work as well as the training of newly appointed Police Officers; acted as supervisor in the absence of the Shift Supervisor.
- **Patrol Officer.** (1978-80). Performed with distinction all duties of a Patrol Officer.

EDUCATION

B.S. degree in Political Science, Los Angeles State University, LA, CA, 1985.
A.S. degree in Criminal Justice, Monterey Community College, Monterey, CA, 1983.
Hold Advanced, Intermediate, and Basic Law Enforcement Certificates.

Date

ACI, Inc.
Dept. B90
98 Caison Road
San Francisco, CA 90712
Re: Job Codes TEL/45/89

**Division President,
Telecommunications
Industry Firm**

Sometimes an early retirement
doesn't quench the appetite for
accomplishment. This top
executive is seeking a lower-level
job than the one from which he
retired, but he misses the
"action" of the corporate world.

Dear Sir or Madam:

I am sending you a resume describing my background with AT&T because I feel there might be a "fit" between your needs for an E & O Manager and my extensive management skills, telecommunications knowledge, and familiarity with Sprint operations.

As you will see, I recently opted for an early retirement from AT&T after serving the company with distinction. In my most recent position as President and General Manager of Engineering and Construction, I was handling responsibilities similar to those listed in your advertisement. While managing 300 personnel including managers, engineers, supervisors, craft, and clerical employees and supervising more than 200 contractors performing large-scale fiber optic/copper installations and maintenance, I was in charge of a $32 million budget. When the company merged with Zenith in 1993, I took over the physical and human resources of Zenith engineering/construction and was given the additional responsibility of reforming their organization into the AT&T Telephone structure. I offer experience in capital planning, negotiating local contracts, and managing capital budgets. I would welcome your investigation of my performance and background with AT&T and invite you to contact Human Resources.

I enjoyed working with AT&T and am very interested in three of the positions you advertised. I would also welcome the opportunity to serve on a contractual or consulting basis whether full- or part-time. Although I've enjoyed pursuing leisure activities since taking an early retirement, I have decided that (1) my golf game is not good enough for me to retire and (2) I am too young to retire! I am anxious to get back in the fast-paced work environment again.

If you can use an astute and energetic executive who is eager to make valuable contributions to your company as I have previously done with AT&T, please contact me and I will make myself available at your convenience. You would find me in person to be a youthful and vigorous manager who could have a great deal to offer your organization.

Sincerely yours,

John G. Ansardi

JOHN G. ANSARDI

1110½ Hay Street, Fayetteville, NC 28305 • preppub@aol.com • (910) 483-6611

OBJECTIVE

To benefit an organization that can use a respected executive with highly refined strategic planning and problem-solving skills who has expertly managed multimillion-dollar budgets, capital expansion projects, and large-scale responses to natural disasters including hurricanes/tornadoes while supervising unionized and non-unionized personnel.

EXPERIENCE

Recently declined a promotion and took an early retirement after a distinguished career and track record of promotion with AT&T:
PRESIDENT, ENGINEERING AND CONSTRUCTION DIVISION. Frankfort, IN (1993-1999). After the company merged with Zenith, was promoted to oversee all engineering and construction activities in the South Region, and assumed responsibility for the physical and human resources formerly under Zenith management.

Management of Human Resources:
- Managed 300 engineers and professionals including district managers; also provided oversight management of 200 contractors who provided engineering/construction services; negotiated and supervised the proper administration of contracts/agreements.
- Gained rigorous experience operating in a union environment and became skilled at union negotiations, handling grievance procedures, and resolving disputes in a timely and fair manner; was entrusted with the independent authority to add or reduce contract work forces and to shift personnel from one district to another.
- After the merger with Zenith, had to plan and implement a reduction in force of former Zenith employees; was commended for my sensitive handling of terminations.

Financial Management:
- Planned and administered a $32 million budget within a corporate system which had a "no excuses" philosophy about cost overruns; managers were strictly evaluated on cost control.
- Was the approving authority for procurement of capital equipment.

Management of Disaster Response Efforts as well as Major Capital Expansions:
- Directed prudent responses to emergency outages and responded to natural disasters such as tornadoes, hurricanes, and accidents that impacted on outside distribution network and physical plant; was Chairperson of the Emergency Restoration Plan and supervised emergency response crews.
- While managing multiple priorities and projects, implemented project management practices such as scheduling tools and Total Quality Management Techniques; supervised the installation of fiber optic systems all over the U.S.

Customer Service and Community/Government Liaison:
- Customer service was considered the company's #1 priority at all times, and I was keenly responsive to customer service demands with critical deadlines.
- Negotiated with federal, state, local government, and private persons and agencies for right-of-way access and other issues.
- Improved the corporate image through my extensive civic involvement; received the prestigious "Old Faithful Award" for community service given by The President's Club.

Exceptional Performance Ratings:
- Always earned commendable performance ratings of my administrative abilities, problem-solving and analytical skills, leadership, and initiative; excelled in a job in which I handled responsibilities similar to those of a CEO of a small company.

Highlights of previous AT&T Telephone Experience:
DIVISION DISTRIBUTION MANAGER. Phoenix, AZ (1982-93).
DIVISION ENGINEER. Davidson, NC (1976-81).
DIVISION COMMERCIAL SUPERVISOR. Frankfort, IN (1974-75).
DISTRICT ENGINEER. Frankfort, IN (1967-74).

EDUCATION

Bachelor of Science in Business Administration, Davidson College, 1966.

Date

Exact Name of Person
Title or Position
Name of Company
Address (number and street)
Address (city, state, and zip)

**President, Manufacturing
Industry Firm**

This manufacturing executive
prefers a low-key style in his
cover letter, although his resume
is loaded with bottom-line
accomplishments.

Dear Exact Name of Person: (or Dear Sir or Madam if answering a blind ad.)

With the enclosed resume, I would like to make you aware of my top management experience and my desire to utilize my background to benefit your company.

As you will see from my resume, I have most recently served as president of a company which we developed into an attractive acquisition candidate and which subsequently attracted the attention of major corporations. When I took over as president in 1990, it had a negative cash flow and was considering Chapter 11. I aggressively reduced costs while negotiating with vendors, and within two years we achieved a positive cash flow. I rose to the position of president after graduating from MIT and excelling in positions as a plant engineer and then plant manager.

Although my engineering background is vast, I believe the key to my success as a top manager is my creativity and ability to anticipate problems before they actually happen. I offer a proven ability to work effectively with people at all organizational levels.

If my considerable skills, experience, and talents interest you, please contact me. Thank you in advance for your professional courtesies.

Sincerely,

Scott G. Kandt

SCOTT G. KANDT

1110½ Hay Street, Fayetteville, NC 28305 • preppub@aol.com • (910) 483-6611

OBJECTIVE

To benefit an organization that can use a highly resourceful manager who offers a proven "track record" of restoring profitability to ailing operations and troubleshooting stubborn productivity and manufacturing problems, as well as designing new processes, tools, and facilities that improve efficiency and output.

EXPERIENCE

ACTING PRESIDENT. Manufacturing Plus, Aiken, SC (1999-present). Since the company was sold, I have continued on a contract basis and have been offered the job as President and CEO, which I have declined; manage plant operations at three plants including maintenance and upkeep of the equipment, buildings, and grounds for this busy manufacturing company.

PRESIDENT. Manufacturing Plus, Aiken, SC (1990-1999). Reported to a board of directors while managing operations of a company which manufactures grinding wheels and ceramic filters; became president in 1990 after excelling in jobs as plant engineer and plant manager.
- After taking over as president of a company which had a negative cash flow, aggressively reduced costs while extending terms with vendors, a strategy which produced a positive cash flow in less than two years.
- Developed operations/production schedules; determined staffing needs, machine and equipment requirements, tooling needs and development methods, and time standards.
- Planned and implemented programs/procedures to ensure compliance with OSHA and EPA regulations regarding plant safety and materials handling.
- Directed research and development projects for new products and equipment.
- Managed the purchasing of raw materials, equipment, supplies, and services, including procurement of capital equipment and negotiation of contracts.
- Developed or refined written procedures in numerous operational areas in order to assure that company procedures "on the ground floor" were consistent with strategic goals for short-term profitability and long-term growth.
- Oversaw every aspect of internal operations and external relationships for a company with $50 million in sales and up to 975 employees.
- As **plant manager from 1984-90,** improved overall output by 15% and, through new equipment which I designed and built, increased one product line by 1000%.
- As **plant engineer from 1981-84,** developed engineering and maintenance controls, developed and built new equipment, and reorganized manufacturing processes with the net result that operating efficiencies improved by 30%.

PRODUCTION MANAGER & PLANT ENGINEERING MAINTENANCE MANAGER.
L.P. Floyd, Inc., Florence, SC (1978-81). Began with this company as a Production Foreman and Maintenance Foreman overseeing 45 employees and responsible for a $1.5 million profit center; promoted to oversee a $6 million profit center with up to 150 employees working in a union shop.

EDUCATION

Bachelor of Science in Industrial Engineering, Massachusetts Institute of Technology (MIT), Boston, MA, 1978.
MBA, University of South Carolina, Aiken, SC, 1984.
Executive development course work sponsored by industry groups and associations.

PERSONAL

Can provide outstanding personal and professional references at the appropriate time. Believe that the kind of creativity and vision I possess give me the ability as a CEO to formulate strategy and anticipate problems before they occur. Am known for my integrity, compassion, and desire to work toward perfection. In excellent health, enjoy gardening and woodworking.

Date

Betty Graber
J.A. Newsome & Associates
Search 235
P.O. Box 28566
Cape Cod, MA 32238

School Superintendent

Mr. Cooperman is applying for a job similar to the one he has now. He is seeking a larger pond in which to test his skills and refine his knowledge.

Dear Ms. Graber:

After reviewing your announcement for the Cape Cod Public Schools Superintendency, I believe I am the ideal candidate for the position, and I would like to formally make you aware of my interest in what sounds like a challenging assignment! I am aware of the major construction program underway in the Cape Cod Schools, and I would like to become a part of your ambitious plans and projects.

As Superintendent at Ft. Riley School System, I have provided the leadership for expansion of technology in the instructional program. During this past year, one of Fort Riley's elementary schools was chosen as a testbed site for President Clinton's Technology Initiative (PTI). This pilot project will afford our students and staff an opportunity to share innovative programs and instructional strategies. As Superintendent, I have also been instrumental in forming partnerships with business and community groups. On my own initiative, I have also developed an early childhood program for children from birth to three years of age: Parents and Children Together (PACT) focused on the early identification of youngsters with special needs.

As the instructional leader of the school system, it is been essential for me to establish an active presence in community life by being both available and visible. Serving as Director on several boards has provided me opportunities to share information about the schools and gain community support for our programs. Sharing the good news about the schools is vital. Seeking greater involvement among all age groups in volunteerism would be a strategy to enhance the "life-long learning" process.

In closing, any professional accomplishments I have achieved during my career have been attained through the combined efforts of many people. If I were to be selected as Superintendent, I would work diligently with all stakeholders in moving Cape Cod Public Schools forward.

Thank you for your consideration. I look forward to hearing from you.

Sincerely,

Larry Cooperman